FAMILY AND FRONTIER IN COLONIAL BRAZIL

Family and Frontier in Colonial Brazil

Santana de Parnaíba,
1580–1822

ALIDA C. METCALF

UNIVERSITY OF TEXAS PRESS, AUSTIN

LIBRARY OF CONGRESS CATALOGING-IN-PUBLICATION DATA

Metcalf, Alida C., 1954–
Family and frontier in colonial Brazil :
Santana de Parnaíba, 1580–1822 / Alida C. Metcalf.
p.   cm.
Includes bibliographical references (p.   ) and index.
ISBN 0-292-70652-9 (pbk. : alk. paper)
1. Family—Brazil—Santana de Parnaíba—History.
2. Frontier and pioneer life—Brazil—Santana de Parnaíba.
3. Brazil—Colonization. I. Title.

HQ594.15.S24M48   2005
306.85'0981'61—DC22   2004053553

To My Parents

Helen Waterman Metcalf
and
John Trumbull Metcalf, Jr.

Contents

MAPS

TABLES

FIGURES

PLATES
FOLLOWING PAGE 119

Seventeenth-century Chapel of Our Lady of Conception, Vuturuna
   Estate, Santana de Parnaíba.

Seventeeth-century wattle-and-daub church from Areias, São Paulo.
   Watercolor by Thomas Ender, early nineteenth century.

Indians captured from the *sertão*. Lithograph by Jean Baptiste Debret,
   early nineteenth century.

Making war on tribal Indians. Debret, early nineteenth century.

Guaraní Indian women on their way to mass. Debret, early nineteenth
   century.

Sparse interior of a wealthy family home, city of São Paulo, Ender,
   early nineteenth century.

Eighteenth-century *taipa de pilão* houses of Santana de Parnaíba.

Abbreviations

The following abbreviations are used in the citations:

Archives

ACDJ   Arquivo da Cúria Diocesana de Jundiaí

ACMSP   Arquivo da Cúria Metropolitana de São Paulo

AESP   Arquivo do Estado de São Paulo

AHU   Arquivo Histórico Ultramarino, Lisbon

AN   Arquivo Nacional, Rio de Janeiro

ATT   Arquivo da Torre do Tombo, Lisbon

Manuscript Collections of Documents

IPO   Inventários do Primeiro Ofício, AESP

IT   Inventários e Testamentos, AESP

LP   Livros de Parnaíba, AESP

MP   Mapas de População, AESP

LPS   Livros Paroquiais de Santana de Parnaíba, ACDJ

Published Collections of Documents

IT   *Inventários e testamentos*, Departamento do Arquivo do Estado de São Paulo

DI   *Documentos interessantes*, Departamento do Arquivo do Estado de São Paulo

         Boletim, Departamento do Arquivo do Estado de São Paulo

         Sesmarias, Departamento do Arquivo do Estado de São Paulo

Preface to the Second Edition

Every spring, a colleague in the history department at Trinity University asks me to come to her class titled "The Historian's Craft." For this course on historical methods, my assignment is to talk to students about how I wrote *Family and Frontier in Colonial Brazil*. My colleague uses my visit as an entrée into a larger discussion on social history and historical demography, but for me the occasion has become a chance to reflect on how and why I wrote the book as I did. As I prepare this second edition of *Family and Frontier*, it seems fitting to share some of these thoughts with my readers.

While preparing my talk for my colleague's students the first time, I realized that the book I had written was not the one that I intended to write. As I would later explain to the students, my initial research interest was the lives of women in colonial Brazil. In fact, when I flew down to Rio to assess the feasibility of such a project, I believed my biggest challenge would be finding sources in the archives on the lives of women. But my first forays into Brazilian archives revealed precisely the opposite: I easily located treasure troves of potential documents, many of which suggested fascinating questions to explore. I found petitions written by women to royal officials, wills dictated by women to notaries, inventories of properties owned by women, censuses that recorded the names of women, and baptismal, marriage, and death records that registered key events in the lives of hundreds of thousands of women. Through these and other documents, I met women who lived ordinary, unremarkable lives, as well as women who filed for divorce, married against the wills of their fathers, fought husbands over their dowries, and languished in jails. I read about women who had been raped, women who had been murdered, and women who were violent themselves. The names and numbers of women recorded in the archives seemed endless. Clearly, a richly detailed history of women in colonial Brazil could be written.

Yet, as I explained to the students, I soon foresaw an insurmountable

problem. Although I knew colonial Brazil to be a highly stratified society, these levels of stratification were not often noted in written sources.
With the exception of slave women, I found it difficult to judge a
woman's social status. And although I judged that many of the documents pertained to women from families of means, I could not separate
the women who were part of the free poor population from those of the
elite. Furthermore, although the civil status of a woman—whether she
was single, married, or widowed—was regularly noted in documents,
I had little sense of what that meant legally or socially. If a widow appeared in a land dispute, did that mean she was poor and vulnerable?
If a married woman signed a contract, did that mean she had power in
her marriage? If a single woman headed a household, did that mean
she had chosen independence? Moreover, I knew that where a woman
lived—on a rural estate, in a village, or in a town or city—had a major
impact on her life. Yet many of the documents I held in my hands in the
national and state archives gave me only snatches of information about
women from all over Brazil. Who were these women? What kinds of
communities did they come from? Which of these women were typical? Which life experiences could I take as representative? Finally, most
of the documents I so easily found on women dated from the nineteenth century. How had women's lives changed? Were the nineteenth-
century documents reflective of women's lives in Brazil during the colonial period?

I came to the conclusion that all of these questions depended to a
large degree on understanding the roles of women in their families
and communities over time. Women did share some common life experiences, but a woman's social class and the parish, village, town, or
city in which she lived, as well as when she lived, shaped her life in
significant ways. The first step to understanding women was to reconstruct family life in colonial Brazil and especially to differentiate
family life by social class. I resolved to write the study that would
make it possible to place women in colonial Brazil in the contexts of
their families, their social classes, and their communities. The study
that I began to formulate in my mind would explain the connections
between marriage and inheritance, family structure and agricultural
production, slavery and family life. It would take into account the
structures of families among the rich as well as among the poor, and
among the free as well as among the enslaved.

With this new sense of purpose, I returned to Brazil and began looking for a community I could study using the methods pioneered by historical demographers and family historians in France, England, and the United States. Historical demographers prize the finely grained reconstructions of family life cycles and individual life courses that can be assembled from parish registers of births, marriages, and deaths. Family historians value sources such as wills and property inventories, as well as community records that reveal aspects of individual and family lives. With the help of two Brazilian historians, I found one large rural community in São Paulo, Santana de Parnaíba, which had an exceptional run of documents in the state archives of São Paulo. These extraordinarily rich sources, which included manuscript censuses, wills, probate proceedings, and town council record books, were complemented by the complete books of baptismal, marriage, and death sacraments maintained by the parish priests. Collecting the data for the study took more than a year, even when I was aided by two research assistants (then undergraduate history majors at the University of São Paulo). I analyzed the quantitative sources at the University of Texas, using the outstanding computing facilities available there. My reconstruction of family structure in eighteenth-century Santana de Parnaíba by social class became my doctoral dissertation, which I defended in 1983.

As often happens in historical research, quite by accident I began to notice that not only did families, and therefore women's lives, vary by social class, but so too did the ways that families interacted with the frontier. This discovery came as I was working in the genealogies compiled by the nineteenth-century genealogist Luiz Gonzaga da Silva Leme. As I followed descendants of families through the brittle pages of his opus, I began to notice not only repeating names but also repeating patterns of migration. As I explored migration in other sources, a pattern of family interaction with the frontier emerged and became so compelling that I resolved to reconceptualize the dissertation and write a book about the relationship between families of each social class and the Brazilian frontier. Like the original dissertation, *Family and Frontier in Colonial Brazil* reconstructs family life by social class: the slaveowning planters, the families of the free poor (or peasantry), and the families of slaves. But in order to uncover larger historical patterns, it extends the time frame to include the seventeenth as well as the eighteenth century. Moreover, it conceptualizes Santana de Parnaíba not as a closed community, but rather as an open one with powerful ties to the frontier. I argue that the roots and persistence of inequality in Brazil derive from the way that the resources of the frontier—land, labor, and minerals—were transformed into private property and possessed by families. I trace this process over 250 years and suggest that it may continue, albeit in different ways, to the present day.

Since 1992, when the first edition of *Family and Frontier* appeared, much new work on the family in Brazilian history has been published. Although my research interests have shifted away from family and community studies, I have followed the field with great interest. *Family and Frontier* is regularly cited in this literature, as are articles I published in academic journals in Brazil, the United States, and Europe. Were I to rewrite the book, I would incorporate the new findings of social historians and historical demographers for comparative purposes, but I would not change the methodology or findings presented. For this reason, and because there is no study quite like this one, when the University of Texas Press decided to bring *Family and Frontier* back into print in a paperback edition, I resolved to let the original book stand as it is. This second edition of *Family and Frontier,* therefore, remains fundamentally the same as the first edition published by the University of California Press. Known errors have been corrected and the maps have been redrawn for greater clarity.

There are always individuals to thank when a book is finally finished. Those who helped me in the writing of this book are still very much on my mind as I write these words. Their names may be found in the acknowledgments. There are a few more individuals whom I wish to thank as this second edition goes to press. Theresa May, Editor-in-Chief at the University of Texas Press; Char Miller, my department chair at Trinity University; my colleague Linda Salvucci, whose class I refer to above; and Mark and Jane Carroll, dear family friends, all encouraged me to bring this book back into print. I owe a special debt to geographer David Stinchcomb, who redrew the maps. It is a great pleasure to dedicate the book once again to my parents, Helen and John Metcalf.

San Antonio, Texas   A. C. M.
December 2003

Acknowledgments

When I first visited Brazil in 1967, we crossed the Amazon by motor-boat from the Colombian town of Leticia and spent the day in the tiny village of Benjamin Constant. I could not have imagined then that one day I would write about the settlement of the vast Brazilian frontier. As my family and I walked down the muddy street among the houses built on stilts, and as we visited rubber tappers, we found ourselves in a world dramatically different from the one we knew. I realize now that the Indians, rubber tappers, hunters, and fishermen whom we met on that unforgettable trip were living as their forebears had lived generations before. Entering that world was stepping back into history, into the world of the individuals whose lives I reconstruct in this book. Although this book is set in a very different town, Santana de Parnaíba, located not in the Amazon but in the state of São Paulo, the families of Santana de Parnaíba sent most of their descendants into the frontier, perhaps some even to the remote village I visited in 1967.

Re-creating the lives of the people of Santana de Parnaíba in the seventeenth and eighteenth centuries has been an intensely challenging task that has occupied me for the last fifteen years. I am deeply grateful to institutions, colleagues, friends, and family who made it possible for me to write this history.

First, I wish to thank the institutions that funded my research. A Fulbright-Hays fellowship from the U.S. Department of Education and a grant from the Social Science Research Council funded the bulk of the archival research in Brazil and Portugal in 1979 and 1980. The Mellon Foundation, the Institute of Latin American Studies at the University of Texas at Austin, the University of Texas at San Antonio, and Trinity University supported research at the Nettie Lee Benson Latin American Collection of the University of Texas at Austin during the summers of 1985 and 1988. The Joullian fund, granted by that family to the Department of History of Trinity University for faculty development, made it possible for me to visit Brazil in 1989 and to hire student assistants. I am grateful to each of these institutions and to the Joullian family for their support of historical scholarship.

Many happy memories of times spent with friends and colleagues in Brazil and the United States are woven into the researching and writing of this book. Richard Graham deserves special recognition for helping this project grow from its earliest beginnings and for offering excellent critical advice at many stages along the way. Sandra Lauderdale Graham first introduced me to the Brazilian archives; her ability to make history come alive from the sources has been an inspiration. Laura Graham helped me to understand the forces affecting Indians in the modern frontier, which has influenced my portrayal of similar forces in the past.

Working in Brazil has been enormously interesting and enjoyable. I am deeply grateful to many Brazilian colleagues who graciously received me in their homes, shared their ideas, and helped me to understand colonial and modern Brazil. The work and friendship of Eni de Mesquita Samara, whom I first met in Austin in 1977, has been instrumental to the development of this study. Maria Luiza Marcílio's studies of São Paulo made it possible for me to place Santana de Parnaíba into a larger context; I am also grateful to her for her excellent counsel as I formulated my research methodology. My understanding of the lives of Brazilian women has been greatly advanced by historian Maria Beatriz Nizza da Silva, whom I also thank for her enthusiastic encouragement of my work. The unfailing good humor of Fernando Novais has made the study of colonial Brazil always a pleasure. Iraci del Nero da Costa has sent me numerous articles to keep me informed of work being done in Brazil. Robert Slenes introduced me to many Brazilian colleagues and to the intricacies of slave family life. Jacy Machado Barletta took my friend Cecilia Pinheiro and me on a memorable tour of Santana de Parnaíba in 1989.

In 1986, as a Fulbright Lecturer, I taught at the Universidade Estadual Paulista in Assis. The generous hospitality of Anna Maria Martinez Correa and the friendship of my colleagues there, especially Manuel Lelo Bellotto, Elizabeth and David Rabello, Olga Mussi da Silva, and Glacyra Lazzari Leite, as well as that of my students, made me feel a part of this institution.

I conducted the majority of my research in the manuscript collections of the Arquivo do Estado de São Paulo, where Dona Glorinha and Dona Azoraidil of the manuscript section helped me to locate

sources and to master paleography. To them, and to the former direc-
tor of the archive, Dr. José Sebastião Witter, who honored many requests, I am most grateful.

Research assistants helped me at many stages of the project. I could
not have finished my research without the excellent assistance of Ines
Conceição de Inacio and Wilma Gomes da Silva. In Austin, Pedro
Santoni entered reams of data into the computer. At Trinity University, Elizabeth Thompson coded the 1820 census, while Deanna Perez
compiled the bibliography.

I wish to acknowledge the support of the chair of my department at
Trinity University, Terry Smart, who facilitated my requests for research
assistance, travel, and library research so essential to the completion of
this book. My colleagues John Martin and Colin Wells read the manuscript and offered valuable suggestions. At the Trinity University library, Carl Hanson answered numerous questions about Portuguese
history and helped me to locate rare books. In the library's Instructional
Media Services, Pat Ullman, Patricia Beneze, and David Garza drew
the maps, produced the figures, and photographed the illustrations.

I also wish to thank the readers for the University of California
Press who reviewed the manuscript; their excellent suggestions,
incorporated into the final revision, greatly improved the book. I
wish to thank my editors at the press, Edward Dimendberg, Shirley
Warren, and Michelle Nordon for shepherding the book through
production.

I have explored some of the ideas presented in chapters 2, 4, and 6
in articles published in *The Hispanic American Historical Review, Estudos Econômicos, The Journal of Family History,* and Mark D. Szuchman,
*The Middle Period in Latin America: Values and Attitudes in the 17th–19th
Centuries.*

In my own family, my uncle, William Van Antwerp Waterman, first
interested me in family history and genealogies. My husband, soci-
ologist Daniel Rigney, carefully read the manuscript and offered numerous suggestions that clarified my ideas and their presentation. Our
young sons, Matthew and Benjamin, have given me a new appreciation
for the meaning of family life. And finally, it is with great pleasure that
I dedicate this book to my parents, Helen and John Metcalf, whose love
has followed me everywhere.

San Antonio, Texas   A. C. M.
April 1991

A Note on Currency

The common currency of colonial Brazil was the *real*, plural *reais*, although many other coins, as well as gold dust, circulated. One thousand reais, or one *mil* reais, was written 1$000. To alleviate confusion in the text, I have replaced the $ with a comma; hence 1$000 becomes 1,000 reais. While it would be difficult to give meaningful modern equivalents, some comparative values might be helpful to the reader. In the eighteenth century, a strong slave in the peak of his or her working years was worth between 100,000 and 150,000 reais.

A Note on Orthography

The Portuguese language has undergone several reformulations to standardize orthography. This poses difficulties for social historians, for the accepted modern spelling of proper names differs from that found in colonial documents. In addition, the notaries who wrote and transcribed these documents often used their own spelling. To complicate things even further, individuals often had several family names, all of which might not be recorded in every document. I have adopted the standard modern usage for prominent historical figures and places—for example, Santana de Parnaíba—regardless of how they were spelled in the documents. I have not, however, modernized the spelling of the names of the people of Parnaíba. Instead, I spell their names as they appear in the documents. Where variations of the same name appear, I have adopted the most common one.

FAMILY AND FRONTIER IN COLONIAL BRAZIL

Introduction

Family, Frontier, and the Colonization of the Americas

This book tells the story of ordinary people who lived simple lives in four adjacent parishes that once formed a large rural town in southern Brazil. Although historians have rarely been interested in these people, the majority of whom were slaves and small farmers, they did have an enormous influence on the colonization of this region of Brazil, today the state of São Paulo. By the manner in which they lived, unpretentious and unselfconscious as it was, they established certain lifeways that directly shaped the character of the society in which they and their descendants lived.

The inheritance of cultural attitudes and economic resources from generation to generation among the people of this community, Santana de Parnaíba, from the time when the Portuguese first landed on the coast of Brazil in 1500 to the birth of the Brazilian nation in 1822, is the subject of this book. Santana de Parnaíba serves as an excellent microcosm for the analysis of how families survived in the world of colonial Brazil. Passed through family life to succeeding generations, their family strategies became a cultural inheritance that shaped the community and the development of the western frontier. Moreover, given the continued expansion of the agricultural frontier into the modern Amazon basin, the survival strategies of these people in the seventeenth and eighteenth centuries explain why similar strategies continue to be used by their descendants in Brazil today.

I argue that the strategies of families, in relation to the frontier, are critical to understanding the colonization of this region of Brazil. Not only does this relationship help to explain the process of colonization but it also holds the key to understanding the origins of social stratification. Power and wealth in this region have come from the frontier, but not all have had equal access to it. Those families and social classes that controlled the development and exploitation of the frontier came to dominate the region economically and politically.

In Santana de Parnaíba, colonization occurred in discrete stages. In the first stage, Santana de Parnaíba was itself a frontier—poised between the wilderness to the west and the city of São Paulo to the east. As colonists came from São Paulo to the region and began to settle there in the late sixteenth century, a society emerged which blended Indian and Portuguese ways. Although it was not an egalitarian society, it was a fluid one, and social mobility was possible for those of Portuguese descent who successfully acquired land and Indian slaves from the wilderness. After Santana de Parnaíba became an established town in the early seventeenth century, it served as a jumping off place for the frontier to the west. Throughout the seventeenth century, men from Parnaíba, but only occasionally women, set off into the frontier in search of their fortunes.

As the town grew and became a more complex community in the eighteenth century, it entered a second stage. Social classes began to emerge. A cash-crop commercial economy took root in the town, as did investments in commerce and mining. The influence of Indians waned. Slavery remained pervasive and unquestioned, but Africans replaced Indian slaves on the agricultural estates of the town. As in the first stage, those of the town who successfully exploited the frontier became or remained the wealthy and powerful in Santana de Parnaíba. The frontier continued to hold the key to social and economic success in the town.

In the third stage of this process, Santana de Parnaíba lost its ties to the wilderness and declined while towns farther west, many of which had been founded by men and women from Parnaíba, flourished. In this last stage, Parnaíba continued to remain a stratified community, with few rich slave-owning planters and an increasing number of small slaveless farmers. Eventually, the town faded into obscurity and became dependent on the growing city of São Paulo. This third stage began in the early years of the nineteenth century in the central parish of the town, somewhat later in the outlying rural parishes, and continued through the nineteenth century as the coffee frontier boomed farther west. Today, Santana de Parnaíba has entered a fourth stage as the region increasingly becomes part of greater São Paulo. The population has grown as city workers have sought inexpensive housing. Wealthy families have built expensive vacation homes there, too. By the next century, Santana de Parnaíba may well be another suburb of the city of São Paulo.

In each of these stages of development, the relationship between families and the frontier played a major role in shaping the lives of their individual members and structuring the contours of community life. Attitudes about how to survive that families consciously and unconsciously adopted affected how they perceived the frontier, raised their sons and daughters, divided their property, and farmed their lands. Many of these attitudes were formed in the first stage of colonization when families adapted and experimented in order to survive. One such attitude was the belief that the wilderness held the riches that individuals and families needed to survive in the town. This attitude had developed during the earliest stage of colonization and continued to characterize life in the later stages because of the proximity of the frontier.

The history of the frontier in Brazil holds much in common with the history of the frontier in North America. Indeed, the most influential work on the role of the frontier in American history describes some of the same features of the Brazilian frontier. In 1893, Frederick Jackson Turner's remarkable paper, "The Significance of the Frontier in American History," argued that America was different from Europe because of the frontier, the meeting point between wilderness inhabited by Indians and an expanding European population.[1] The existence of the frontier, and its continued colonization by wave after wave of colonists, was what in Turner's eyes made America unique. While in their first settlements along the Atlantic coast colonists did re-create much of their European culture, as they moved west they had to adapt to the wilderness and be transformed by it in order eventually to master it. Turner writes, "Moving westward, the frontier became more and more American. . . . Thus the advance of the frontier has meant a steady growth of independence on American lines. And to study this advance . . . is to study the really American part of our history."[2] For Turner, the "really American" part of American history was the growth of individualism and democracy on the frontier. These values created the basis for an American nationalism. Turner's thesis has been developed[3] and critiqued[4] by later historians, but his work remains provocative because of the questions he posed and the issues he raised.

Brazilian historians such as Sérgio Buarque de Holanda also perceived the frontier to have been a critical factor in Brazilian development.[5] Like North America, Brazil began with a handful of coastal settlements that faced the Atlantic while behind them extended a vast, and to them unknown, wilderness. Brazil has expanded west, devouring the lands of Indians and creating a new, distinctly Brazilian culture. Brazilian development has depended on the cheap lands and resources of the frontier. But there is a big difference. The frontier in Brazil has rarely bred democracy or individualism. While many historians of North America now question whether the frontier in the United States really fostered democracy or individualism,[6] the contrast with Brazil is nevertheless striking. In northeastern Brazil, huge cattle ranches effectively colonized the frontier and concentrated immense tracts of lands into the hands of a few. In the south, sugar and coffee planters sought virgin forests to fell and transform into large agricultural estates worked by slaves. Relatively few parts of the Brazilian frontier were colonized by the yeoman farmers so eulogized by Turner—the hardworking entrepreneurial families who carved their homesteads out of the wilderness by the sweat of their own brows. While small farmers did move into the frontier in Brazil, they rarely legally owned the lands they claimed. As a result, when large agribusinesses arrived, they pushed out the small farmer, who either moved west, became a sharecropper, or migrated to the city.

As I will illustrate, the frontier provided the resources that allowed a small elite to form and to become wealthy and powerful in a town such as Santana de Parnaíba. Because of the way this elite perceived the frontier and made it an integral part of their family lives, succeeding generations of elite families were launched into the frontier, where they too found the resources to make themselves wealthy and powerful in their respective local communities. Other social groups did not benefit equally from the resources of the frontier and did not successfully incorporate strategies for developing the frontier into their family lives. Small farmers subsisted off the frontier but did not use it to make themselves wealthy, while slaves did not have the opportunity to acquire its resources. Thus, the way the frontier has been developed in Brazil is one of the roots of inequality in Brazilian society and continues to be to this day.

A second source of inequality in Brazilian society springs from family life. Historians of Latin America are increasingly aware that the family, particularly the elite family, has been one of the most powerful forces in colonial society. Though the region's economic and political institutions were planted in the colonies by Spain and Portugal, the families of the Creole (native-born) elites managed to infiltrate these institutions and to use them to their advantage. In the process, they deeply affected the character of colonial society itself.

After the discovery and conquest of Latin America, the colonies offered many opportunities to individual Spaniards and Portuguese who found the means to come to the New World. As these individuals settled and eventually formed families, they increasingly chafed at the many restrictions placed on them by Spain and Portugal. In particular, Spain regulated the colonies excessively, always with the intent of squeezing as much revenue from them as possible. These regulations continually hampered the aspirations of early conquerors and settlers. Such an environment meant that families that did succeed economically—through investments in agriculture or mining, for example—had to be exceedingly crafty to maintain their power and influence.

Historians of colonial Mexico and Peru have documented the exceptionally complex strategies that elite families pursued to preserve their status and influence. Studies by David Brading, Doris Ladd, and Richard Lindley (among others) for Mexico and Susan Ramírez, Fred Bronner, and Robert Keith for Peru illustrate how an elite formed in the sixteenth and seventeenth centuries and how, through their families, they maintained their power and influence.[7] They did so by carefully marrying their daughters, by grooming their sons for careers in the church or government or as managers of agricultural estates, by maintaining an extended kin network, by establishing fictive kinship ties to other influential families, and by planning for the transmission of property through inheritance. These strategies made the landowning elite rich and powerful and made it difficult for other social groups to achieve upward social mobility. Spain's colonial caste system, based on purity of blood (*limpieza de sangre*), further strangled the aspirations of the poor mestizos, blacks, and Indians.

In Brazil, a colonial society less rigid than Spanish America, a similar process occurred. In the sugar-growing region of the northeast, a powerful landowning elite emerged in the late sixteenth and early seventeenth centuries. This elite relied on family strategies to maintain itself economically and to guarantee its political power. By marrying their daughters to wealthy merchants, landowners bought themselves new capital. Marriages to powerful royal officials gave them influence. Family life in colonial Brazil, as in Spanish America, was critical to the formation and perpetuation of the elite.[8]

The behavior of elite families in Parnaíba similarly affected the evolution of a socially stratified town. Because wealthy families owned valuable resources of land and labor, how these families acquired property, held it in their families, and distributed it to their heirs affected not just their own families but the community as a whole. The dominance of elite families in local institutions—the town council, militia, and church—likewise contributed to social inequality. Such institutions reflected the interests of the elite, not those of the whole population, and thus served to reinforce the power of wealthy families.

As a few families successfully concentrated resources into their own .hands and influenced local institutions to their advantage, they helped to create and reinforce social classes. The social world of Parnaíba was stratified in many different ways. Wealth, race, family ties, age, sex, and marital status all influenced how the townspeople perceived themselves and each other. Yet, increasingly in the seventeenth and eighteenth centuries, three social classes evolved in Parnaíba: planters, peasants, and slaves. Planters owned land and slaves and produced commercial crops, such as sugar, for sale. Peasants owned no slaves and primarily produced food crops for their own use and for local markets. Slaves had few resources beyond what they received from their masters. The majority of slaves did not own anything, not even their own labor. Each class had a unique relationship to the principal resources needed for survival in the town—land and labor. Each class had fundamentally different family lives. Each class interacted with the frontier in distinct ways.

Any typology invariably oversimplifies the social world experienced by individuals. In Parnaíba, a family with one slave was hardly much better off than a family without any slaves. Similarly, a freed slave who continued to serve her former master probably did not experience a radical life change from what she had known as a slave. Yet in terms of how families perceived themselves, it did matter to a former slave that freedom had been purchased, awarded, or promised. To a poor family with one slave, the possession of that slave accorded a status in the community that families without slaves did not have. Thus, while the boundaries between social classes might seem crude, they do serve to define the ranks of Parnaíba's society. In that society, the lives of planters (who owned slaves) differed fundamentally from the lives of peasants (who did not), and the lives of slaves similarly diverged from those of peasants and planters.

Historians of colonial Brazil disagree over what terminology to use to characterize the social structure of the colony.[9] Some argue that the colonial world was a society of castes; others, that it was a society of classes. Still others prefer the concept of estates. The proponents of the term "estate" borrow it from old regime France, which was divided into three estates: those who prayed (clergy), those who fought (nobility), and those who worked (peasants, artisans, the bourgeoisie). The term "caste" derives from studies of India wherein individuals were born into a caste and remained in it all their lives. I use the term "class" because it best describes the historical reality I find expressed in the sources. "Estate" does not rightly characterize a society that had no titled nobility, a weak clergy, and a large number of slaves. "Caste" implies a rigid society with no social mobility, yet the extensive ties to the frontier provided the residents of Parnaíba with such avenues. Even slaves could obtain their freedom. In contrast, "class" suggests a society in which large groups of people are differentiated by their relationship to material resources. Planters possessed land and labor; slaves did not. Peasants owned more resources than slaves, but fewer than planters. These simple facts increasingly differentiated the lives of individuals in the seventeenth and eighteenth centuries. Thus, I conceptualize Santana de Parnaíba as a class society composed of planters, peasants, and slaves.

Family life varied by class. Families of the planter elite lived in large hierarchical households where the interests of many had to be subdued and conflicts avoided. The importance of property in maintaining their status meant that family customs explicitly regulated events such as marriage and inheritance. These customs worked to keep women from wanting independent lives or from marrying the men of their choice. Other customs worked to minimize conflicts between brothers. Similarly, the paternalistic and benevolent ways in which these families treated their slaves and other servants served the very important function of smoothing over the inequalities that existed in such households.

For the peasantry, family life revolved around the cultivation of small plots of land by family members. They had to cooperate with each other and share in the work that provided the sustenance for all. The vast majority of these families lived in small nuclear households composed of parents and their children. Mothers and fathers taught their children how to work in the fields and in the house from a young age. These families valued cooperation between men and women, brothers and sisters, and families and neighbors.

Slave family life differed substantially from that of planters or peasants. Slavery afforded little room to create autonomous family lives. The economic fortunes of masters and the attitudes of masters toward slave families determined many aspects of slave family life. Other factors, such as the demographic characteristics of the slave population or the size of the estates on which slaves lived, also influenced the chances that slaves would marry and form families. Slave families tended to be less stable than those of planters and peasants because of constant change, occasioned not just by marriage, birth, or death but by transfer of ownership. Thus, of the three social classes of Parnaíba, slaves had the least control over their family lives.

Not only did family life vary by class but each class interacted with the frontier in different ways. Families of planters saw their survival in terms of acquiring property from the wilderness frontier and preserving it for future generations. This property could be land, Indian slaves, or gold. Moreover, when these families divided their property each generation, they expected some of their children to migrate west. Thus, they favored some heirs at the expense of others by allowing the favored heirs to inherit the bulk of the family resources and the social position of the parents in Parnaíba, knowing that other children would make their fortunes in the frontier. Heirs who remained in Parnaíba but were not favored paid a price: downward social mobility. They became small planters with few resources. Such customs of family life among the planter elite promoted the development of the frontier, maintained large agricultural estates in Parnaíba, and created a growing substratum of the planter class composed of poor planters.

The peasantry also relied on the frontier for their survival. Primarily, they desired land to provide for themselves and their children. But because they often lacked the ability to protect their lands over time, they moved on with the frontier. These peasant farmers became the first wave of frontier settlement, often battling with Indian tribes for virgin forest to clear and plant. Those peasant families who were able to retain their lands in Parnaíba turned their attention to the developing city of São Paulo, which they furnished with their food surpluses and in which they worked as mule drivers and laborers. Many of the young men and women from peasant families migrated to the town center to become artisans or servants, and to the city of São Paulo.

Although some slaves did escape to the frontier where they formed runaway slave communities (*quilombos*), and many others were taken to the frontier to cultivate new sugar and coffee estates, the majority of slaves did not see the frontier as a place they might use to their advantage. Beyond running away to the frontier, slaves devised no strategies to exploit it. Their strategies for the survival of their families and kin networks developed in Parnaíba and its immediate environs, where they formed a black community. Slaves sought privileges from their masters which might make their lives more bearable. This might take the form of the right to plant a garden, the right to save for purchasing their freedom, or the right to marry a free person or a slave from a neighboring estate. Slaves formed religious brotherhoods with other slaves and free blacks; these associations created the basis for a black community in Parnaíba. Slaves thus devised their family lives in a very different context than the slave-owning planters or the slaveless peasants.

To summarize, frontier family life in this region of colonial Brazil developed in several contexts. First, family life varied for each social class. Second, families perceived the frontier in diverse ways and used it accordingly. Third, the frontier had a dissimilar impact on the families of each social class. Families of planters, for example, used the frontier to their advantage; slaves generally did not.

Through their varying strategies for survival, families participated in and reinforced the formation of social classes in Parnaíba. The resulting structure of power and authority reproduced itself in this community over many generations. The social structure of the community was neither preordained nor imposed from afar. Rather, it evolved as colonists in this region of the Portuguese empire made choices about how to live in and interact with the empire, choices that would shape the community inherited by their children and by their children's children.

Through the study of a small and ordinary town, a wide variety of issues, events, and processes characteristic not only of Brazil but of the Americas during the great age of colonization can be examined. The intent of this study is not to elevate the importance of this town but to use it as a lens so that one process of colonization can be magnified and revealed in detail. Since the different character of colonization in the Americas has produced very different results, an understanding of modern American societies must rest on an analysis of their colonial roots. The history of Santana de Parnaíba helps us to understand the historical roots of modern Brazil, especially the region dominated by São Paulo, the industrial, financial, and technical hub of Brazil today, and its modern frontier, the western Amazon basin.

To write the history of colonization from the point of view of the people who lived it is not easy. The vast majority of the people who lived in Santana de Parnaíba did not read or write. Many did not even speak Portuguese very well. Because Santana de Parnaíba did not interest the Portuguese kings or their Brazilian governors, they sent few officials to this community to observe the people and to write about them. The sources that historians traditionally have used thus do not exist. But the history of this community can be written and the contributions of its people to the colonization of Brazil assessed because many other sources do exist which can be developed by historians.

Many diverse sources, pieced together, reveal glimpses of San tana de Parnaíba as it evolved over time. The most important sources for this study are the manuscript censuses that capture, as in a snapshot, the entire population at one moment in time. From the census, it is possible to calculate a demographic profile of the population that would include such factors as its size, its age structure, and the ratio of women to men. Because the censuses of the second half of the eighteenth century for the state of São Paulo are so exceptionally detailed, historians can see clearly who lived in each household, what families planted on their farms, and the composition of the labor force. From this information, it is possible to define the social classes that inhabited the community. Unfortunately, the censuses only exist for the late eighteenth century, when the region of São Paulo caught the attention of the crown's ministers because of its strategic location close to the Spanish colonies of the Rio de la Plata. The officers of local militia, ordered to canvass their districts beginning in 1765, conducted yearly censuses until the 1840s. Three of these censuses, those of 1775, 1798, and 1820, provide the statistical backbone of this book.

The property inventories and wills from seventeenth- and eighteenth-century Santana de Parnaíba are the second major source for this study. This collection includes several hundred manuscript and published inventories and wills. Through the analysis of the inventories, it is possible to reconstruct the material culture and the inheritance customs of the people. The inventories of property, conducted after the death of an individual according to Portuguese law, meticulously recorded every item owned by the deceased. Perhaps the most important part of the inventory was the division of property (the *partilhas*) among the legal heirs, which was carefully recorded in these documents. Some of the inventories included wills dictated by men and women who wished to record certain last wishes to be carried out after their deaths. These wills are an especially rich source of information on individual lives, family ties, community life, religious customs, and family property.

The wills and inventories document the many changes that took place in Santana de Parnaíba over two hundred years, but they do have their limitations. One major flaw is their bias in favor of the wealthy. People who did not own property did not need to inventory it; nor did they have the opportunity to summon a notary to whom they might gasp, in their dying breaths, their last testament to the living. Sometimes the poor can be glimpsed in the wills and inventories, as for example when bequests were left to the destitute. Slaves can be traced through inventories because as property, very valuable property, they always appeared in them.

Parish registers of births, marriages, and deaths kept by the priest of one parish, Santana, through the eighteenth century are another source extensively used in this study. Parish registers, like the censuses, include the whole population, not just the wealthy. Records of marriages and baptisms are used not only to calculate the rate of marriage or the fertility of women but to understand how families linked themselves to others. Since at marriage and at baptism, godparents and witnesses presented themselves, such records provide important clues to how families constructed their wider world of relations and acquaintances.

The town council of Santana de Parnaíba kept a huge volume of records on local government, many tomes of which are preserved in the state archive of São Paulo. Of special import to this study are the notary books that list land sales, slave sales, and slave manumissions. The records of cases brought before the local justice of the peace are especially interesting because they contain the testimony of individuals on a variety of conflicts that erupted in the town. The ledger of the jailer recorded every prisoner sent to the jail in the second half of the eighteenth century. Finally, communications from royal officials, the letters of Jesuit priests, maps, and genealogies of prominent families have all been used to reconstruct the history of this community and the people who lived in it.

Although the innermost thoughts of the people of Parnaíba are rarely recorded, the sources do allow the historian to reconstruct the outward characteristics of individual and family life. For this reason, this book describes behavior rather than thought, the exterior rather than the interior. But even if such introspective sources did exist, one of the central tenets of this work is that the family strategies used to survive and succeed in Parnaíba were not always conscious; rather, they were part of the unacknowledged and even unquestioned way of living. Thus, the behavior of families as a group, is, in this analysis, more important than the thoughts of individual members.

The methodology of this study was designed to reconstruct the evolution of the community over time while also analyzing in detail the relationships among individuals, families, and social classes at particular moments in time. Thus, the study has both a horizontal and a vertical dimension. Many of the sources yielded information on both axes. A single census, for example, provides a plethora of information on households in the population and the class structure of the community at one point in time, while the study of three censuses at fifty-year intervals reveals the changes in household and class structure over time. The methodology also incorporates both quantitative and qualitative sources. The censuses, the parish registers, and the property inventories lend themselves to quantitative analysis. Easily coded for computer manipulation, they can reveal certain statistical characteristics of the community—its size, class structure, economic character, and demographic profile—as these change over time. The statistical analysis of these sources creates the framework for the qualitative analysis of other sources, such as wills, testimonies, and letters, which provide information that helps to explain the patterns found in the quantitative analysis. For more detailed information on sources and methodology, see the Appendix.

The units of analysis for this study are family, class, and community. Family is the most basic unit of analysis. The term is, however, difficult to quantify. In censuses, the "family" appears as a group of individuals living together at the moment of the canvassing, but in a will or an inventory, the "family" refers to a larger group of related kin. For this reason, demographers and family historians distinguish between the household and the larger family.[10] The household refers to the individuals who actually live together at one moment in time, while the family encompasses a wider group of individuals, such as those who have left home, relatives, and biologically unrelated kin. For quantitative analysis, the delineation of households in a census defines at the most basic level what a family is, but the broader sense of the term is also employed. This is especially true in the qualitative analysis.

Here family life has been evaluated within the larger context of social class. Social classes, which gradually emerged during the seventeenth century, eventually differentiated the community and came to create a vast distance among the family lives of the people. Because slaves were the most visible and valuable measure of status and wealth, the ownership of slaves is used in the quantitative analysis to demarcate the boundaries between social classes. Thus, the dividing line between peasant farmers and planters is the ownership of slaves.

The third level of analysis in this study is the community, Santana de Parnaíba. In the early seventeenth century, Parnaíba became a *vila*, a term difficult to translate into English. Literally "town," in actuality it encompassed a large rural area composed of four parishes. In the original settlement, which became the parish of Santana, stood the administrative institutions of the town—the town council (*câmara*) and the mother church (*igreja matriz*). Residents of the community conducted their business here, and for that purpose, the most important families built townhouses. In the seventeenth and eighteenth centuries, the parishes of São Roque and Araçariguama sprang up around large estates. Barueri was the site of an Indian community founded in the early years of the seventeenth century. In the eighteenth century, São Roque and Araçariguama grew steadily. By the nineteenth century, these two parishes had become large enough to be cut away from Parnaíba and become independent *municípios* (municipalities) after Independence. São Roque and Barueri, now both on the railroad line, have become small cities, while Parnaíba and Araçariguama (not on the railroad) have remained sleepy rural towns despite their proximity to the burgeoning city of São Paulo. Today, Santana de Parnaíba refers only to the old parish of Santana and is therefore much smaller than the community studied in this book. Thus, community here does not refer to a closely knit hamlet of a few families but to a rather large rural area that had a common administrative center in the original settlement, the parish of Santana.

When writing a social history based on the experience of a single community, historians and their readers must ask themselves a very important question: How typical is this community? Stated otherwise, how useful is this detailed history for understanding the experiences of larger groups of people? The work of North

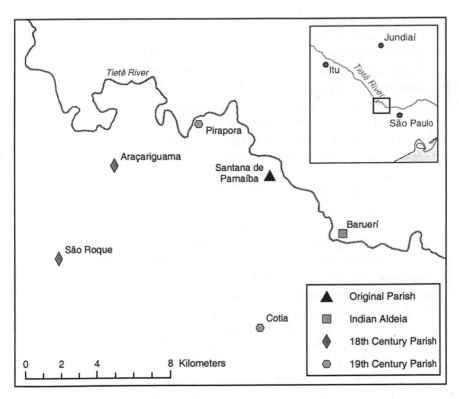

Town of Santana de Parnaíba

American historians on colonial America is especially instructive for answering this question. Beginning in the 1970s, the history of colonial America was revolutionized by the appearance of two community studies on the New England towns of Dedham and Andover.[11] These studies sought to show in concrete detail how the Puritan colonists put into practice their religious ideas; historians Lockridge and Greven turned their attention from what the Puritan religious leaders thought and preached to how the families of Dedham and Andover actually constructed their communities. Lockridge found that Dedham in its early years was a closed corporate community bonded by shared religious beliefs that expressed a utopian ideal. Life in Dedham was better than life in Europe had been: mortality was low, inequality less pronounced, and the farming economy adequate for the sustenance of the community. Later, Lockridge argues, the utopia ideal died in Dedham as the community grew, as land became scarce, and as younger generations lost the religious fervor of the town's founders. The closed agrarian world of the seventeenth century gave way to a more complex, provincial town in the eighteenth century.

Greven also found continuity between England and America in the early history of Andover and a substantial change from the seventeenth to the eighteenth century. In the first two generations, Andover resembled an English village. A strong patriarchal family had taken root, and fathers maintained control over their sons by withholding land from them until late in their lives. Like Lockridge, Greven characterizes these early years as times of stability and order. Compared to England, individuals lived longer and women had more surviving children. In the third and fourth generations, these patterns changed as sons began to challenge their fathers' authority. Many left the community in search of lands elsewhere.

These two studies, with their characterization of the seventeenth century as a time of order, harmony, stability, and prosperity and the eighteenth century as a time of growth, change, lessening community values, and greater individualism, dramatically influenced the work of later historians of colonial America.[12] The transformation of a closed agrarian, relatively harmonious world into an open, commercial, individualistic, and conflict-ridden world seemed to lay an appropriate foundation for the explanation of the American

Revolution at the end of the eighteenth century. But as more historians began to adopt the community study approach of Greven and Lockridge, their results diverged. Stephen Innes's Springfield, Massachusetts, a river town founded in 1636, never resembled the closed, corporate, utopian communities of Andover and Dedham. In his introduction, Innes notes, "few historians have . . . queried whether the experiences of Dedham and Andover really typified early New England. Particularly striking is the willingness to generalize with such confidence from the examples of two subsistence farming communities, especially since . . . [t]he majority of seventeenth-century New Englanders lived either in ocean ports or in major river towns."[13] Innes documents that materialism, not spiritual unity, characterized Springfield, where men were judged more often by their financial worth than by their piety. Artisan crafts, manufacturing, commerce, and agriculture created the base of the economy of the region. Springfield, hardly a utopia, fostered conflict, violence, and social inequality. One family monopolized the resources of the community and dominated its political institutions. And whereas Andover and Dedham became more individualistic and stratified in the eighteenth century, Springfield became less so as the American Revolution approached.

Innes's study of Springfield thus seems to contradict in virtually every way the picture of life in Andover and Dedham painted by Lockridge and Greven, even though the towns in question are all from the same region and indeed the same state, Massachusetts. Which is the more accurate description?

Gradually, what has emerged from this fascinating literature is an awareness of the importance of regions in colonial America. Innes argues that Massachusetts alone had three distinct regions: an urban coastal region with its center at Boston; a surrounding subsistence farming region (in which Andover and Dedham were to be found); and a third area of commercial agriculture in the Connecticut River towns, such as Springfield. Each region, he argues, "had different patterns of social relations, economic opportunity, and political behavior."[14]

If Massachusetts has to be studied in terms of its distinct regions, all the more important is the distance between New England and the communities that emerged in the American South. There the environment, economy, and social institutions such as indentured servitude and African slavery created very different communities. Historians have found that the high mortality rate in seventeenth-century Maryland, due largely to malaria, coupled with the influx of immigrant indentured servants, most of whom were men, created dramatically different patterns of family life. In a society where 70 percent of men would die before the age of fifty and where men outnumbered women by three to one, spinsters married and widows remarried quickly and easily. "Blended" families were formed, composed of stepchildren from previous marriages and new children. Because of the high death rate, thousands of children became orphans and wards of community institutions.[15]

Unlike their northern counterparts, southern communities were not rent with conflict between fathers and sons because the adult lives of fathers and sons rarely overlapped. When fathers did live to see their sons to adulthood, they transferred property and authority to them at a young age.[16] As Lorena Walsh argues, families in New England successfully transferred a patriarchal family structure to their communities, but in the Chesapeake, they could not.[17]

The very different pictures of community life in colonial America has led to much questioning of the genre of community studies. A proponent of the method himself asks, "Collectively do they add up to anything?"[18] This same scholar submits that despite the many different panoramas of life in America that the studies depict, there are some common features. Almost everywhere the fundamental social institution was the nuclear family, which survived by farming. Families tended to form long and lasting ties to their neighbors, with whom they cooperated in order to survive. The pace of life was slow, and the large events of history "crept upon the towns and counties all unawares."[19]

Jack Greene further proposes that it is possible to integrate the findings of diverging community studies to reach a synthesis. In Greene's view, the first settlements in the New World were disorderly because colonists had a hard time adapting their European culture to the American environment. But slowly, as the settlements grew, they became stabler, more orderly, and more complex. By the eighteenth century, elites consciously began to try to replicate British society in their lives and communities. For Greene, the progression of development in colonial America followed the patterns found by historians in the Chesapeake rather than those of New England. Moreover, American societies became more, not less, like Europe over time.[20]

Greene's "developmental model" and the community studies of the Chesapeake are particularly evocative for colonial Brazil. Colonial Brazil held much in common with the U.S. South. The formation of cash-crop agricultural economies based on slave labor and the creation of sharply stratified communities are characteristics shared by both. Like the towns of the Chesapeake, the residents of Santana de Parnaíba did not share a common dream of religious utopia. The study of this town reveals not the genesis of a community united by religious ideals but the birth of a town rent with social inequality.

As has occurred among historians of colonial America, historians of colonial Brazil also question the significance of a single interpretation or model for understanding the past. For decades, the portrayal of Brazil's colonial past has been dominated by the work of one anthropologist, the late Gilberto Freyre. Freyre characterized the colonization of Brazil as a process in which a plantation society typified by miscegenation took root. In this process, it was the family, not the individual, the state, a commercial company, or the church, that played the major role. The family was "the great colonizing factor in Brazil, the productive unit, the capital that cleared the land, founded plantations, purchased slaves, oxen, implements; and in politics it was the social force that set itself up as the most powerful colonial aristocracy in the Americas."[21] For Freyre, colonial society evolved in the *casa grande*, the big plantation house, the seat of the colonial aristocratic family, and in the *senzala*, the slave hut. In the big house, families were large, extended, and patriarchal. The slaves of the huts outnumbered the whites of the big house and transmitted to them much of their African culture. Surrounding the plantation, but dependent on it, lived a racially mixed but marginal population of free men and women. While Freyre recognizes that this model of colonization principally characterized Pernambuco and the Recôncavo of Bahia, he argues that wherever sugar cultivation spread in Brazil, "there grew up a society and a mode of life whose tendencies were those of a slaveholding aristocracy, with a consequent similarity of economic interests."[22] Because sugar cultivation and slavery did dominate Brazil's colonial economy in the sixteenth and seventeenth centuries, and continued to spread during the great gold rush of the eighteenth century, historians have used Freyre's model of colonization to characterize colonial Brazil.[23]

When social historians in Brazil, influenced by the work of European historical demographers, began to study the family, they uncovered startling evidence that Brazilians had not, by and large, lived in the great families described by Freyre. The analysis of censuses for the city of São Paulo in the second half of the eighteenth century and for the city of Vila Rica in Minas Gerais in the early nineteenth century reveal few large extended families. In São Paulo, Elizabeth Kuznesof found that nuclear families predominated and that households were small. Households headed by women became increasingly common as the city grew, accounting for 45 percent of all urban households in 1802.[24] In Vila Rica, Iraci del Nero da Costa found that likewise very few, less than 10 percent, of the households were extended or complex households in 1804. Forty-four percent conformed to what Peter Laslett calls the simple family (a household of one or both parents and children), and a surprisingly high number (39%) of the households were formed of single or widowed individuals living alone or with retainers or slaves.[25] Donald Ramos, analyzing the same census, was struck by the large number of households headed by women.[26] At first glance, this high number of female-headed households appeared to be explained by the fact that they were an urban phenomenon: the cities attracted poor women who survived there as artisans, servants, street sellers, and seamstresses.[27] But on closer analysis, female-headed households were also found in the rural areas.[28] Even in rural Bahia, family historians confirm the existence of female-headed households.[29]

These findings, so incompatible with the traditional image of the Brazilian family, have caused scholars to question seriously Freyre's model of the large, extended, patriarchal family as the Brazilian norm.[30] But while historians are willing to agree that the characteristic family of Brazil was not the extended patriarchal family envisioned by Freyre, not all are willing to give up Freyre's model as a description of elite families. They intimate that while Freyre's family type is inappropriate for the majority of the population, it may well characterize the family life of the upper classes.

Two scholars who do not entirely reject Freyre's portrait of the

family are Linda Lewin and Darrell Levi, who studied two influ
ential families in nineteenth-century Brazil, the Pessoa oligarchy
of northeastern Paraíba and the Prado family of São Paulo.[31] While
neither of these historians argues that Freyre's description of the
family is accurate, nor do they employ the demographic analysis
of households favored by historical demographers, they clearly
illustrate the importance of the elite family's extended and intricate
kin network. Colonial Brazilians may have lived primarily in nuclear families, Lewin and Levi imply, but the larger kin network
deeply affected family life and is key to their social and economic
power. From these two studies, it would appear that such extended kin networks, which are not usually visible in censuses, are
crucial to the understanding of elite families.

Demographic analysis of elite families based on manuscript censuses, however, suggests that Freyre's model must be used with
care, even when applied only to elite families. Ana Silvia Volpi
Scott[32] illustrates that nuclear families predominated among the
elite of São Paulo, accounting for 60 to 75 percent of all elite households between 1779 and 1818. Family size was small: 6.3 members
in the towns of the Paraíba River region and 4.7 members in the
towns of the region of and around the city of São Paulo. Because
Scott bases her analysis on families as they appear in the manuscript censuses, she is unable to establish the kinship ties of
families from her data. But if it were possible to combine a demographic analysis of elite families with family histories like Lewin's
or Levi's, such analysis might reveal that the extended, patriarchal,
elite family proposed by Freyre was not a demographic fact but
rather a description of elite family kinship relations. Further studies on elite families that combine a demographic analysis with a
social and economic inquiry into elite family life will eventually
allow historians to describe accurately the elite family in Brazil.[33]

Before rejecting Freyre's family model, historians must consider
change over time. Elite families may have been more extended and
more complex in the first centuries of colonization—that is, in the
sixteenth and seventeenth centuries—than in the nineteenth century. While the most reliable demographic data exist for the late
eighteenth century and the nineteenth century, historians must
not assume that patterns of elite family life found then characterized the whole of the colonial period.

But what of the family lives of other social groups in colonial and nineteenth-century Brazil? Slowly, historians are fashioning a picture of the urban poor, a group whose demographic history points to very high levels of female-headed households, illegitimacy, and consensual unions.[34] Clearly this population did not live in or even near the large extended families portrayed by Freyre. While historians have come a long way in documenting the demographic contours of this social group, very little is known about the families of the rural poor in the historical past. Maria Luiza Marcílio's path-breaking study of the peasant farmers and fishermen of the coastal village of Ubatuba in São Paulo begins to define the family lives and survival strategies of Brazil's peasantry. As she shows, peasants in their traditional life-style successfully used the labor of family members to support themselves and to interact in local economies; but lacking political power, they proved unable to retain their lands as agriculture commercialized.[35] This pattern, also found in Parnaíba, may well be a common characteristic of the peasantry throughout Brazil.

Spurred by the celebration of the 100th anniversary of the abolition of slavery in Brazil, many new studies on the slave family have been undertaken there. But, given the fact that slavery existed for over three hundred years in Brazil in regions as diverse as that of the sugar-producing northeast, the mining regions of the interior, or the Amazon River, historians are a long way from defining "the slave family." Clearly slave life differed in these distinct areas and changed over time. In the cities, for example, slaves had more independence and autonomy but less stable family lives.[36] In the countryside, slaves had little autonomy, but because many lived on large plantations, they were able to form nuclear and extended families that endured over time.[37]

Thus, the work of many historians on Brazilian families has forced scholars to seriously qualify the universality of Freyre's vision of the Brazilian family in the past. As more and more studies are completed, it will become possible to come to a synthesis of what family life was like in colonial Brazil. This book works toward that goal by studying family life in the context of social class, the larger community, and the frontier.

The study of family life in Santana de Parnaíba reveals that the roots of inequality in this community stem from the way that families interacted with the frontier. Virtually all families of the free population in Parnaíba in the seventeenth and eighteenth centuries depended on the resources of the frontier for their survival. Those families that exploited the frontier for a larger Atlantic economy became part of the planter class and renewed their wealth each generation by continuing the exploitation of the frontier. Those families that depended on the resources of the frontier for the survival of their immediate family became part of an independent but ultimately vulnerable peasantry. Slaves, prevented from sharing in the wealth of the frontier, remained at the bottom of the social ladder. These conclusions suggest profound questions about how family strategies in colonial Brazil have influenced the evolution of a stratified social order in this American frontier society.

Indians, Portuguese, and Mamelucos

The Sixteenth-Century Colonization
of São Vicente

In 1628, the lady widow Suzana Dias lay sick in her bed in her son's house in a tiny hamlet known as Santana de Parnaíba. The village was located on the edge of the Brazilian wilderness, several leagues to the west of the town of São Paulo. Fearing her death, Suzana summoned a scribe to her bedside to record her last will and testament and a priest to perform the last rites. First, she asked the priest to "commend her soul to God our Lord who created her" and prayed that "through the death and suffering and worthiness of his Son our Lord Jesus Christ, that he have mercy on her soul and pardon her sins." She begged for the intercession of the Holy Virgin, the apostles, and all the saints before God so that she might attain the rewards of glory.[1] Suzana declared that she believed in everything that was and is the Holy Mother Church of Rome and that she would die a loyal and true Christian. Then, having taken care of salvation, she turned her attention to her temporal life, to the family she had reared, the property she had accumulated, and the settlement she had founded on the remote edge of the Portuguese empire.

Suzana had married twice and bore seventeen children. She owned Indian slaves who served her and who would serve her heirs after she died, even though as she herself knew, these Indian slaves were legally free according to the laws of the Portuguese empire. A shawl, a skirt, a cloak, and the material for a skirt were important enough to be mentioned in her will as special bequests for her daughters and granddaughters. Suzana asked her two sons to have thirty masses said for her soul "so that God Our Lord might have mercy on her" and stated that she wished to be buried in the chapel of St. Anne that she had founded and around which the settlement had grown. Last, she asked the priest to sign the will for her, as she did not know how to read or write.

This seemingly simple document marks the end and the beginning of the history of Santana de Parnaíba. When Suzana Dias was born, Santana de Parnaíba did not exist. The area was wilderness, as yet unsettled by the Portuguese or by those of Portuguese and Indian descent, known as *mamelucos*. By the time Suzana died, however, the Portuguese had claimed and colonized this area of the wilderness.

Who was Suzana Dias? According to historical and genealogical reconstruction, she was one of the granddaughters of Tibiriçá, the Indian chief of the Piratininga plateau when the Portuguese first landed on the coast of Brazil in 1500.[2] The Piratininga plateau, site of modern São Paulo city, is nearly 800 meters above sea level. It is drained by the Tietê River, which flows west, deep into the interior, to the Paraná River. The climate is mild, with an average temperature of 68.4 degrees Fahrenheit and an average rainfall of 52.2 inches per year.[3] Tibiriçá first met the Portuguese through João Ramalho, a Portuguese sailor or convict who had been shipwrecked or dumped ashore during the early years of the sixteenth century, probably between 1511 and 1513.[4] Although Tibiriçá could not know what his encounter with this Portuguese castaway portended, it was the first step in a long chain of events that would radically transform the world he knew.

In Spain and Portugal, the last years of the fifteenth century and the first years of the sixteenth century were heady times. When Christopher Columbus "discovered" islands in the Caribbean in 1492, Portugal was on the verge of achieving a long-sought sea route to India. In anticipation of this, in the Treaty of Tordesillas of 1494, Spain and Portugal divided the non-Christian world in half, with the east going to Portugal and the west to Spain. Six years after Columbus's attempt to reach India by sailing west, the Portuguese explorer, Vasco da Gama, rounded Cape Horn and sailed into India. In 1500, Cabral set off for India intending to lay the foundation for trade between India and Portugal. Cabral set his course slightly different from that of Vasco da Gama, and blown farther west, he reached Brazil by accident. Unlike Columbus, Cabral had not left Lisbon on a voyage of discovery and did not have any rights to lands that he might discover. The discovery of

Brazil thus held no immediate reward for him. He would not become the viceroy and governor over any lands he discovered, nor would he be known as the "Admiral of the Ocean Sea," privileges promised to Columbus by Ferdinand and Isabella.[5] Instead, this remarkable discovery was treated as an unexpected delay on the more important voyage to India. Far more interested in the opening of trade to India, the Portuguese made no immediate plans to explore or colonize Brazil, although it clearly lay within Portugal's sphere, according to the treaty.

Cabral remained in Brazil only eleven days, but the first Portuguese impressions of Brazil were captured by Pedro Vaz de Caminha, a royal clerk on the expedition bound for Calicut. In a letter written to the king of Portugal, Caminha described a vast new land and people of "good and of pure simplicity." "From point to point," he wrote, "the entire shore is very flat and very beautiful. As for the interior, it appeared to us from the sea very large, for, as far as the eye could reach, we could see only land and forests, a land which seemed very extensive to us."[6] He described the inhabitants of this land as "dark, somewhat reddish, with good faces and good noses, well shaped. They go naked, without any covering; neither do they pay more attention to concealing or exposing their shame than they do to showing their faces."[7] Caminha marveled at the innocence and beauty of the Indians. He wrote, "They are well cared for and very clean, and in this it seems to me that they are rather like birds or wild animals, to which the air gives better feathers and better hair than to tame ones. And their bodies are so clean and so fat and so beautiful that they could not be more so."[8]

Caminha's observation of the Indians convinced him that they had no religious beliefs and that they could be easily "tamed" and "stamped" with "whatever belief we wish to give them."[9] While Caminha saw the possibility of using the new land for agriculture, he thought the evangelization of these people would, in and of itself, be a noble achievement for the king of Portugal to undertake, even if the new land proved to be not much more than a stopping place on the way to India.

Caminha finished his letter on May 1, 1500, the night before the fleet set sail for India. That day, two sailors stole a boat and deserted from Cabral's command, disappearing somewhere along the coast. In addition to these, Cabral left behind two prisoners to learn the Indian language to facilitate further encounters with the Indians, should there be any. Then without further ado, Cabral weighed anchor and headed east for Africa and India. Caminha's letter, along with the parrots, bows, arrows, headdresses, and the like, collected from the new land, were sent directly back to Portugal on one of the ships of the fleet. Perhaps no one who witnessed this simple eleven-day visit realized how dramatically it would change the future of the land the Portuguese now called "Santa Cruz."

At the moment when Spain and Portugal first made contact with the vast New World, each country had very different ideas about how to proceed with colonization. The Spanish had completed the work of centuries, known as the reconquest, when they defeated the Moors of Granada in 1492. The marriage of Ferdinand of Aragón and Isabella of Castile began the process of the unification of Spain. The religious zeal with which the Spaniards conquered the Moors and allotted their lands to military commanders overflowed into the New World. Spain embarked on a similar quest to spread Christianity, to make vassals of the Indians, to reward the conquerors who delivered this new empire, and to strengthen the power of the crown.[10]

Portugal was a trading nation that for decades in the fifteenth century had pioneered the navigation of the southern Atlantic and the charting of the African coast in pursuit of a sea route to India. The Portuguese sought to enter the profitable spice trade from the Orient, a trade completely controlled by Arab traders across land routes through the Middle East. In 1498, they succeeded in establishing the long awaited sea route, and thus for the first time, Europeans had direct access to the spice trade.[11] Cabral's discovery of Brazil, therefore, was treated differently in Portugal than Columbus's discovery was treated in Spain. Portugal saw the value of trade with the newly discovered natives of Brazil, not colonization. For this reason, Portugal made no immediate plans to colonize Brazil.

For thirty years after the discovery of Brazil, from 1500 to 1530, the Portuguese saw Brazil as simply another entrepôt, similar to the many trading posts along the coast of Africa where Portuguese ships stopped on the way to and from India to trade for slaves. At the few coastal trading posts in Brazil, the Portuguese traded with local Indian tribes for the *pau brasil*, or brazilwood, a tree trunk much in demand in Europe because of the deep red color that could be extracted from it and used to dye cloth. Each of the trading posts had a factor and a small garrison of soldiers to protect it. The factor conducted trade with the Indians, bartering iron tools, combs, mirrors, beads, and the like, for brazilwood. The Indians cut, carried, and stacked the logs at the trading post so that cargoes would be ready for ships to load when they put into port.

The Portuguese were not the only ones to trade in Brazil. The French were also active in the brazilwood trade, arguing that since Portugal had not colonized Brazil, she could not prevent others from trading with the Indians. Thus, while Portugal claimed Brazil by virtue of Cabral's discovery, she exercised virtually no sovereignty over it.

During these early years of the sixteenth century, only a handful of Europeans, like João Ramalho, lived in Brazil. Convicts left ashore by sea captains, shipwrecked sailors, and the factors who manned the small trading posts were the only Portuguese there.[12] Many went "native" to survive. Such was the case of Ramalho.

Men like Ramalho adapted to a radically different world than they had known in Europe. The huge area of Brazil, covered largely by forests, was sparsely inhabited by hundreds of Indian tribes. While it is difficult to estimate the size of the Indian population of Brazil in 1500, John Hemming presents a reasoned estimate of 2.4 million.[13] These tribes belonged to four major language groups: the Tupi, the Gê, the Carib, and the Arawak. The Tupi lived primarily along the Atlantic seaboard, the Gê lived in the central plateau, the Arawaks inhabited the upper Amazon, and the Caribs lived in the lands to the north of the lower Amazon River delta. Despite differences among these major groups, the Indians of Brazil shared some common lifeways. They lived in independent tribes composed of several villages ruled by councils of elders, chiefs, and shamans. They fed themselves by hunting, fishing, gathering fruits and other edibles, and simple agriculture. In small clearings made by cutting trees and burning the brush, they planted the basic staples of their diet: corn, manioc, pumpkins, beans, squashes, and peanuts. A clear division of labor separated men and women: the men hunted, fished, and fought, while the women farmed, prepared the food, and cared for the children. The tribes moved their villages frequently to take advantage of new hunting grounds and new land for farming. Possessions were few, easily packed, and carried on tribal migrations. Compared to the large and complex Indian civilizations of central Mexico and Peru, the Indian tribes of Brazil were mobile, autonomous, and egalitarian.[14]

Among all tribes, but especially among the Tupi, warfare was a common occurrence and an unquestioned part of tribal life. Competition over hunting grounds often sparked intertribal wars. Among the Tupi, intertribal feuds caused a virtual state of war between hostile tribes, such as that between the Tupiniquin and the Tupinambá. These wars often began over the need to avenge the honor of the tribe because of atrocities committed against them in the last war. Usually these insults centered on the practice of ritual cannibalism, committed with prisoners of war. In an elaborate ceremony, prisoners were killed and their flesh "tasted" by the tribe. In return, the tribe of the prisoner would retaliate by performing a similar ceremony with a prisoner from the guilty tribe. This created an unending cycle of warfare between the Tupi Indians.[15]

Because few Portuguese lived in Brazil during the thirty years following Cabral's discovery, the vast majority of the Brazilian Indians had little contact with the Portuguese. Those who did either assimilated individual men or had limited, intermittent contact with the traders. On the Piratininga plateau, Ramalho became a part of the extended family of Tibiriçá. He married one of the chief's daughters and became a respected and powerful member of the tribe. Since the Portuguese did not establish a trading post near Piratininga, Tibiriçá's people did not go to work for the Portuguese cutting brazilwood.

This isolation changed in 1530 when, concerned over the increasing interest in Brazil by French traders, the Portuguese king directed Martim Afonso de Sousa to establish Brazil's first colony. Martim Afonso's expedition, charged with patrolling the coast of Brazil and exploring the southern coast in addition to founding a colony, left Portugal toward the end of 1530. Royal officials, soldiers, priests, gentlemen, mechanics, laborers, settlers (some with their wives), and sailors made up the expedition, which numbered about 400 persons and four ships. Martim Afonso sailed along the coast of Brazil attacking French ships before heading south to establish a colony. He selected an island at a latitude of 24°30" and there ordered his men to erect a fort and construct the rudimentary beginnings of Brazil's first colony, São Vicente. Leaving behind the colonists, Martim Afonso continued on with his soldiers to reconnoiter the southern coast of Brazil, particularly the Rio de la Plata. On his return, Martim Afonso distributed the first land grants to the colonists. Later he imported sugarcane and built the first sugar mill. The colony quickly spread from the island onto the narrow shelf of land, covered with a dense tropical forest, between the steep mountains and the Atlantic Ocean.[16]

Martim Afonso envisioned a colony dedicated to the production of sugar, similar to the Portuguese colony of Madeira, and to the extraction of precious minerals, should any be found. Thus, he built São Vicente on the coast so that it would remain closely linked by sea to Portugal. Above the colony, on the Piratininga plateau, lived Tibiriçá's tribe of Tupiniquin Indians, known as the Guaianá. They lived in several villages near the present-day city of São Paulo. The Indians preferred the plateau, which had a cooler and drier climate than the coast, and only descended to the sea at certain times of the year to fish and hunt. Hence, as long as the Portuguese remained on the coast and allowed the Indians to fish, the relations between the colonists and the Guaianá progressed smoothly, aided by the intercession of Ramalho. Greatly outnumbered by Indians and isolated from Portugal, the colony was extremely vulnerable to Indian attack. Ramalho persuaded his father-in-law, Tibiriçá, to protect the fledgling Portuguese colony. Indeed, Tibiriçá allowed himself to be baptized, adopting the name Martim Afonso Tibiriçá to emulate the colony's leader, and married several of his daughters to Portuguese men. One of his daughters took the name Beatriz at baptism and married a Portuguese man, Lopo Dias. These were the parents of Suzana Dias.[17] The good relations between Portuguese and Indians in São Vicente played a major role in the early success of this colony. Uninterested in the interior and determined to make the sugar economy work, Martim Afonso prohibited his colonists from visiting the plateau without his permission.[18] To Ramalho, he gave the monopoly of supplying the colony with Indian slaves from the plateau.[19]

Very soon after Martim Afonso founded São Vicente, the crown of Portugal decided to pursue further colonization in Brazil. The crown wanted to reinforce its claim to Brazil, but it did not wish to expend the funds necessary to establish royal colonies. Thus, between 1533 and 1535, regardless of the nearly two and a half million Indians who lived in Brazil, the Portuguese crown divided Brazil into fourteen horizontal strips and granted each to an individual to colonize at his own expense. Each of the recipients of these grants (*donatários*) had extensive legal powers. Each could appoint officials, administer justice, create towns, license mills, and grant land to colonists. Each received extensive tracts of land for himself, and each received the right to collect rents from his colonists. These grants were hereditary and followed the principle of primogeniture, passing intact from father to oldest son. The crown expected the holders of these grants to raise the capital to colonize the region and that in time, such colonization schemes would generate handsome incomes for the holders and their heirs.[20] Martim Afonso received the grant of the colony he had founded, São Vicente. Although he spent little time there himself, the colony survived under the stewardship of his wife and lieutenants.

Of the fourteen donatários, only ten were actually colonized, and of these, only two, São Vicente and Pernambuco, met with any immediate success. All of the settlements faced many obstacles. Poor leadership, the difficulty of attracting settlers, the lack of capital, and wars with neighboring Indian tribes doomed many of the early colonies. The economies of these early settlements rested on the cutting of brazilwood and early attempts to establish sugar plantations. Labor was a perennial problem. Most of the brazilwood trade continued to be conducted through barter with the Indians. As the coastal stands of brazilwood were cut, however, it became progressively harder for the Indians to cut and carry the wood from the forests of the interior. Barter with the Indians broke down when the Indians no longer needed or desired Portuguese trading goods or when they resented the ceaseless demands placed on them. The labor problem was even more acute on the sugar plantations and sugar mills that needed a reliable work force. Increasingly, the Portuguese began to enslave Indians, especially for work on the sugar plantations. Indians who were captured by other tribes in tribal wars and exchanged for goods with Portuguese traders became the slaves of the Portuguese, and any Indians captured by the Portuguese in wars between the Portuguese and Indians also became slaves.[21] As Indian slavery emerged as the solution to the colonists' labor problems, conflicts between the colonists and Indians intensified.[22]

In São Vicente, one of the two successful donatários, sugar plantations expanded along the coast. By 1548, the colony had six sugar mills, 600 Christian "souls," and 3,000 slaves.[23] The majority of these slaves were Indians from the plateau captured and sold by Ramalho and his allies to the Portuguese.[24] Yet Martim Afonso's dream of creating a Brazilian Madeira proved illusive. The Portuguese settlers were increasingly drawn to the plateau, the source of Indian labor. In 1544, when Martim Afonso was in Portugal, his wife formally revoked his order against visiting the plateau without permission.[25] As more and more colonists went there, the Portuguese began to alter the economic focus of the colony. The Portuguese settlers became enamored with the temperate climate inland and began to establish wheat and cattle estates. Thus, while sugar continued to be produced in São Vicente, it did not remain the central driving force of the economy of this southernmost colony.

The failure of most of the donatários in Brazil caused the crown to rethink its colonization policy. By the middle of the sixteenth century, it realized that private initiative alone could not colonize Brazil. Thus, in 1549, the crown appointed the first royal governor of Brazil, Tomé de Sousa. The new governor's primary task was to aid the faltering colonies by giving them military assistance. In addition, he was to increase the crown's revenues and to build the colony's capital, Salvador da Bahia. With Tomé de Sousa came the first Jesuits, the order chosen by the king of Portugal to evangelize and pacify the Indians.

During the second half of the sixteenth century, the quickening pace of Portuguese colonization began to devastate the traditional lifeways of the Indians. All of the Portuguese had plans for the Indians of Brazil. The Jesuits hoped not only to convert the Indians to Christianity but to replace their traditional life-style with one more in keeping with European notions of religious, family, and community life. The Jesuits established *aldeias*, or Indian missions, where they moved Indian tribes to facilitate their conversion. There they taught the Indians new cultural values and new forms of subsistence and introduced them to new social institutions. The congregation of Indians into these villages, their conversion to Christianity, and their exposure to a new life-style all began to unravel the fabric of Indian tribal society in the areas of Portuguese colonization.[26]

The Portuguese colonists saw the Indians as the solution to their labor problem. Slavery and forced labor on their sugar plantations destroyed Indian tribal society even more rapidly than the Jesuit missions. Indian slavery was considered legal by the Portuguese crown if the Indians were captured in "Just Wars" or if they practiced cannibalism.[27] These restrictions, liberally interpreted by the colonists, led to numerous slaving expeditions into the interior.

All Europeans unknowingly brought with them diseases to which the Indians had no natural immunity. The great epidemics that decimated Indians elsewhere in the Americas also ravaged the Indians of Brazil. Beginning in the 1550s, influenza, dysentery, smallpox, and plague swept through the Indian villages, killing many. Indians who lived among the Portuguese, as well as those in the forest, contracted the diseases and died in great numbers. Famine followed on the heels of disease, further weakening the survivors.[28]

These changes in the first half of the sixteenth century forever altered the history of the indigenous peoples of Brazil and paved the way for Portuguese colonization. As Indian society disintegrated following contact with the Portuguese, Portuguese society took root. While the Portuguese saw this transformation as unbearably slow, Indian groups had virtually no time to adapt to or to prevent these changes that would eventually destroy their way of life.

In São Vicente, moreover, it is clear that the characteristics of this very early stage of colonization set the stage for the future development of the region. How the Jesuits, the Portuguese colonists, and the growing group of mamelucos survived in São Vicente in the sixteenth century influenced the behavior of subsequent generations who carried those survival techniques deeper into the interior. Patterns visible in the sixteenth century on the coast could be found deeper in the interior one hundred years later. The colonization of São Vicente was a repeating cycle of events that gradually rolled west. The key aspects of this colonization cycle were first enacted on the plateau in the middle of the sixteenth century.

The Jesuits played a major role in the early colonization of São Vicente. In 1553, Father Manuel da Nóbrega, leader of the Jesuits in Brazil, arrived in São Vicente. At that time, seven Jesuit brothers had built a church and a house on the coast near the settlement founded by Martim Afonso de Sousa. They had begun to teach a community of between fifty and sixty Indian children.[29] Nóbrega reported great initial success with "the Indians of this land," the "sons and daughters of Christians, mamelucos, of whom there are many, and slaves." He wrote of their "great fervor" at confession when many came "crying" and "in great pain." Moreover, he observed that the Indian catechumens "know the doctrines better than many Old Christians" and "discipline themselves with such great fervor that it creates confusion among the whites."[30] In the school, the Jesuits taught the boys to read and write, to sing, and to play the flute. The more able studied grammar. Some boys learned trades. But life was difficult for the Jesuits, who lived off the alms given to them by the Indians.

Despite the fact that the Jesuits had little income with which to care for the children (most were still naked, as the mission was too poor to clothe them), Nóbrega envisioned a great future in São Vicente. He saw that from São Vicente the Jesuits could spread up onto the plateau and from there into the interior, where they could bring the Indians salvation. The Jesuits had heard of the Guaraní Indian civilization located beyond São Vicente, toward the Spanish settlements of Paraguay. There the Jesuits hoped to establish missions. For Nóbrega, São Vicente would be the great base for the Jesuit evangelization of Brazil.

To this end, Nóbrega wished to establish a Jesuit mission above the small coastal settlement on the plateau of Piratininga. The Jesuits created their plateau mission, which they called São Paulo, with the help of Tibiriçá, in 1553. As on the coast, they opened a school for the children and traveled into the wilderness to preach to Indian tribes.

Uplifted and yet weighted with the responsibility for saving the Indians, the Jesuits alternated between hope and despair. Invariably optimistic after surviving the terrifying sea voyage to arrive at São Vicente, and the dangerous ascent up the steep escarpment to Piratininga, the new brothers delighted in the plateau. José de Anchieta described it as "a healthy land where men lived to be old and robust,"[31] while Balthezar Fernandes wrote in 1556 that "it is land like that of the Kingdom [Portugal], cold and temperate" and that "this land is like the best that there is in the Kingdom and it produces everything which can be produced there."[32] Yet, Nóbrega, discouraged, reflected, "We are in a land so poor and miserable that nothing can be gotten from it, because it is the people who are so poor, and poor as we are, we are richer than they. . . . Here there is neither wheat, nor wine, nor vinegar, nor meat (except by a miracle); that which there is in the land is fish and the food from roots, and as much as we have, we are still poor."[33]

Driven by a faith and a responsibility that few understood, the Jesuits clearly suffered in their work. José de Anchieta described the travail of missionary work among the Indians as the Jesuits "harvested many souls in Brazil for Christ."[34]

> In the Captaincy of São Vicente it is sometimes so cold that we find Indians frozen along the trails. One cannot sleep in the forest because of the intense cold. Without shoes or socks and with no fire, our legs are frequently frostbitten. Continuous and heavy rains flood the rivers, and many times we wade up to our waists or chests through stretches of very cold water. After an entire day in the rain and rivers, we spend most of the night drying our garments by a fire, since we have no change of clothing.[35]

While the Jesuits had one idea for the way Brazil should be "harvested," the Portuguese settlers in São Vicente had another. Many identified with the mameluco culture—a blend of Portuguese and Indian ways. A growing number of mamelucos and Portuguese settlers lived on the plateau by the 1550s. In the small village of Santo André lived Ramalho, his mameluco kin, and a few Portuguese settlers. Far from seeing Ramalho as an ally, as Martim Afonso de Sousa had in 1530, Nóbrega felt him to be an obstacle to the Jesuit vision for Brazil. He wrote of Ramalho in 1553:

> In this land there is a João Ramalho. He has been here many years and his life-style and that of his children is Indian and is a *petra scandali* for us, because his life is a great hindrance for the Indians we have; he is well known and well connected by kinship to the Indians. He has many women. He and his sons have relations with sisters and have children by them. . . . They go to war with the In-

dians and their festivals are those of the Indians and they live naked as the Indians.[36]

Ramalho had become powerful on the plateau not only because of his ties to the Indians but because Portuguese officials recognized his power. The royal governor of Brazil in 1553, Tomé de Sousa, ordered Portuguese settlers on the plateau to live in Ramalho's town of Santo André and made Ramalho their captain.[37] Twenty years before, Martim Afonso also acknowledged his authority on the plateau and had given to Ramalho the monopoly of supplying slaves to the Portuguese settlers on the coast. Ramalho's years of slave trading, which consisted of selling Indians captured in traditional tribal wars as well as out and out slave raiding, provided the Portuguese settlers and their mameluco descendants with laborers for their fields and servants for their homes. Mamelucos followed Ramalho's example and became slave traders. They excelled at Indian slaving because they could negotiate both the Indian and the Portuguese worlds. The increasing scope of the Indian slave trade reverberated throughout the interior of São Vicente and destabilized Indian intertribal relations.

The Indians of the plateau found themselves caught between many worlds—their traditional society, the strict religious ways of the Jesuits, and the mameluco culture. Some Indians and many mamelucos passed back and forth between the Indian and Portuguese cultures. Nóbrega wrote of Indian boys who studied with the Jesuits but who, when adults, returned to the Indian ways of their parents. Then, he reflected, having returned to nudity, the Indians were too ashamed to go to church. Nóbrega understood that although they once wore clothes, they had no means of making the clothes they needed to be respectable in Christian society.[38] Anchieta lamented that "of our old pupils with whom we worked with so much toil and pains we have no news. Dispersed in various localities where they cannot be taught, they soon lapse into the ways of their fathers."[39] He remarked approvingly, "Our Savior, however, has punished many with sickness and death."[40]

While the Indians attempted to understand what was happening to their world and culture, the first plagues broke out in São Vicente. In 1554, Jesuit Pero Correia wrote that among the Indian converts, "death struck three chiefs and many other Indians" and that "almost every day we lost some."[41] Others described the fever: "it struck with such violence that as soon as it appeared it laid them low, unconscious, and within three or four days it carried them to the grave."[42]

In 1562, another epidemic erupted, this time, smallpox. Not understanding the disease, Anchieta bled the feverish victims, cut away their rotting flesh, and attempted to nurse them back to health. He described the disease as a "malignant type, frightful, covering the entire body from head to foot with a leprous eruption similar to sharkskin."[43] But the Indians, possessing no immunities, frequently died.[44]

Between the epidemics that swept across the plains hung the threat of annihilation from war. The small Jesuit settlement at São Paulo, the surrounding Indian villages, and Ramalho's village of Santo André were all vulnerable to attack by hostile Indians. These included the traditional enemies of the Tupiniquin as well as disaffected Indians who resented the colonists and the Jesuits. In 1561, these two groups attacked São Paulo. One of the leaders of the rebellion, Jagoanharo, or "Fierce Dog," was Tibiriçá's own nephew and a former pupil of the Jesuits. Fed up with plagues and Indian slaving, he led many Indians in revolt. The rebels were joined by the Tamoio, a federation of Tupinambá tribes allied with the French along the coast of Rio de Janeiro. The Tamoio were traditional enemies of the Tupiniquin Indians of the Piratininga plateau. The siege of São Paulo very nearly succeeded. But Tibiriçá, loyal to the Jesuits, fought off the attack and saved the settlement.[45]

The conflict between these traditional Indian enemies had become entangled with the larger imperial rivalry between Portugal and France over Brazil. France had established a small colony on an island in the Guanabara Bay in 1555. Both the governor of Brazil, Mem de Sá, and the Jesuits wanted the French out—Mem de Sá because the presence of the French challenged Portuguese hegemony and the Jesuits because the colony included Protestants whom the Jesuits viewed as capable of spreading heresy among the Indians. While Mem de Sá and the Jesuits dislodged the French from their colony in 1560, the hostilities between the Tamoio and the Portuguese continued. Numerous expeditions harassed the Tamoio until they were virtually extinct by the end of the sixteenth century.[46]

After the rebellion, the Portuguese and mameluco settlers of the plateau moved from the village of Santo André to a new site alongside the Jesuit college, creating the town of São Paulo. The old chief, Tibiriçá, died from an outbreak of dysentery in 1562. Ramalho, his son-in-law, now accepted by the Jesuits, took over the chief's role of defending the Portuguese settlement of São Paulo. The town grew to become a small walled settlement of 120 households inhabited by Portuguese, mamelucos, and a multitude of Indian slaves. The Jesuit mission consisted of five or six brothers and their Indian catechumens. Surrounding the town lay a sweep of fields that produced wheat, corn, olives, wine, and fruits. Cattle, horses, and pigs grazed freely on the open plains.[47]

Outside of São Paulo, the Jesuits had established a ring of satellite Indian villages such as Pinheiros, São Miguel, M'Boi, and Guarulhos. In these aldeias, the Indians lived a regimented life of work and catechism punctuated by the ringing of the mission's bell. At dawn, the bells summoned the girls for religious teaching, after which they spun and wove cloth so that the Indians could have clothes to wear. Then the Jesuits taught the boys their lessons, after which they were dispatched to hunt and fish. The adults worked in the fields during the day, but before sunset, a bell rang for them to come have their religious instruction.[48]

Beyond São Paulo, its surrounding fields, and the ring of Jesuit aldeias lay the wilderness. There, deep in the interior of Brazil, Indian tribal society remained intact.

By the end of the sixteenth century, the Portuguese had forever altered the coasts and plains of São Vicente. Portuguese institutions and mameluco lifeways had taken root and had choked out the original indigenous ways. The mameluco culture freely borrowed from the Portuguese and the Indian. It was a frontier culture, created by the need to survive in a world only recently linked to Portugal. While the independent and self-sufficient tribes of the plateau no longer lived as they had in 1500, many of the Indian lifeways continued on the plateau. The mamelucos spoke Tupi, ate a predominantly Indian diet, and adopted only the outward manifestations of Christianity.

In between the world of the interior, where Indian tribal society remained intact, and the established Portuguese colonies of the coast lay a buffer zone—a frontier—where colonization was still in progress. There Jesuits, mamelucos, and Portuguese colonists met new Indian tribes and set into motion once again the events that had already transpired in the settled coastal areas. The conquest and colonization of Brazil thus occurred in cycles as each new frontier became part of Portugal's colonial empire.

The colonies created by the Portuguese in Brazil varied from region to region. In northeastern Brazil, the settlements of Bahia and Pernambuco began to flourish by the 1570s. The growing and milling of sugarcane drove these areas. The first sugar plantations used Indian slaves, but as disease, mistreatment, and overwork decimated Indian tribes, the Portuguese planters turned to Africa as a source of labor.[49] By the end of the sixteenth century, the African slave trade, controlled and developed by the Portuguese, supplied the sugar regions with a steady stream of laborers. In the middle of the 1580s, approximately one-third of Pernambuco's slaves were African.[50] Africans held the skilled positions in the sugar mills, replacing Indians as the sugar masters, purgers, blacksmiths, kettlemen, and craters.[51] The transition to African slavery gave the Indians a respite. Indians lived in Jesuit aldeias and grew food crops for the Portuguese towns. They became a free peasantry.[52]

The climate, the availability of labor from Africa, and the demand for sugar in Europe all caused the sugar economy to flourish in the northeast. By 1570, Brazil had 20,000 Portuguese or white inhabitants and sixty sugar mills. Most of the mills (41) and the majority of the population (60%) could be found in the captaincies of Pernambuco and Bahia.[53] The sugar economy brought a prosperity to the northeast unknown in São Vicente. In 1593, whites in Pernambuco earned on the average 9,660 reis, while in São Vicente they earned only 2,770 reis.[54] Pernambuco produced a gross product of 116,000,000 reis in 1593, all subject to the royal tithe, while São Vicente produced only 5,000,000 reis.[55] São Vicente had the distinction of being Brazil's first permanent settlement, but it was not a wealthy one.

By the end of the sixteenth century, the Portuguese colonization of the northeast rested on a plantation model—that is, the exploitation of land and labor to produce sugar for sale in European markets. In other areas, however, this plantation society developed more slowly or never fully took root. São Vicente is one such region.

Several factors set São Vicente apart from the northeast of Brazil. High on a temperate plateau, the major settlements of São Vicente were cut off from the Atlantic by a very steep coastal range that could be virtually impassable. Since the inland town of São Paulo lacked easy access to the sea, it made the transport of sugar to Portugal difficult. As a result, the economy there became more self-sufficient. Lacking the capital to buy slaves from Africa, the Portuguese and mameluco settlers of the plateau continued to enslave Indians from the interior and put them to work on their agricultural estates. In São Vicente, unlike Bahia and Pernambuco, the free Indians of the plateau remained the allies of the Jesuits, the colonists, and the mamelucos. Their cultural contribution, therefore, was far greater to the society forming in São Vicente than it was in the northeast.

The family of Manoel Fernandes Ramos, a Portuguese immigrant, and Suzana Dias, one of Tibiriçá's granddaughters, suggests how families lived on the plateau in the late sixteenth century. The couple married in 1570 and lived in São Paulo, where Suzana bore seventeen children. Manoel, being Portuguese and therefore fluent in that language and familiar with Portuguese civil institutions, held several positions in São Paulo's municipal government.[56] In 1580, Manoel left São Paulo and followed the Tietê River downstream some seven leagues west (about 40 kilometers). There he reached a waterfall known to the Indians as "paranaiba."[57] Presumably, he was looking for land to claim and farm, for he petitioned the governor of São Vicente for the hilly lands around the river. Manoel died several years later, but this area, which his wife later received in a royal land grant, became the nucleus of a new settlement, Santana de Parnaíba.[58]

The basic contours of this family suggest some of the survival strategies used by the people of São Paulo in the late sixteenth century. Manoel married a mameluca, Suzana. Since the plateau was not suited for sugar production, he did not seek to establish a sugar plantation as his compatriots did in Pernambuco and Bahia. Rather, he wanted virgin forest lands on which to begin a farm worked by his Indian slaves. He set off into the interior to find suitable lands. He thus entered the buffer zone between the unknown Brazilian wilderness and the known Portuguese town of

São Paulo. He began again the process of colonization that would bring a new area into the Portuguese colonial world.

It is unclear exactly when the family developed the lands, but in 1597, discoveries of gold were made outside of São Paulo, some of them in a place called Vuturuna in Parnaíba.[59] Certainly by 1597, then, the area was well known in the town of São Paulo. Mining claims were soon staked out and a settlement of sorts must have begun. Suzana Dias and her son constructed a small chapel, dedicated to St. Anne, near the waterfalls called "paranaiba." Thus, the settlement became known as Santa Anna de Paranaiba, which over the years became Santa Anna de Parnaíba, Sant'anna de Parnhyba, and today, Santana de Parnaíba. Despite high hopes for gold mining, the alluvial deposits never yielded much. But the area grew as an agricultural site, using the Indians living in the nearby aldeia of Baruerí, which was founded in the early seventeenth century and had a population of 500 or 600 Guaraní Indians by 1612.[60] In 1625, the settlement of Santana de Parnaíba was large enough to be raised to a town, which gave the settlers the right to create their own town council to take charge of local government.[61]

Three years later, in 1628, Suzana Dias wrote her will. From her will we realize how far Portuguese colonization had progressed during the sixteenth century. Suzana, a devout Christian, identified with Portuguese society, despite her Indian mother and her own mameluco ethnicity. From her will we know that she wore clothes, that she lived in a house, that she confessed to a priest, that she married in a Christian ceremony. We may surmise from the names of her children that they were baptized by a priest and from Suzana's discussion of her daughters' marriage dowries that they married according to Christian doctrine. Cognizant of her responsibility as a Christian woman in the wilderness of Brazil, she founded a chapel. But in other aspects of her life, she may have retained Indian customs. She undoubtedly spoke Tupi, the common language of the plateau. Possibly she slept in a hammock, for although her will begins with the phrase "sick in bed," beds were scarce and valuable.[62] Most probably, her diet followed Indian rather than Portuguese traditions. Into her Catholicism, too, probably crept vestiges of her mother's tribal beliefs and superstitions.

Thus, Suzana Dias, like her uncle, João Ramalho, straddled the

Portuguese and Indian worlds. Carrying this dual heritage, she, with her Portuguese husband, made her way into the Brazilian wilderness. In so doing, she began the colonization of the region to the west of São Paulo.

While historians usually hold up Pernambuco and Bahia as the classic examples of the Portuguese method of colonization in the New World, it is important to remember that not all of Brazil can be understood through their experience. As the most important and richest centers of Portuguese colonization, Pernambuco and Bahia dominated the attention of the crown. Yet, compared to the vastness of the colony, these two captaincies were, in a sense, islands surrounded by a much less developed, more frontierlike colony. Colonization in other regions of Brazil, like São Vicente, took different forms. Colonization outside the zones of plantation agriculture depended on a fluid interaction between the settlement and the wilderness. Families compensated for their inability to create sugar plantations by exploiting a vast frontier. These actions, in turn, encouraged the settlement of the west in the seventeenth, eighteenth, and nineteenth centuries.

Fifty years after Martim Afonso founded Brazil's first European colony, Manoel Fernandes Ramos and Suzana Dias brought the area that would become Santana de Parnaíba into the orbit of the Portuguese colonial world. At that time, the small settlement lay on the edge of the wilderness. Over the next two hundred years, as the town grew, the descendants of Manoel and Suzana would, like their parents, grandparents, and great-grandparents, move farther and farther west. The experience of Santana de Parnaíba provides important clues about how that frontier was settled. Let us look more closely, then, at the role of a frontier town in the conquest of the Brazilian wilderness.

2

Town, Kingdom, and Wilderness

From the earliest days of colonization, the Portuguese and mameluco colonists of Santana de Parnaíba lived in three worlds: the town, the kingdom, and the wilderness. Each affected families in profound ways. How families interacted in these areas largely defined their future wealth and social position. Moreover, the way that some families in Parnaíba dominated all three worlds in the seventeenth and eighteenth centuries explains how social classes emerged and perpetuated themselves in the town.

Everyone in Santana de Parnaíba belonged to the vila, or "town," a legally established community within the Portuguese American empire.[1] The culture created in the vila drew from both old and new world traditions. The laws of Portugal, European Catholicism, and Iberian municipal institutions each shaped the town, just as the Indian diet, language, and farming methods became part of daily life. Santana de Parnaíba boasted all the outer trappings of a Portuguese town: it had its mother church (igreja matriz), a town council (câmara), a militia (ordenança), common lands (rossio), and the officials who represented Portuguese society—priests, aldermen, militia captains, and notaries. Yet, placed as it was in colonial Brazil, a town such as Parnaíba contained many attributes of the wilderness, such as uncut forests and a large population of Indians. In many ways, the town became the synthesis between the kingdom and the wilderness: for in the town, a hybrid; mameluco culture formed in the seventeenth century. A Brazilian town did not completely replicate a Portuguese town but merely certain of its institutions. It became a new and different world.

The word reino, "kingdom," when used in colonial Brazil referred to Portugal.[2] From Portugal came the impetus for colonization, the policies that structured the colonial empire, and the

43

dominant cultural values. The kingdom represented the home base of Portuguese civilization—the place where authority in matters spiritual and temporal lay. It was the source of political power, the laws that governed the colony, religious institutions, and the traditions that shaped family and community life.

Not everyone in the town understood the meaning and significance of the kingdom. Only a handful of Parnaíba's residents ever visited Portugal. But for a small minority who comprehended the relationship of the town to the kingdom, the reino provided a source of power. Those who upheld the sovereignty of the kingdom over the town and those who marketed Parnaíba's agricultural products for the kingdom recognized that their ties to the kingdom increased their authority and status in the town.

The word *sertão* designated the frontier, the unknown, the vast wilderness.[3] On maps, sertão specified the interior of Brazil, the territories under Indian control, and the virgin forest that might still exist around and between Portuguese settlements. If the reino represented one pole on a continuum that extended from the Old World to the New World, the sertão epitomized the opposite—America in its natural state. Tall rugged forests, only sparsely inhabited by Indian tribes, covered most of the wilderness. Rivers that rose in the mountain ranges, meandered through the forests, and eventually emptied into the Atlantic Ocean provided the only reliable entrances to the wilderness. Virtually everyone in Parnaíba in the seventeenth and eighteenth centuries had firsthand experience with the wilderness. For Indians, the wilderness was a familiar world. Mamelucos easily moved between the wilderness and the town. But to a newly arrived man from Portugal, the wilderness appeared incomprehensible. To the Portuguese, the wilderness begged to be colonized, exploited, and transformed.

For 250 years, the history of the town of Santana de Parnaíba unfolded in relation to the ebb and flow of the competing influences of kingdom and wilderness. In the sixteenth century, the wilderness to the west of the town of São Paulo included what would later become Santana de Parnaíba. As the town grew in the seventeenth century, the values of the kingdom took root. By the eighteenth century, Parnaíba had lost its frontier identity, and more and more of its families emulated Portuguese attitudes and traits. After independence in 1822, Parnaíba came to resemble a small Portuguese town populated largely by peasant farmers who produced for the nearby city of São Paulo. But although a very gradual evolution from the characteristics of the "wilderness" to those of the "kingdom" took place in the town of Santana de Parnaíba, it was not a complete progression. Parnaíba never perfectly replicated a Portuguese town, because it did not share the same historical past. Rather, colonists successfully transplanted certain Portuguese cultural institutions into this (and many other) Brazilian towns.

In 1625, Santana de Parnaíba formally became a town. A small town center began to take shape along the banks of the Tietê River. On the steeply sloping central square, Indian laborers began to build the mother church in the 1640s. Using large blocks of pressed earth, they constructed a simple one-story sanctuary. Along one side, a tower went up which later held the three bells that summoned the people to mass. Inside the cool and dark church was the main altar, five smaller altars along the sides of the sanctuary, and a baptismal font made of wood.[4] Across from the church stood the chambers where the town council met. These two institutions, one representing the religious heritage of the town's founders and the other the civil traditions of Portuguese local government, symbolized the identity and aspirations of the first colonists.

Yet, beyond the tiny urban core extended the vast forests of the town which dwarfed the small urban nucleus. Here and there, families cleared small patches of land and built farms (*sitios*). The great distances made it virtually impossible for the town council's aldermen to enforce edicts from the kingdom, especially if unpopular. The priest of the mother church found it difficult to summon the people of the huge rural town to mass. The majority of the population spoke the Indian language, Tupi. In the beginning, the wilderness far eclipsed the influence of the kingdom in Santana de Parnaíba.[5]

The wilderness not only dominated the character of life in Parnaíba in the early seventeenth century but the entire economy of the town rested on its exploitation. Colonists depended on the free land and labor found in the wilderness to create and make possible the growth and prosperity of the town.

From the first days of settlement in Parnaíba, men from this town made war against the Indians of the wilderness, submitting those whom they captured to a life of slavery. The Indians from the wilderness created the wealth that sustained the first generations of colonists.[6] Bands of men entered the wilderness to attack Indian tribes at war with the Portuguese, the Jesuit missions to the south and west, and individual tribes.[7] Like the early Spanish conquests of the Caribbean, Mexico, and Peru, these military expeditions assaulted Indian tribes, plundered Indian villages, and abducted men, women, and children for war booty and personal slaves.[8] Just as the Spanish conquistadors invested their lives and meager resources in such expeditions with the expectation of being rewarded with large grants of Indians (*encomiendas*) or the spoils of conquest, so, too, did the men of São Vicente seek Indians for their estates on the Piratininga plateau.[9]

Men from the established mameluco families of the Piratininga plateau organized *bandeiras*, large companies of armed colonists and Indian warriors.[10] From São Paulo and Santana de Parnaíba, most of the bandeiras marched south after the Guaraní Indians. The slave hunters sought the Guaraní, known in São Vicente as "domestic" and "civilized" because of their skill as agriculturalists.

Beginning in the late sixteenth century, expeditions left the plateau and headed southwest to the region then known as Guairá (today the state of Paraná in Brazil) where the Guaraní lived. In Guairá, the Jesuits had launched their great evangelization drive, first envisioned by Father Nóbrega. There the Jesuits congregated the Guaraní Indians into large agricultural missions. The bandeira soldiers, or *bandeirantes*, coveted the Indians in these prosperous but poorly defended missions. In the 1620s, the bandeirantes began frontal assaults against the missions and enslaved the Indian neophytes. By the 1630s, repeated offensives had destroyed thirteen Jesuit missions in Guairá.

The sacking of the missions of Guairá and the inability of the Jesuits to effectively halt the slave hunters convinced the Jesuits to move their missions. The Indians of the two surviving missions of Guairá and their Jesuit fathers relocated in 1631. Sailing down the Paraná River, they portaged past the Guairá Falls and reestablished their missions in what is today Rio Grande do Sul, the Missiones Province of Argentina, and southern Paraguay. The Jesuits rebuilt a few missions much farther north along the Paraguay River at Itatín, now part of Mato Grosso do Sul, the far western province of Brazil.[11]

These migrations bought the Jesuits only time. The slave hunters stalked the Jesuits and their Indians, following them to their new locations. Slaving expeditions ventured into the Tape province (Rio Grande do Sul) in the mid-1630s and destroyed three missions there. These attacks fueled a counterattack by the Jesuits, who finally received permission from their superiors to arm their Indians. Later bandeiras to Tape met armed resistance, and in 1641, the mission Indians repulsed an expedition of 300 colonists and 600 Tupi Indian allies.[12] The defeat of this and other bandeiras in Tape brought to an end the years of the large organized slave-hunting bandeiras against the Guaraní and the Jesuit missions.

Men from Parnaíba participated in and led many of the infamous bandeiras. André, Domingos, and Baltezar Fernandes, the mameluco sons of Manoel Fernandes Ramos and Suzana Dias, participated in the pillaging of many Guaraní missions. Of the three, the Jesuits regarded André as a particularly ferocious and brutal Indian hunter. The Indians whom the three sons claimed as their booty from these raids became the basis of their estates in Parnaíba and the area, initially part of Parnaíba, that later became the towns of Itú and Sorocaba, farther west.[13] Pedro Vaz de Barros, also from Parnaíba, commanded one of the companies on the expedition led by veteran slaver Antonio Rapozo Tavares, which left São Paulo in 1628 and returned with many Indians. Pedro Vaz de Barros's estate became the nucleus of one of the parishes in Parnaíba, São Roque.[14] Paschoal Leite Pais and Fernão Dias Pais, two other Indian hunters from Parnaíba, laid the foundation for their agricultural estates in Parnaíba by joining and leading bandeiras.[15]

For the Indians of the wilderness, life in the towns on the plateau spelled slavery. The majority went to work on the large wheat estates in the towns of São Paulo and Parnaíba.[16] The colonists did not consider these Indians slaves—they called them servants (*servos*) or free slaves (*peças forras*)—yet Indians clearly lived in an institution similar to slavery. Colonists in Parnaíba, as elsewhere on the plateau, subjected the Indians to a kind of labor service known as "obligation" (*obrigação*). In return for being fed, clothed, and catechized, Indians were "obliged" to give their labor

São Vicente in the Age of the Bandeiras

to their masters. In the eyes of the colonists, this represented service, not slavery. Still, colonists described Indians as property in their wills and divided them among heirs at inheritance.[17] But unlike slavery elsewhere in Brazil, colonists in São Vicente rarely sold their slaves, nor did they supply Indian slaves to other regions of Brazil.[18]

The attacks of the bandeiras against the Jesuit missions created a state of war between the colonists and the Jesuits. At stake was the control of the Indian population. The colonists sought the Indians for labor; the Jesuits wanted to save their souls. Literate, educated, and articulate, the Jesuits vociferously complained to the king and pope about the de facto enslavement of Indians, illegal according to royal law.

This state of war came to a head in 1639 when the Jesuits persuaded the pope to issue a bull that reiterated the freedom of Indians and penalized with excommunication by the church those who kept Indians in servitude.[19] In response, the town council of São Paulo formally expelled the Jesuits from São Vicente in 1640.[20] In a petition to the pope, the town council expressed the position of the colonists of the plateau. The Indians from the wilderness who served the colonists, they argued, were not slaves but free men. Moreover, when Indians lived with them, in their households, they maintained, colonists could oversee their Christian spiritual education and cure their illnesses. If left free, the Indians might rise up in rebellion. The papal bull should be revoked, the letter concluded, "because it is against the common good, spiritual and temporal."[21]

Pope Urban VIII's bull coincided with the end of the bandeiras, for after 1640, large expeditions rarely left São Paulo or Parnaíba. But the years of Indian hunting were not yet over. Men from the towns of the plateau continued to hunt for Indians in the wilderness to the north and northwest, but in smaller groups. These expeditions, commonly referred to as *armações*,[22] were smaller, more compact, and more frequent than the bandeiras. Financed from the towns, the Indians brought back on these expeditions went to the estates of the backers, known as *armadores*, and to the men on the expedition. For example, Antonio Gomes Borba of Parnaíba stated in his will, "[I] came on this expedition with an armação of Francisco de Alvarenga Ribeiro with the [understood] division that of the Indians which I brought from the wilderness, I would pick two and the rest we would divide equally between us, and for this he gave me three blacks and a black woman and all the accessories that I needed."[23]

The crown had passed laws to regulate armações. A royal edict of 1570 stated that such expeditions must be licensed by royal governors, that two or three Jesuit fathers should accompany each to persuade Indians to come voluntarily into Portuguese society, where they would be paid for their work by colonists, and that when Indians were divided, royal officials must be present to ensure that Indians would not be forced to serve colonists against their will.[24]

Inventories and wills from Parnaíba reflect the fact that armações more nearly resembled economic ventures and military expeditions of conquest than peaceful expeditions to "persuade" Indians to come down to the towns of the plateau. In small companies led by a captain, the bands made their way through the wilderness. The colonists and their Indian guides and porters lived off the land and the stores of manioc flour they carried with them. They ported gunpowder, shot, and long metal chains with collars, used to overpower the Indians unwilling to be lured down to the Portuguese towns. Life on these campaigns was hard for colonists as well as for Indians. With crude maps, the men made their way down the rivers and the Indian trails largely from memory. Some expeditions disappeared without a trace. Men died from hunger and sickness. When one of the men died, his companions buried him in the wilderness and auctioned off his possessions among themselves. Antonio Gomes Borba, a resident of Parnaíba, died in the wilderness in 1645, and to his captain fell the responsibility of conducting an inventory of his possessions. Antonio had with him a hammock, a blanket, a leather fighting jacket,[25] two shirts, a pair of breeches, some thick stockings, a hood, a pillow, several lengths of cloth, a butcher's knife, and a shotgun. Deep in the interior, the captain assigned high monetary values to them, and his companions willingly paid the high prices.[26]

The Indians of the wilderness, hunted, captured, and subjected to a life of service, provided the labor that built the town of Santana de Parnaíba and its agricultural economy in the seventeenth century. Although Indians knew the wilderness intimately, they did not share in the wealth it brought to the town. Instead, the colonists of Parnaíba transformed the Indians of the wilderness into property.

A second seemingly limitless resource of the wilderness that also underlay the growth and prosperity of the town was land. The colonists easily obtained land in the seventeenth century. The agents of the proprietor (donatário) of São Vicente handed out land grants, usually one league square, or 43.56 square kilometers, to those who had the means to farm them. These grants, *sesmarias*, carried few obligations for the colonist beyond cultivating them and paying the tithe, a 10 percent tax on agricultural production given to the church. Since the Indians who had once used the lands around Parnaíba for hunting, fishing, and planting small gardens had been decimated by disease, slavery, and conquest, there were few, if any, Indian tribes who could challenge the allocation of lands to the colonists. Moreover, the policy of the crown with respect to the Indians was to congregate them into villages (aldeias) and give each village a grant of land. This provided the Indians with access to land but freed up the rest of the land for colonization.[27] Thus, colonists quickly became the owners of large tracts.

Land grants transformed the forests of the wilderness into lands "possessed" by individuals according to the rules of Portuguese law. Some of these grants went to the sons and daughters of the founders of Parnaíba—Vicencia, Benta, André, Domingos, and Baltezar Fernandes—but others went to early settlers of no relation to the founders.[28] To receive a land grant, one petitioned the donatário. The petitioners often cited their long-term residence in the captaincy, their family ties to early colonists, their ability to cultivate land, and their need for land to support themselves as reasons for deserving land.[29] To use one such petition as an example, João Missel Gigante stated that he was a son and grandson of settlers and conquerors of the captaincy, that he had a wife and children to support, and that he had not yet received any land. He specifically asked for two tracts in Parnaíba: one piece lay between the lands of Jeronymo de Brito and Jorge Fernandes, one league (6.6 km) deep, and the other was the usual one square league. Gigante received the lands "for himself, his wife, and his children . . . forever" with the sole obligation of paying the tithe.[30]

Colonists who did not receive land grants still participated in the transformation of the wilderness. Most residents of Parnaíba simply occupied lands in the Indian way—owning the fruits of their labor rather than the land itself. These families cleared and planted the unclaimed or unoccupied lands of the town.

Once the wilderness land began to be claimed and owned by settlers, other forms of land tenure emerged, more reminiscent of Portuguese practices. For example, the mother church and the small chapels of the town owned lands, bequeathed in perpetuity to them by their founders, that were rented out at nominal sums to local residents.[31] Also, land could be purchased, inherited, and received as gifts or in marriage dowries. These transactions became increasingly common as the second and third generations of settlers in Parnaíba sought land.

With the labor provided by the Indians captured from the wilderness, and the lands along the Tietê River, the settlers of Parnaíba created their town. In the seventeenth century, families lived simply, with few material possessions. One of the first inventories conducted in the town depicts the fragility of the early farms entirely surrounded by wilderness. The inventory recorded a straw house, a field of cotton and a field of manioc, thirty-four Indian servants, basins for panning for gold, gunpowder and shot, and trading goods for barter with the Indians.[32] Twenty years later, in the 1640s, the inventories reflect the growth of a farming community. At the time of his death in 1642, Ambrosio Mendes had beans, corn, and wheat stored in his barn. Twenty Indians worked for him, growing wheat, cotton, and foodstuffs and raising pigs and chickens on his farm.[33] Still, life on these farms remained simple, as Manuel de Lara's inventory makes clear. Manuel owned virtually no furniture. He slept in a hammock with a blanket (a custom adopted from Indians), and in his house could be found only several large chests that doubled as tables and storage bins.[34]

The largest estates of the seventeenth century had dozens of Indians and larger houses and produced ample harvests of wheat that were traded in the port of Santos for items not produced in São Vicente. Only these families could trade for the woolen cloth, silk, taffeta, fine cottons, thread, buttons, braid and trim, hats, soap, wine, paper, salt, gunpowder, iron chains, and lead imported from Portugal. The accounts kept between Antonio Castanho da Sylva, a resident of Parnaíba, and Diogo Rodrigues, a merchant in Santos, illustrate the high costs of such goods. Antonio's purchases, nearly 30,000 reis, reached 66 percent of the total value of his property when it was evaluated at his death.[35]

While the resources of the wilderness, land and Indians, provided the two basic underpinnings of Parnaíba's economy in the seventeenth century, the property inventories of the colonists rarely reflected their true value. Land and Indians invariably received minimal appraisals in the inventories in the first century of colonization.[36]

Grants of wilderness land usually received no valuation at all in property inventories.[37] Assessors appraised only land that had been improved, that is, cleared and planted. For example, the two cotton fields of Antonio Furtado de Vasconcellos were evaluated in 1628 at 5,000 reis and 2,000 reis, respectively, while his two land grants, which would have measured 43.56 square kilometers each, received no value at all in the inventory.[38] Only land that could produce, particularly crops like wheat, had value in the early seventeenth-century inventories.

Late in the seventeenth century, as Parnaíba ceased to be a frontier outpost, land began to acquire value in the inventories. In 1664, assessors estimated the value of Paschoal Leite Pais's farm, which consisted of his house and one square league of land, at 150,000 reis. The very next year, in 1665, appraisers rated Maria de Oliveira's very similar farm, described as "one square league of land, most forested, some cleared, and its cotton fields, sugar mill, and houses," as worth 100,000 reis.[39] Thus, the evaluations of farms increased in the second half of the seventeenth century, especially in the most settled areas of the town, as the population of Parnaíba grew and competition increased for land.

Assessors also neglected to measure the monetary value of the Indians, whose labor made possible the town's growth. Like grants of wilderness land, colonists viewed Indians as their property—but as a kind of property that could not be measured according to monetary standards. This stemmed from the custom on the Piratininga plateau of calling Indians "servants" and not "slaves."[40] Since legally Indians could not be enslaved, appraisers could not evaluate Indians in property inventories, because to do so would be to acknowledge that the law had been broken. Instead, the Indians appeared in the inventories as "servants" who "freely" served the succeeding generations. Assessors simply named each Indian in the inventory, and later the probate judges divided the Indians among the heirs of the deceased.

The custom of treating Indians as property but not evaluating them as slaves can be seen in Antonio Bicudo's will and inventory. He stated to the notary in his will, "I have several slaves [peças] of the people of this land, these are free and as such I ask them to serve my heirs because of the good treatment that I have always given them . . . and likewise, I ask my heirs . . . to treat them well."[41] These Indians nevertheless found themselves distributed among his heirs after he died. This suggests that Antonio knew his Indians were not slaves but that he expected his heirs would benefit from their labor after he died, as he had done. Colonists thus perpetuated the custom of de facto Indian slavery in Parnaíba.

In the second half of the seventeenth century, however, appraisers increasingly valued Indians, especially for individuals who died with large debts. In such cases, heirs sold Indian servants to repay creditors, royal laws notwithstanding. In one such situation, which occurred in 1697, the average value of an Indian servant was 16,000 reis. The highest valuation went to an Indian weaver (22,000 reis) and the lowest to a sick Indian (10,000 reis).[42]

Compared to Indians and land, property from the kingdom received extremely high valuations in property inventories. Assessors evaluated Paschoa Leite's black silk dress, for example, at 21,000 reis, nearly the value of an Indian weaver. They estimated her taffeta shawl at 6,000 reis and her red wool slip at 3,000 reis. Yet the assessors decided that her farm, which consisted of three houses and land that extended one and a half kilometers along the road and back two and a half kilometers into the wilderness, was worth only 16,000 reis, less than her black silk dress.[43] Similarly, the assessors described a bed belonging to Paschoal Leite Pais as "one bed of blue taffeta with curtains and a canopy with an embroidered silk fringe, . . . two mattresses, . . . a silk comforter, . . . four linen sheets." This amounted to 68,000 reis and was equal to almost half of the value they assigned to his farm, which contained 43.56 square kilometers of land and was worked by more than two hundred Indians.[44]

Fine clothing and bedding, then, were among the most precious items that individuals could own, even more valuable than land, houses, and Indian servants. The valuations assigned to property suggest how the colonists perceived their material possessions in the seventeenth century. What came from the wilderness and appeared to exist in abundance, they considered less valuable and perhaps less "ownable" than what came from the kingdom. Residents of Parnaíba held this view consistently, even though the land and Indians that came from the wilderness formed the productive base of their economy.

To be sure, these attitudes reflected the matter of the availability of goods in a small town on the fringes of the Portuguese empire. Items from Portugal, transported over great distances and at great cost, must have been treasured precisely because they were so scarce. Land and Indians, however, existed in abundance, even overabundance, in the eyes of the early colonists. Although the resources of the wilderness provided the means by which the first families of Parnaíba survived, families did not perceive them in this way, at least not in their property assessments.

The extremely high valuations given to property from the kingdom conveys how important the kingdom was to the early colonists of Parnaíba. Although the colonists rejected some of the laws of the kingdom—such as those that outlawed Indian slavery—some did seek, nevertheless, to acquire at great cost clothing and furniture from Portugal. Such items symbolized the ties between the town and the kingdom. Those that could purchased such luxuries to reinforce their Portuguese descent.

The majority of the population in the seventeenth century did not attempt to identify themselves with the kingdom. They could not afford the costly silks and beds from Portugal which marked the status of those who claimed Portuguese ancestry. But like the wealthy, the poor depended on the free resources of the wilderness. Venturing into the world of the wilderness became the key strategy used by families to survive in Santana de Parnaíba in the seventeenth century.

During these first one hundred years, Parnaíba's ties to the frontier and to the larger colonial world created the twin axes on which life in the town revolved. Commercial links to other towns and cities in the Portuguese empire provided markets for Parnaíba's major products and supplied luxuries and tools. The frontier yielded the Indians and the lands that produced the town's livelihood. Thus, Parnaíba's orientation was both inward toward the wilderness and outward toward the kingdom. Both were essential to the town's survival.

By the end of the seventeenth century, not only had most of the lands of the town been handed out to colonists but the number of Indians living in the town began to decline rapidly. The Indians captured by the slaving expeditions suffered not just from the virtual slavery to which their captors subjected them but also from disease and the loss of their cultural heritage. The common cycle of contact between Europeans and Indians, played out virtually everywhere the Portuguese went in colonial Brazil, also occurred in Parnaíba. Conquest soon followed contact, slavery followed conquest, and disease, cultural loss, and death came with slavery.[45]

A glimpse of the alarming mortality rate for Indians in Parnaíba can be seen in Isabel de Barcelos's inventory. Since she died when her husband was in the wilderness, the probate judge conducted her inventory in his absence, in December 1648, and turned the property over to Isabel's mother until her husband reappeared from the wilderness. When Isabel's husband arrived seven months later, seven Indians had died in the interim. A receipt appended to the inventory matter-of-factly reported the losses suffered because of these deaths:

> Afonso is dead. He belonged to the share of the heir Manuel Favacho. His daughter is dead. A girl named Aniceta is dead. She belongs to the same heir. Maria is also dead. She belongs to the same heir. The black woman Luiza is dead. Two young children of hers are dead and two more are alive.[46]

Put simply, the town was a death trap for the Indians of the wilderness.

With the claiming of wilderness lands and the decline of the Indian population, it would seem that the traditional strategy of looting the wilderness for the benefit of the town had run its course, but this was not to be so. In the last decade of the seventeenth century, the first discoveries of gold in the Brazilian wilderness had a profound impact on all of São Vicente and especially on the towns of the plateau, such as Santana de Parnaíba. This new rich resource of the wilderness revitalized the economic life of the town as men made their way into the wilderness in search of gold and precious minerals.

The Brazilian gold rush occurred in three phases. The first discoveries of gold surfaced in Minas Gerais with the major excavations at Sabará, Vila Rica, and São João del Rei. Men from São Paulo, Parnaíba, and other nearby towns prospected in these fields until many lost their claims there in the civil strife known as the War of Emboabas of 1708.[47] The second phase of the gold rush took place in Mato Grosso, where prospectors found gold along the Cuiabá River in 1718 and then along the Guaporé River in 1734.

These fields were very remote, and travel to them was hazardous. The third phase of the gold rush transpired in Goiás, in the highlands to the north and west of Minas Gerais. Bartolomeu Bueno da Silva of Parnaíba discovered gold there in 1722. These three phases prolonged the gold rush, for just as gold production began to wind down in one area, prospectors discovered gold anew somewhere else. Individuals and families from Parnaíba prospected in all three regions.[48]

Parnaíba, like other towns on the Piratininga plateau, easily took advantage of the gold rush of the eighteenth century because of its historic ties to the interior. Men from Parnaíba who had formed armações or participated in bandeiras readily made the transition from Indian hunter to gold prospector and merchant. From Parnaíba, Bartolomeu Bueno da Silva and his two partners petitioned the crown in 1720 before embarking on their famous search for gold in Goiás. They argued that their experience as bandeirantes had prepared them to undertake the expedition, for which they wanted to receive in advance certain favors from the crown. They stated that they "had cultivated and explored part of the American wilderness on various expeditions; that wilderness being populated by the villages and kingdoms of various tribes of savage Indians . . . which first they must conquer so that they can discover mines of gold and silver." The men asked the king to grant them the right to control the passage along the rivers and to collect tolls from those who would enter the region as well as "the honors and favors which Your Majesty is willing to grant in remuneration."[49] Convinced that the men did know the wilderness, the crown granted them permission to undertake the expedition and awarded them the right to collect tolls for themselves and their heirs. Fernão Dias Pais, another well-known Parnaíba bandeirante turned prospector, spent the last years of his life on a quixotic quest for gold and emeralds in the wilderness.[50]

The discovery of gold in the interior drew new generations of men from Parnaíba into the wilderness. Because it was near all three principal routes to the mining regions—the fluvial route to Mato Grosso,[51] the overland trail to Goiás, and the old road from São Paulo to Minas Gerais—Parnaíba functioned as a gateway into the interior during the Brazilian gold rush. Men from Parnaíba became merchants, sending tobacco, cane brandy, slaves, horses,

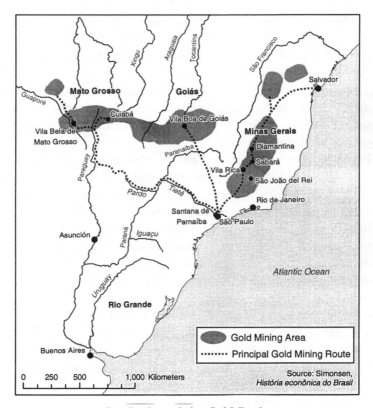

São Paulo and the Gold Rush

cattle, and other goods to the mining camps. Wealthy families established ranches in Rio Grande, near where their fathers and grandfathers had once hunted the Guaraní Indians, to raise cattle, horses, and mules for the mining towns. Others staked out mining claims that they worked in addition to maintaining their farms in Parnaíba. The very wealthy loaned money to men in the mining towns, collecting interest. The mining boom also provided a market for the produce of Parnaíba's large estates. Families began to plant sugar, construct sugar mills, and distill cane brandy (*agua ardente*) for sale in the mining areas.[52]

Parnaíba still remained the home base for many families. Rather than picking up and moving to the mining regions, men of the family periodically left Parnaíba to do business in the interior. Like their fathers and grandfathers before them, these men spent many years of their lives outside of the town. When Francisco Bueno de

Camargo wrote his will in 1736, he stated he had sent his son to the Guirixas mines with eighteen slaves. Similarly, Domingos Rodrigues de Fonseca Leme's son was in Goiás with twenty-seven slaves when his father died in 1738. Luis Pedrozo de Barros alluded in his will to the fact that his son returned from Cuiabá owing five kilograms of gold. To settle the debt, he sent his son out again with a cattle drove to be sold in Goiás.[53]

Just as the elite had financed the slaving expeditions into the wilderness in the seventeenth century, so, too, did the wealthy back the ventures to the mining frontier. Father Guilherme Pompeo de Almeida, a wealthy priest, acted as a financier based in Parnaíba. According to his detailed account book, in one year alone, he received 90 kilograms of gold sent by more than twenty men from the mining regions.[54] Similarly, Domingos Rodrigues de Fonseca Leme lent sums to many men who sought their fortunes as miners, merchants, and prospectors in the mining regions.[55]

The infusion of gold into Parnaíba, the third great resource of the wilderness, profoundly affected the town. The decline of the Indian population forced the elite to look for new sources of labor, and the availability of gold made it possible for them to purchase Africans, who, unlike Indians, could be legally owned as slaves.[56] Father Guilherme sent five shipments of gold to a merchant in Bahia in a two-year period specifically for African slaves.[57] African slaves began to replace Indians as the labor force of choice in the first decades of the eighteenth century. Indians still continued to live in the town, many as wards (*administrados*) of colonists. As wards, they lived in the homes of the colonists where they worked in exchange for food and religious instruction. Other Indians became independent subsistence farmers.

Like the Indian slaves before them, Africans interacted in both the town and the wilderness. The majority of the Africans slaves worked in the town on the large farms of the richest families. The wilderness was not a familiar world for Africans, but sometimes it brought them a measure of wealth and autonomy. Some accompanied their masters to the gold fields where they dug and panned for gold. Because of the scarcity of labor in the mining areas, slaves successfully negotiated with their masters for control over some aspects of their lives there. They might accumulate gold, for example, and purchase their freedom.[58] In the south, slaves worked on

the cattle and horse ranches owned by wealthy families in Parnaíba. Runaway slaves sought shelter in the deep forests of the
wilderness. Although slaves might have more autonomy and independence in the wilderness than in the town, the wealth of the wilderness rarely benefited them.

The pursuit of gold and the new economic ventures inspired by
the gold rush made agriculture less important to elite families in
Parnaíba. They abandoned the large wheat farms of their forebears, which needed substantial numbers of workers, in favor of
smaller farms with fewer workers which produced basic subsistence crops (corn, beans, and manioc) and sugarcane for cane
brandy. The largest slave owners of the eighteenth century owned
fewer African slaves than their seventeenth-century Indian slave-
owning counterparts. The size of their lands also diminished as
families divided their original land grants between their heirs every
generation. Still, the extensiveness of the original grants precluded
any immediate land shortage, for heirs simply cultivated a greater
proportion of the lands. Domingos Rodrigues de Fonseca Leme's
will conveys these changes in the productive base of elite families.
He stated in his will that he owned three parts of a land grant—the
first, which was his by inheritance, the second, which belonged to
his brother and for which he had traded five slaves, and the third,
inherited by his other brother who sold it to him for 1.4 kilograms
of gold. On his farm, he grazed cattle and horses and planted
sugarcane. But he had invested most of his capital in the nearly
one hundred African slaves he owned and in the mines of Minas
Gerais and Goiás where he sent his slaves, loaned monies, and
financed trade.[59]

Parnaíba's rich families became more worldly and more integrated into the Portuguese colonial economy in the eighteenth century. They accumulated property unknown to their grandparents
in the seventeenth century. What would have been considered
positively luxurious in the seventeenth century became the norm
in the eighteenth. The homes of residents in Parnaíba lost their
frontier simplicity. A typical home of a rich family, such as that of
Jozé Madeira Salvadores, by no means the wealthiest man in Parnaíba, shows the newly found comforts of town life. At his death
in 1733, his farm consisted of a league of land (probably a square
league, thus 43.56 sq. km), fifteen slaves, and all the necessary

farm implements and tools. In his house could be found books, such as two books of sermons by the Jesuit, Father Vieira, a painted wooden buffet, two leather trunks, several wooden chests with strong locks, two cots, wooden benches, eight pewter plates, three tablecloths with table napkins, three pairs of silk stockings, and a black wool suit.[60] By the early eighteenth century, the elite families of Parnaíba had moved closer to the kingdom. They adopted a more European life-style. The influence of Indians over their daily life had waned.

The poor families of Parnaíba, however, remained tied to a world more reminiscent of the seventeenth century. On the fringes of the town where dense forests still stood, the poor farmed small cleared fields and lived in simple houses constructed from sticks and mud. They had little contact with the affairs of the town or the kingdom. The captain of the militia of Parnaíba tried to explain the lifeways of the poor in a reply he wrote after receiving an order to prepare his company for a military campaign in 1736. He wrote that "the majority of my regiment is made up of bastards[61] descended from Indians" who "desert the small farms on which they live, and with their wives and children go into the forest." "By no means can I have them ready for royal service," he complained, because they do not live in one place, "but are divided, each in his place within forests so thick" that "I do not know how to bring them together, since they flee before they are even called."[62]

Thus, while the elite became more a part of a Portuguese colonial world in the eighteenth century—active in the economic opportunities it offered—the poor remained isolated and distant. They lived as the first settlers of Parnaíba had, in a mameluco world where the influences of the wilderness still outweighed those of the kingdom. But whether poor or rich, the bounty of the wilderness still supported the colonists of Santana de Parnaíba in the eighteenth century.

During the eighteenth century, the old captaincy of São Vicente passed out of the hands of its proprietor and into those of the crown. The crown renamed it "São Paulo and the Mines of Gold" and included within it not just the old territory of São Vicente but also the new mining regions. Thus, the orientation of the captaincy continued to face west, to the wilderness. But as time passed, the crown gradually cut the mining regions from São Paulo, making each a separate captaincy to facilitate the collection of taxes on gold. São Paulo became a mere southern appendage to the captaincy of Rio de Janeiro in 1748.[63] These acts deprived São Paulo of its vast wilderness. Many historians see this as a time of decline and decadence in São Paulo. Lacking the mining regions of the interior and even a royal governor, they argue, São Paulo became a poor and distant backwater of the Portuguese empire.[64] But as Maria Luiza Marcílio clearly shows, the eighteenth century was a time of growth there. Not only did the population increase but towns throughout the region continued to lay the foundation for a modest prosperity. This is certainly true in Santana de Parnaíba.[65]

In 1765, the crown restored the captaincy of São Paulo and set about to encourage economic development in the area as a way of protecting Brazil's southern frontier from the territorial designs of the Spanish. The actions of the crown, particularly those of a series of royal governors, intensified the pace of the region's integration into the Portuguese empire. Dom Luís Antonio de Souza, known by his title as the Morgado de Mateus, came to São Paulo as the new royal governor in 1765. He immediately saw the tension in São Paulo between the wilderness and the kingdom. The vastness of Brazil and the isolation in which the population lived amazed him. From his perspective, the small towns of São Paulo were but frail barriers against the power of a vast wilderness that threatened to impede the development of São Paulo. He wrote in 1766, his second year in São Paulo:

> There are 38 parishes in this Captaincy. Of these, there are some that consist of 12, 20, and more leagues . . . and in this area the parishioners are dispersed. . . . Rare is he who hears mass, nor can the parishioners come to Church. . . . They fail to keep lent . . . and the young are baptized as adults, all because of the impossibility of the distances in which they live.[66]

For the governor, who sought to transform São Paulo into a prosperous province tightly interwoven into the Portuguese empire, the wilderness represented backwardness and savagery, not avenues for wealth. "When men live away from villages, off in the forest," he wrote, "one cannot expect any usefulness from them, neither for the Kingdom of God nor for that of your Majesty."[67]

The governor's vision for the future of São Paulo placed a high priority on the creation of a strong commercial agricultural economy. He ordered the planting of new crops, such as cotton and indigo, and demanded that each town produce a surplus to feed the army and to outfit territorial expeditions. He hoped to create a commercial infrastructure—roads, warehouses, and a port—that would allow São Paulo to export sugar, cotton, indigo, and hides to Portugal. The governor also had in mind the defense of Portugal's southern territories. He organized a new state militia, the auxiliaries, and strengthened the local militia in each town.[68]

Stimulated by the reforms of the governor, the focus of São Paulo's economy in the late eighteenth century became agricultural products destined for export. By the end of the century, ships stopped regularly in the port of Santos to load the produce of the region. Sugar, cane brandy, rice, hides, coffee, cinnamon, wood, honey, and gum spirits were all products that one ship, the *Mercúrio*, carried from Santos in 1791.[69]

In spite of the perception of São Paulo's governor that the wilderness hindered development, the rapid spread of the sugar economy in the last decades of the eighteenth century rested on the age-old pattern of exploiting the wilderness. Instead of searching for Indians or gold in the wilderness, families in Parnaíba groomed their sons as the colonizers of new lands into which the sugar economy would expand in future generations. Sons left Parnaíba for the towns of Itú, Sorocaba, and Campinas, an area that became the core of the sugar economy of São Paulo.[70] Children of poor families also moved west where they claimed forest for their own farms. These farms produced subsistence crops with a surplus for trade in local markets.

Although Parnaíba's families continued to rely on the frontier for their prosperity, by the end of the eighteenth century, they no longer lived in the world of the wilderness. The elite adopted the fashions of Europe. Men wore English shirts with ruffles, frock coats, silk stockings, and breeches. Women continued to dress simply, in long dresses with shawls, but their homes, once spare and plain, now housed beds, cupboards with china plates, pewter cutlery, and glassware, tables and chairs, razors, mirrors, and so on.[71] Even the poor gradually accumulated property such as simple tables, benches, cots, and chests.[72] Few spoke Tupi or identified with the customs of tribal Indians.

As the nineteenth century dawned, most of the lands in the

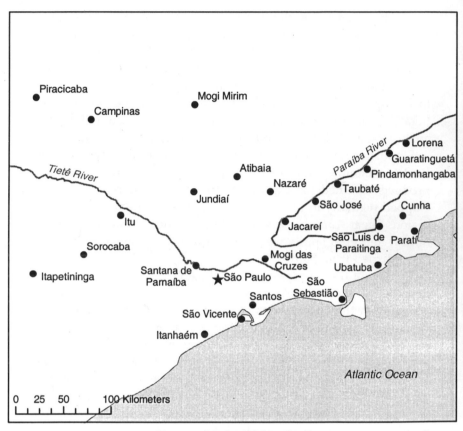

Towns of Colonial São Paulo

town were already being farmed, and the vast resources of the wilderness, which had guaranteed the prosperity of the town, were no longer in sight. Those who lived in Parnaíba reflected on their "poverty" compared to the days of yore.[73] The wealthy did manage to stave off complete ruin by seeding a new cash crop, coffee. In 1820, farmers in Parnaíba harvested virtually no coffee, but by 1836, Parnaíba became the fourth largest producer—812,000 kilograms, or 9 percent of all the coffee produced in the province of São Paulo.[74]

In the second half of the nineteenth century, Parnaíba, well inside the coffee frontier, did finally lose its ties to the wilderness. For the first time in its history, families in the town no longer could exploit the wilderness. Those who remained in Parnaíba saw their resources dwindle with each passing generation. The lands of the town became subdivided among many descendants. By the end of the nineteenth century, Parnaíba fell under the shadow of the burgeoning city of São Paulo. But as the coffee economy boomed in the nineteenth century, the old patterns of the colonial period did not die. The success of the coffee economy in the state of São Paulo rested on the old formula of looting the wilderness (now the far western virgin forest lands) for the benefit of the kingdom (now independent Brazil). Lacking virgin lands or a vital commercial or financial center, Parnaíba could not remain active in this nineteenth-century economy. But the city of São Paulo, so much like Parnaíba in the seventeenth and eighteenth centuries, continued to prosper by exploiting the wilderness.

As the history of Santana de Parnaíba in the colonial period shows, the ways that families interacted with the kingdom and the wilderness critically affected the development of the town. The most successful families knew how to use each of these worlds to their advantage. Whether it was exploiting the resources of the wilderness, or controlling the institutions of local government, or becoming representatives of the kingdom, elite families understood the importance of each of these spheres to their survival in Santana de Parnaíba. Poor families also took advantage of the wilderness. But as some families successfully developed strategies that combined all three worlds while others could not, an unequal division of power and resources occurred in the town which laid the foundation for the emergence of social classes.

3

The Origins of Social Class

From the beginning, life in the town of Santana de Parnaíba differed from life in the kingdom of Portugal because the wilderness to the north, west, and south provided colonists with an unending supply of valuable resources. Yet Parnaíba never became an egalitarian community. Instead, a large portion of the residents of the town lived in slavery, while a minority monopolized the resources of the wilderness and used them to accumulate wealth and power. The roots of this inequality lay in the way the first colonists perceived the wilderness and exploited it. The Portuguese and mameluco residents of seventeenth-century Parnaíba believed that the remedy for their poverty lay in freely claiming for themselves resources of the wilderness. They transformed land into private property and Indians into personal slaves. These acts, carried out throughout the seventeenth century, cast the foundation for a hierarchical social order in Santana de Parnaíba.

The custom of Indian slavery on the Piratininga plateau created the first class divisions in the town. As Thomé Fernandes, grandson of Suzana Dias, matter-of-factly told the notary, who, in turn, recorded the statement, "between he and his wife they own some free slaves, whom he says he leaves to his wife and children as is the custom."[1] The custom of slavery, legal or not, radically differentiated the lives of slaves from those of masters.

Colonists reinforced the distance between masters and slaves by labeling slaves as "black" and masters as "white." Paschoa Leite, like many others in Parnaíba, referred to her Indian slaves as "blacks of the people of this land."[2] Antonio Nunes had only to say, "a black woman by the name of Luiza," for the notary, judges, and townspeople to know that Luiza was his slave.[3] To masters, to be "white" meant that one was free. Ambrosio Mendes made a point of noting in his will that the young mameluca girl

who served him in his house was free "because she is white," and
Domingos Fernandes also declared in his will, "I have in my house
a white boy named Ignacio, son of a girl of my service by name
Suzana . . . free because she is white."[4]

Although colonists equated "black" with slavery and "white"
with freedom, in reality, they lived in a more complex world.
Not all Indians in the town served as slaves, nor did all "whites"
own Indian slaves. Moreover, most of those who considered themselves "whites" in the town had parents, grandparents, or other
kin who were Indians; some even had kin who lived as slaves.
Antonio Nunes, a master of twenty slaves, for example, freed his
uncle, his mother's brother, in his will, "for the good services he
has given me."[5] Because so few Portuguese women emigrated to
Brazil, Portuguese and mameluco men in São Vicente chose Indian
and mameluca women as their wives. Masters of Indian slaves in
seventeenth-century Parnaíba were in effect mamelucos.

Regardless of their color or ethnicity, mamelucos who identified
with Portuguese culture, such as it existed in São Vicente, saw
themselves and were seen by others as "white." Maria Bicuda revealed this in her will. She stated, "I declare that I have two black
women of this land in my service who have several bastards of
whom it is said that they are [children] of white men. I order that
if the fathers should appear, my heirs will give them over to their
fathers . . . and if they do not appear, for the love of God [my
heirs] shall treat them as whites and give them the necessary education."[6] Colonists saw mamelucos as "whites" who belonged to
the class of the free, even if their mothers had been slaves.

The Portuguese and mameluco masters of Indian slaves comprised a large and very differentiated group in the seventeenth
century. There were a few extremely wealthy families who became
rich from exploiting the wilderness. The men of these families were
slave hunters such as Paschoal Leite Pais or André Fernandes. In
addition to the Indians they captured from the wilderness, they received extensive land grants from royal officials. These families
built farms on which they planted their cash crop, wheat, grew
their own food, and grazed livestock. But very poor men and
women also owned Indian servants. These were men like Pedro
Fernandes, who died leaving only a black serge suit, a sword and
dagger with a belt and baldric, a shotgun, and three Indians to his

son.[7] Men such as Pedro served in slave expeditions but never became wealthy from them. Nonetheless, they identified with other masters and served as their allies.

Neither land nor Indians were distributed equally among the Portuguese and mameluco colonists of Parnaíba. The two fundamental resources needed to produce crops for a broader market fell into the hands of some but not all. This inequality can be seen in the property inventories that largely depict the mameluco class of slave owners in the seventeenth century. Inventories reveal that the largest estates had dozens of Indians. Indian slaver Francisco Pedrozo Xavier, who led an attack against the Jesuit missions of Itatín and Paraguay shortly before his death in 1680, had amassed 112 Indian slaves.[8] Another bandeirante, Paschoal Leite Pais, held 229 Indian slaves at his death in 1664.[9] Diogo Coutinho de Mello could only estimate that he owned 150 Indians "more or less" when he wrote his will in 1654.[10] The inventories of others, however, reveal that large estates such as these were not the norm. When Pedro Fernandes died in 1649, his inventory listed three Indians; when Domingos Alvres died in 1650, his inventory reported six.[11]

According to John Monteiro, Indians were never distributed equally among the residents of the towns of São Paulo and Parnaíba in the seventeenth century. Estates with 100 or more Indians held 27 percent of all Indian slaves. The richest 10 percent of the population controlled 41 percent of all Indians from 1630 to 1700.[12]

Similarly, property inventories indicate that some families received several land grants, while others received no land at all. Domingos Fernandes, son of Suzana Dias, listed five land grants in his will; Clemente Alveres indicated that he had received three land grants himself and had bought another from its original grantee; yet João de Gomes Camacho, like most residents in Parnaíba, did not receive a single one.[13] Some of the early colonists may never have seen the need to petition for a grant because land seemed infinite; yet as the settlement grew, competition for land increased. This process gave those with land grants a distinct advantage and inevitably forced those without legal land titles to seek less desirable lands or even to abandon the town entirely. Thus, the origins of the planter class can be seen in the consolidation of land and slaves into the hands of a few families in the seventeenth century.

A variety of Indian tribes captured from the wilderness by the bandeiras formed the slave class. Indians clearly outnumbered their Portuguese and mameluco masters by a wide margin. A Spanish resident of the town of São Paulo in the middle of the seventeenth century estimated the population of several towns in São Vicente in 1676. Juan de Mongelos calculated the Indian population of São Vicente at 20,000 Indians. He reckoned that there were almost 1,500 households in the province, and if we assume about five free persons per household, the size of the free population in the province would have been approximately 7,500 (see table 1). Not surprisingly, São Paulo and Parnaíba had the most Indians, for it was from these two towns that the slave hunting expeditions were organized.[14]

Indians captured in slaving expeditions went into personal service for their Portuguese and mameluco masters. They lived on the farms of their masters in family units. Female slaves worked as house servants and farm laborers, while male slaves labored as porters, artisans, and warriors on the expeditions into the interior.[15]

The Indians of the aldeias, however, were not slaves. They had been congregated into these communities by the Jesuits and officials of the Portuguese crown. Each community had a large grant of land that the Indians farmed. Colonists were allowed to hire Indians from the communities to work on their estates, a privilege that was widely abused as yet another form of de facto slavery. Yet colonists distinguished between the "Indians of obligation" (i.e., Indian slaves) and the Indians of the aldeias. The latter they regarded as free and therefore did not divide them among their heirs at inheritance. Antonio Furtado de Vasconcellos's wife declared that they owned nineteen Indian slaves and then stated that "there are no more people of obligation and if there are others, they are Indians acquired from the Indian aldeia, which I, in good conscience, cannot list in the inventory."[16]

A middle group between masters and slaves began to form slowly in the seventeenth century. From this intermediate group, the class of peasants emerged. Free Indians and poor mamelucos,

Table 1. Population of Principal Towns of São Vicente, 1676

Towns	Free Households	Indian Slaves	Ratio of Indians per Household
São Paulo	800	15,000	19
Parnaíba	180	3,000	17
Sorocaba	75	500	7
Itú	40	500	13
Jundiaí	50	250	5
Mogi	50	200	4
Santos	250	500	2
São Sebastião	40	100	3
Total	1,485	20,050	14

Source: Estimates of Juan de Mongelos, 1676, in *Bandeirantes no Paraguai*, 112.

often the "bastard" children of men of established families, found themselves in this social space. Considered "free" from servitude, they could come and go and live where they pleased. But they did not belong to the ranks of the *homens bons*, the men of good standing in the town, who elected the officials of the town council.

The way that Portuguese law treated bastard children contributed to the emergence of the peasant class. It distinguished between children born in marriage and children born out of marriage. But among children born to unmarried parents, "natural" children had higher status than "spurious" children. "Natural" children, according to law, were those born to an unmarried couple for whom no impediment existed which might prevent marriage in the future. Commonly, these were the children of single or widowed men and their mistresses. "Spurious" children, in contrast, had been conceived in sin. These would be the children of couples who could not ever marry. Such children were born of adulterous, incestuous, or sacrilegious liaisons.[17]

Natural children appear to have been commonly accepted into families and reared as close family members. Isabel de Barcelos called her husband's natural daughter her "stepdaughter" and in her will made her a present of an Indian couple "for the good service . . . received from her."[18] Antonio Bicudo stated in his will, "I have a natural son, named Bernardo Bicudo, and his brothers treat him as a brother."[19]

According to Portuguese law, natural children had rights at inheritance equal to those of legitimate children, except among the nobility, but spurious children could not inherit.[20] Few in Parnaíba could claim to be members of the nobility; therefore, their natural children did have the right of succession along with legitimate children. Wills indicate that the rights of natural children were often respected. Domingos Fernandes declared in his will, "I leave a girl of seven or eight months that I had of a free Indian woman after I became a widower. She is also an heir to my estate with my other children."[21] Bernardo Bicudo also asserted that his natural daughter, Luzia Nunes, would inherit equally with his other legitimate daughters after his death.[22] Thomé Fernandes declared likewise that his natural daughter Maria "is an heir of his estate because he had her before he married his wife."[23] But not all men in Parnaíba wished to allow their natural children to share in the division of their estates. Ambrosio Mendes explicitly stated that his natural son would not inherit equally with his legitimate children. However, Ambrosio did leave him a small bequest from his estate.[24] Spurious children fared worse than natural children at inheritance. They could only expect to receive property if their fathers wrote wills and earmarked gifts for them. Such gifts could not be challenged by the legitimate children.[25] Aleixo Leme de Alvarenga, for example, stated in his will that he had five bastard (spurious) children by an Indian slave woman who would not inherit along with his legitimate daughter. However, he stated that he wanted his bastard daughter, Paula, to receive two Indians, as well as her own mother,[26] after he died. He indicated that his bastard son José was to be allowed to keep whatever he brought back from a trip into the wilderness because he went without Aleixo's financial backing.[27]

These provisions of Portuguese law clearly intended for natural children to be accepted into families, to receive equal inheritances, and to (one might presume) share the social status of the family. For the natural children of Parnaíba who were recognized by their fathers, this sometimes did occur. But for spurious children, as well as many natural children, the future appeared far bleaker. These children inherited an ambiguous social space between planter families and their slaves. While spurious children might receive bequests from their father's estates, they did not

usually share in the equal division of property among the legitimate children. They inherited some resources but not many. They
were free but poor.

Indians became part of this free but poor population when
masters freed them. Ambrosio Mendes specifically freed several
Indians in his will stating that "from the day of my death on they
may go where they wish without anyone stopping them, because
they are free and I wish to pay them for their services and company."[28] Other masters also freed Indian slaves in recognition of
good service, and these Indians likewise became part of the free
population.[29] These persons gradually developed into a class of
peasants who lived from subsistence farming on small plots of
land.

The relationships between these groups can be partially reconstructed from seventeenth-century sources. The point of view of
slave owners emerges quite clearly from the wills they wrote. They
saw the interaction between masters and slaves as one that rested
on reciprocal obligations. With respect to Indians, they believed
that "savage" Indians gave their labor in return for "civilization"
and salvation. Isabel de Barcelos described it when she dictated her
will as follows: "She declared that she and her husband own some
free servants, which she leaves to her husband and children as is
customary. [They shall] give them the treatment which until now
they have received, paying them for their work, dressing them so
that they can enter the Church to hear mass without shame, and
teaching them the Christian doctrine."[30] Antonio Castanho da
Sylva put it even more clearly: "I have some people of this land
who serve me," he wrote. "I ask my heirs to serve themselves of
them as free persons, which is, to give them the treatment of free
persons, to teach them the doctrines necessary for their salvation,
and to dress them in payment of their service so that they can have
the clothes to hear mass."[31] From the point of view of Isabel and
Antonio, there was an agreement between master and servant: in
return for good treatment, religious instruction, and payment (by
which they both seem to have meant clothing and probably also
food and shelter), servants "freely" gave their services to their
masters.[32]

The point of view of the Indian slaves is harder to reconstruct,
but what evidence exists indicates that Indians rarely saw the slav-

ery in which they lived as resting on reciprocal obligations. A few slim references to the independent actions of Indian slaves suggest that, on the contrary, they did not freely give their services to their masters and that if provided a choice, they would act quite differently. One episode occurred during the lifetime of Suzana Dias's daughter, Benta Dias. After her second husband died, she left several Indians in charge of their estate in Birachoiassava. But without her knowledge or permission, the Indians destroyed the estate and sold the corn, stock, and other foodstuffs to men leaving for the wilderness.[33] In this case, the Indians did not seem to see themselves bound by a reciprocal relationship with Benta and instead took advantage of her absence to lay waste to her estate. In another episode, after Isabel de Barcelos died, the probate judge decided to turn her estate over to her mother until her husband returned from the wilderness. His rationale was that the estate would be safer if the Indians were not "upset" and if they remained "quiet and peaceful." This could be achieved best, he thought, by having Isabel's mother live on the estate until her husband returned.[34] Both references seem to indicate that Indians, if not properly supervised, failed to keep up their "obligations." From the Indian point of view, this meant that they worked only because they were compelled to do so.

Indian slaves resisted service when they could. Anna de Proença sold several Indians in desperation because "they did not want to serve nor do anything for her."[35] Several inventories chronicle the simplest form of resistance: running away. Simão Minho's widow declared that after her husband's death, four "blacks" had run away into the wilderness.[36] A story survives of some Indians turning on their master deep in the wilderness. Luis Castanho, a veteran bandeirante from Parnaíba, entered the wilderness for the last time with his four sons in 1671. With them they took a group of Guaraní. Tired of the hardships they endured, the Guaraní rose up in rebellion and shot Luis with an arrow. He died, but his sons survived and barely made it back to Parnaíba with their father's bones.[37] Rebellion, running away, and forced slavery all belie the idea of "free" servitude promoted by the elite.

The perceptions that the poor free had of themselves and of the world they lived in are extremely difficult to resurrect. Those natural children reared in wealthy families learned from a young age

how race and ethnicity divided the free from those with the "obligation" of service, even among those of the same family. After her
father's death, Maria, a natural daughter, lived with her grandmother. Maria's mother, an Indian woman, also lived with the
same family. But when Maria's grandmother wrote her will, she
had to spell out her wish that Maria's mother remain with Maria
"free from any suggestion of servitude."[38] Otherwise, Maria's
mother would be considered a slave and given to one of her heirs.
Although Maria was considered "white" and therefore free from
the "suggestion of servitude," her mother was not. Moreover,
Maria could not help her mother; rather, she, like her mother,
remained dependent on the goodwill and favors that she might
receive from her father's family.

Natural children who lived with their fathers' families offered
companionship and personal service to family members. In Felippe
de Campos's family, his bastard[39] daughter, Felicia, lived with him
during his life. After his death, he expected her to serve his heirs.
Felippe further requested that his two bastard sons, Feliciano and
Gervasio, live with the family and serve in the house after his
death. In return, he asked his heirs to see that both sons received an education.[40] Similarly, Antonio Castanho da Silva's natural daughter lived with his mother. In his will, he requested that
this daughter continue to remain with his mother and after her
death, serve his wife and children.[41]

Since natural and spurious children could inherit property,
either in the form of simple bequests or as recognized heirs, and
because natural sons participated in armações and bandeiras,
many did become property owners. Agostinha Dias, the natural
daughter of a priest (presumably before he took orders) and an
Indian woman, married twice before she died in 1648. At her
death, she and her husband owned eighteen Indian slaves, a small
farm, and some farm tools. One of her most valuable possessions
was her silk shawl, which she undoubtedly wore to mass. Although "natural" at birth, Agostinha attained the status of a respectable free white woman during her life. One would expect,
therefore, that she identified with the colonists of the town—
those who exploited the wilderness for the benefit of the town and
kingdom.[42]

In the seventeenth century, then, the seeds of a class society had emerged in Santana de Parnaíba. A differentiated group of Portuguese and mamelucos obtained land and Indian slaves from the wilderness and became a planter class. Indian servos, the majority of the population, worked for them as slaves. In between, an amorphous group, with ties to both worlds, came into focus: a poor free peasantry.

In the eighteenth century, first the gold rush and then the spread of commercial agriculture stimulated the town's economy and the growth of its population. These opportunities in the wilderness again offered the prospect of wealth and social mobility. Nonetheless, success in either mining or commerce or later in sugar production required capital investment in supplies, slaves, merchandise, and agricultural estates. Those who had such resources, or who could obtain them through loans, partnerships, and family contacts, stood in a better position to benefit. It comes as no surprise, then, that the riches from mining, commerce, and cash crop agriculture were not evenly distributed among the families of Parnaíba.

In the first half of the century, during the mining boom, the social structure of Parnaíba continued to evolve from the foundation laid in the seventeenth century. Society remained divided between planters and slaves and an intermediate group of peasants. Slavery prevailed as an unquestioned part of life, as did the unequal allocation of resources among the colonists. But many important changes did occur in the eighteenth century. African slavery slowly replaced Indian slavery. Forced Indian servitude eventually disappeared. The peasant population mushroomed.

The influence of Indians in the town began to decline in the first decades of the eighteenth century as Africans appeared in Parnaíba. In part, the waning presence of Indians resulted from their high mortality rate in the town and the end of the bandeiras and armações. As men in Parnaíba turned their attention to mining and commerce, they gave up the practice of Indian slaving and therefore forcibly settled many fewer Indians there.

Forced Indian service continued during the first half of the eighteenth century in a relationship known as *administração*. This was the crown's solution to the problem of Indian slavery in São Paulo. According to a royal charter of 1696, colonists who had brought Indians from the wilderness had the right to administer them as wards. This right passed to their descendants as well. But the law placed restrictions on colonists: the Indians must live in the Indian communities (aldeias) established by the Jesuits or the crown, they must be paid, and children and women were exempt from service.[43] This royal order seemed to legitimate Indian service, but its legality continued to be debated. In 1725, the town council of São Paulo spoke for all the colonists of the plateau when it summarized their position to the crown. The council cleverly argued that without Indians, colonists of São Paulo could not make new discoveries of gold in the wilderness or "destroy" the "barbarous" Indians who might "infest" the mining areas. The "brown people," the council continued, "know how to cut through the wilderness and navigate the rivers . . . they know how to feed the backwoodsman both from the rivers and from the land." Without them, the petition concluded, there would be no one to accompany the colonists into the wilderness.[44] To this petition, the king replied to his governor in São Paulo that he must inviolably uphold the king's laws concerning the liberty of Indians. On occasion, however, the governor might grant licenses to colonists to take Indians for service on the condition that the Indians be well treated and receive their proper stipend, as set out in royal edicts, because "only thus will Indians willingly embrace such service."[45]

While the debate raged over the morality and legality of Indian service, colonists in São Paulo continued to keep Indian wards in their households. A petition of an Indian family to the governor of São Paulo in 1733 clearly reflects that they believed administração to be slavery. The plaintiffs stated to a notary that they were descendants of Indians from São Paulo and therefore free from slavery[46] but that they had been living practically in slavery under administração "which is different from slavery in name and not in character." They accused their administrator of "always giving them the harsh treatment due to slaves." The suppliants asked to be removed from the house of their master and placed in an Indian community.[47]

In 1733, the governor of São Paulo and the Mines ordered all inhabitants to return Indian wards to the Indian communities. Administrators could only keep Indian wards in their homes with special permission from the governor, and only if they agreed to return the Indians to the communities when requested by the crown. A flood of petitions from administrators soon greeted the governor in São Paulo. For example, Jozeph Bernardinho de Souza asked for permission to keep an Indian ward of the Bororo nation who had lived with him since childhood. Jozeph pointed out that he had baptized the Indian, had taught him the doctrines of Christianity, had cared for him when ill, and had him married according to the laws of the church. The governor granted Jozeph's request, provided that he agree to return the Indian to an Indian community if requested by the crown.[48]

Many colonists received permission to keep their wards. In Parnaíba, Jozé Madeira Salvadores had two wards in his house in 1733.[49] Anna Vieira stated in 1734 in her will, "I own Gonçalo, a black of my administração who will serve me as long as I live and after I die he will follow the wishes of the deceased Anna Fernandes, as stated in her will."[50] João Marques de Araujo had five Guaraní under administration when he died in 1736. In his will, he stated that these wards "would follow the orders of His Majesty."[51] The colonists of Parnaíba continued to call their Indian wards "blacks," to will them to their heirs, and to freely use their services.[52]

From a register of burials performed by the priest of the parish of Araçariguama in the 1720s, it is possible to discern the social structure of Parnaíba in the early eighteenth century. The parish priest used three labels in his book of deaths: Indian wards (administrados), slaves, and the poor. A fourth group he did not label; these were the free residents of his parish whose estates easily covered the burial fee. From this register, a very rough view of the social groups of the town comes to light. Sixty-six percent of all those who died in the parish had been either Indian wards or African slaves during their lives. Administrados made up 46 percent of all those buried in the parish during the 1720s. Twenty percent of those who died were identified as slaves (*escravos*) and were of African origin.

The Indians and Africans who died belonged to forty-three different masters, some with quite large households. Bartolomeu Bueno da Silva, the discoverer of gold in Goiás, buried nine Indian wards in the ten-year period; Fernão Bicudo de Andrade buried six slaves and two Indian wards. Other households were smaller, such as that of Domingos Lopes, who buried only one slave in ten years, or Izabel Lara, who buried one Indian.

Thirty-four percent of all those who died in this ten-year period were not referred to as slaves or wards by the parish priest. These were the colonists of Parnaíba, the free population. Among these free persons were the masters of Indians and Africans as well as those whom the parish priest called "notoriously poor"—a reference to the peasant population that continued to grow in the eighteenth century.

It is not possible to reconstruct either the population of the parish or the mortality rates of social groups from the register, for without knowing the size of the population, one cannot arrive at a mortality rate for each group. Likewise, since Africans and Indians most probably had a higher mortality rate than the free, deaths alone are not an accurate measure of the proportion of each social group to the larger population. Nonetheless, the entries do offer a glimpse of the groups that made up the social structure of Parnaíba in the early eighteenth century (see table 2).

Indian servitude continued until 1758, when the crown completely abolished all forms of Indian administração. The crown also forbade the use of the word "black" to refer to Indians.[53] Thereafter, colonists rarely mention Indian wards in their wills. In the second half of the eighteenth century, Indians seem to disappear from all parishes in the town except that of the Indian community, Barueri.

Many of the Indians became part of the peasantry that grew rapidly in the town in the eighteenth century. Peasants were unable to afford the steep purchase price of African slaves and relied on their families, neighbors, kin, and occasional servants for labor. They lived in the rural districts of the town and planted on unclaimed lands. Some shared land and houses instead of dividing them every generation. João da Cunha, for example, owned half of his family's house in the town center and part of the family lands on the other side of the Tietê river. Luiza Gonçalves inherited one-fourth of her family's farm and its town house. By not dividing the land, heirs managed to keep the farm intact and increased the number of family members who worked on it.[54]

Others owned land outright, for example, Gabriella Ortis de

Table 2. Deaths among Social Groups, Parish of
Araçariguama, 1720–1731

	N	%
Free persons	40	21
Poor free persons	25	13
Indian wards	87	46
African slaves	38	20
Total	190	100

Source: Parish Book of Araçariguama, LP, 104, 6069–21, AESP.

Camargo and her husband, who owned a substantial piece consist-
ing of 220 meters along a road and back into the wilderness, or João
da Cunha, who owned 660 meters along a road back one-half
league into the wilderness.[55] But these families with enough property to justify an inventory were undoubtedly among the richest
of the peasants. As Luiza Gonçalves's inventory makes clear, they
lived relatively well. She owned three hammocks, three pillows,
two pairs of glasses, two wooden chests with locks, two pewter
plates, a pewter basin, a silver tray, household linens, and a
golden medallion. On the farm, she owned a hoe, two copper cal-
drons, a saw, and two wooden troughs.[56]

Individuals of this group were acutely aware of their status.
Domingas de Godoy Bicudo made this quite clear in her will. She
stated that she had been born in Parnaíba, the "natural" child of
Baltezar de Godoy Bicudo and Ursula, an Indian woman. She
stated, "It is my last wish that I be buried in this church of Parnaíba
under the holy water font, wrapped in a sheet, that two blacks
carry me to the church in a hammock, that the Reverend Vicar shall
be called to recommend me [to God], and to him shall be given
his candles and his fee." Domingas's funeral requests tell us much
about her and about the world to which she belonged. She carried
her father's name and asked his sister, her aunt, to be the executrix
of her estate. She felt that she belonged to the world of whites and
desired to be buried as they would be, in the church. She saw herself as superior to blacks, whom she ordered to carry her body to
the church. What little property she had left, after paying for her
funeral, she left to Anna Maria de Godoy, an abandoned orphan
being raised by her aunt, someone not unlike herself.[57]

The success of the commercial agricultural economy, based

primarily on sugar in the second half of the eighteenth century, brought places like Parnaíba into a wider orbit. Their populations began to grow, and new opportunities opened up in the town centers for artisans and shopkeepers. Yet the spread of this economy intensified competition for resources within Parnaíba. Once again, only a small minority benefited from the distribution of these resources.

The censuses initiated by the governor of São Paulo are remarkable documents that allow us to see the four parishes of Parnaíba in the late eighteenth century with remarkable clarity. These censuses list every individual in the town and describe what every household produced. They portray a small town center, inhabited by artisans, storekeepers, clergymen, and beggars, surrounded by rural districts inhabited by farmers. Slaves worked the farms of planters which produced sugar, rum, and cotton for sale and corn, beans, and rice for household consumption. Peasants owned no slaves and produced enough to feed the immediate family and a small surplus for exchange.

Slaves, the largest and most costly investment a farmer could make,[58] represented the ownership of labor, always a key resource in Parnaíba, even more important than land. In the late eighteenth century, slaves gave planters the means to extract a surplus of value. The more slaves planters owned, the more likely they grew sugar for a larger Atlantic market. However, those without slaves, the peasants, produced for household consumption and for a local market. Corn, beans, and pork fat comprised the bulk of their agricultural production. The two agricultural economies are summarized in table 3.

The ownership of land also differentiated planters who owned slaves from peasants who did not. Not surprisingly, planters enjoyed more stable access to land. According to the 1775 census, 91 percent of planters with more than ten slaves owned land, and 64 percent of all planters owned land (see table 4). The majority of peasants, however, did not own land. Instead, they planted "by favor" (*a favor*), that is, freely on unclaimed lands or on the uncultivated lands of others. As long as no one stopped them or as long as they had permission, they planted where they wished.

Three agricultural classes are clearly visible in the late-eighteenth-century censuses. Each had a very different relationship to

Table 3. Two Agricultural Economies: Income from Crops
by Class of Farmer, 1798

	Peasants		Planters	
	(N = 716)		(N = 263)	
	Average Income per Household (in reis)	Percent of Total Income	Average Income per Household (in reis)	Percent of Total Income
Food crops[a]	1,760	85	11,980	10
Cash crops[b]	320	15	110,910	90
Total	2,080	100	122,890	100

Source: 1798 census, Parnaíba.
[a]Corn, beans, pork fat.
[b]Cotton, rum, sugar.

Table 4. Landownership by Class of Farmer, 1775

	Peasants		Planters	
	N	%	N	%
Owns land	111	31	99	64
Joint ownership/ rents land	52	14	28	18
Plants "by favor"	196	55	27	18
Total	359	100	154	100

Source: 1775 census, Parnaíba.
Chi-square = 64.3; DF = 2; probability = 0.000.

the key resources of land and labor. Through the ownership of slaves, planters concentrated many laborers in their hands. They had extensive control over their slaves and forced them to work where and when they wished. They owned land. They grew crops, such as corn or beans, to support their large households, but they also cultivated cash crops, such as sugar or rum, for sale. The planters can be subdivided into two groups: large planters, who owned more than ten slaves, and small planters, who owned fewer than ten slaves. While the small planters produced less, owned less, and lived simpler lives, many were closely related to the larger planters through family ties. Others simply identified with the large planters.

Peasants relied on a labor force composed of their immediate family members, neighbors, kin, and live-in servants. They did not own laborers and depended on cooperation, rather than force, to work the land. Less than half of the peasants owned or rented land. This meant that the majority did not have stable access to it. Instead, they were squatters, planting where they could. They produced primarily for household consumption but sold their surpluses in local markets.

The third agricultural class, slaves, had the most limited access to labor, for their labor was almost completely owned by their masters. Only on their days off could slaves own the fruits of their labor. Neither did slaves possess land. Some slaves probably did cultivate gardens on the estates of their masters, and the food they grew supplemented the diet supplied by their masters. They may even have sold or exchanged the surplus harvest. But the differences between the slaves and free peasants are clear: held in bondage, slaves did not benefit from their own labor, while peasants did.

According to the censuses, the vast majority of the households in Parnaíba in the late eighteenth century (73%) were farmers who did not own slaves, the class I refer to as peasants. Slaves formed the second largest class. By the end of the century, 1,688 slaves (or 27% of the population) lived in the town. The slave-owning planters of Parnaíba formed the smallest class. Twenty-seven percent of all households at the end of the century owned slaves, but only 5 percent owned more than ten slaves, and only one household owned more than fifty.[59]

Where did Indians fit into this social order? Before the crown abolished the Indian aldeias in 1803, a final census of Baruerí offers some clues. In 1803, the official in charge of the community canvassed a population of 1,581 individuals living in 133 households. One-third of these households worked as farmers, one-third as laborers, and one-third as artisans. The farming families grew corn, manioc, and beans for their own subsistence; a few grew cotton and sugar and grazed cattle. No families owned slaves. The artisan families spun thread and made ceramic pots. Those who worked for a daily wage did so because they lacked lands to farm. Fifty-nine young men and women had left the community altogether for the city of São Paulo, the town center of Parnaíba, or the nearby towns of Itú and Sorocaba. The official in charge of the Indian community wrote, "The majority of this aldeia has deserted because the neighboring whites have taken all of their fields and farms and graze horses and mules on the lands farmed by the Indians and for this reason, they cannot cultivate."[60]

Indians were a "disappearing people" in eighteenth-century Parnaíba. So important to the survival of the town in the seventeenth century, their role diminished in Parnaíba as their numbers declined, as colonists purchased African slaves, and as the frontier moved west. Persons of Indian descent continued to live in the town but gradually vanished from the historical record. By the nineteenth century, what remained of the Guaraní, the Guaianá, the Bororo, and other Indian tribes who had once been the majority of the population of Parnaíba were to be found among those classified as *pardo*, "brown," in the town's censuses. The Indians in Parnaíba had clearly become part of the peasant class.

By the end of the eighteenth century, the center of Parnaíba had grown to a point at which it began to resemble a town. The town had a social structure, too, one that paralleled that of the rural areas. There was a good deal of overlap between the town and the rural area. Most of the planters owned a house in town (in addition to their farmhouse), and some of those who lived primarily in the town, such as merchants or the clergy, also owned farms. Still other urban groups were coming into existence, such as artisans, store- and tavernkeepers, civil servants, and beggars.

Each of the principal groups in the town center can be closely associated with a class in the rural area. The merchants, civil servants, and clergy owned slaves and identified with the planters. Shopkeepers, artisans, and mule drivers occasionally owned slaves, but most did not. They were an intermediate group, in between the small planters and the peasants. The poor free in the town center worked as domestic servants and laborers; they correspond to the peasantry. The existence of slavery in the town paralleled slavery in the countryside, but slaves often had more opportunities in the town. One slave even owned his own store.[61] Compared to the countryside, the town offered a wider range of occupations. For some, that meant a rise in social status. Becoming an artisan, a small storekeeper, or even a slave for the parish priest was a step up from life in the countryside as a peasant or an agricultural slave. But the town center also had its share of beggars and poor families who lived by collecting alms and by odd jobs (see table 5).

From the records of the town's jailer, it is possible to catch a glimpse of the differences among these three social classes that inhabited Parnaíba at the end of the eighteenth century. The jailer entered a description of each of his prisoners before he locked them up. The planters showed off the tastes, manners, and fashions of Lisbon. The jailer described João da Costa Silva, a Portuguese small planter, as having "long hair, brown eyes, a black beard, and a small nose." He was dressed in an English shirt with lace cuffs, scarlet pants, white stockings, a blue tunic bordered with yellow, and a dark blue cloak with silver buttons and peach-colored trim. The dress of peasants, in contrast, reveals that they were practical men and women who wore simple utilitarian clothing. Manuel Neves, a peasant from the rural parish of São Roque, wore the costume of many men: a cotton shirt, cotton pants, and a blue vest. Maria Gertrudes de Borba went to jail in 1817 wearing a blouse, a purple cotton skirt, leather sandals, and a blue cloak. The eighteenth-century slaves of Parnaíba wore clothing similar to that of peasants, but only a few had shoes. The slave woman Margarida wore a linen blouse, a blue skirt of coarse cotton, a green cloak, and no shoes when she entered the jail in 1764. Bartolomeu wore a cotton shirt and long loose trousers. A runaway slave named Manoel, remitted to the jailer in 1790, was described as "wrapped in an old hammock, his hair all disheveled."[62]

Perceptions of race and color reinforced this social order. As in the seventeenth century, planters perceived themselves and were seen by others as white; African slaves, as black or mulatto. "Blackness," in the minds of many residents in the town carried the connotation of slavery. In 1779, João Leite Pais testified that "it is well known in this town of Parnaíba that I am white and free by my very nature." João and his family had been imprisoned and forced to work for the rich and powerful planter Policarpo Joaquim de Oliveira. João complained, "[It] is well known, by all the people, that which happened to me, being a white man, and to my family, who even if they are not white, still are emancipated, free from slavery."[63]

To be "white" in Parnaíba also implied a certain social status. In 1787, Joze Branco Ribeiro, the procurator of the town council,

Table 5. The Town Center in 1798

	Households		Slaves Owned	
	N	%	N	%
Clergy/merchants/ civil servants	39	18	105	78
Artisans/mule drivers/ storekeepers	93	42	22	16
Laborers/domestics/ poor	86	39	7	5
Independent slaves	3	1	0	–
Total	221	100	134	99

Source: 1798 census, Parnaíba.

petitioned to annul the election of Joze Ignacio Gonçalves as an alderman because "various republicans say that he is not white and that the cane of office should be taken from him and another named in his place."[64] The members of the town council agreed and refused to let Joze Ignacio assume his position.

The degree to which color reinforced the class structure in Santana de Parnaíba emerges very clearly in the 1820 census. In that census, 97 percent of the planters appeared as "white" and 80 percent of the slaves as "black." In between, the "browns" accounted for 33 percent of the population: 46 percent of the peasant class, 21 percent of the slave class, and 3 percent of the planter class (see table 6).

In the eighteenth century, as in the seventeenth century, perceptions of color were fluid in Parnaíba. João Leite Pais who testified to the crown that he was "white" and therefore "free by his very nature" appeared in the census of 1775 as a retainer on the former Jesuit estate of Araçariguama. The retainers of the estate were those descended from former Indian administrados and freed African slaves. Joze Ignacio Gonçalves [Pais], whose colleagues on the town council refused to let him take office "because he was not white" was nevertheless presumed "white" by the census takers who only recorded the color of those deemed "brown" or "black" in the 1798 census. Joze Ignacio was not among them. In the 1820 census, which recorded race for all individuals, he and his family appeared as "whites."

Still, as table 6 so convincingly portrays, race and class were in-

Table 6. Race and Class in Parnaíba, 1820

	Planters		Peasants		Slaves	
	N	%	N	%	N	%
White	1010	96.9	2104	51	1	0.1
Brown	29	2.8	1921	46	386	20.5
Black	3	0.3	126	3	1500	79.5
Total	1042	100	4151	100	1887	100.1

Source: 1820 census, Parnaíba.
Chi-square = 5704.1; DF = 4; probability = 0.000.

exorably entwined. Only three blacks owned slaves in 1820 and can be considered part of the planter class. Only one white appeared as a slave, a six-year-old girl, listed in the census as Creole (*crioula*) and probably incorrectly designated as white. Only the peasant class was racially integrated. But even among the peasants, only 3 percent appeared as black. Many peasants listed as brown in the census undoubtedly were mulattoes, but the fact that they considered themselves and were considered by others as brown and not black underscores the degree to which those who were free wished to disassociate themselves from the word "negro," which for two centuries had been synonymous with slavery in the town.

From the small wilderness settlement of the 1580s to the racially stratified town of over 7,000 persons in 1820, Parnaíba had radically changed. But although the town in 1820 seemed very different from its first incarnation as a frontier village, the origins of its social structure lay deep in the past. How the first colonists exploited the wilderness, established slavery as a way of life, and planted the seeds for a poor free peasantry in the seventeenth century created the Parnaíba visible in 1820. On the eve of Brazil's independence from Portugal, Parnaíba was a society characterized by three classes: planters, peasants, and slaves. As we shall see in the following chapters, family life differed for each class, and patterns of family life contributed to the formation of social classes in the town.

4

Families of Planters

Who were the planter families of Parnaíba, and how did they live? The censuses initiated by São Paulo's governors in the late eighteenth century paint, in quick, broad strokes, a vivid picture of these families. The first household listed in these censuses was always that of the captain major (*capitão mor*), the commander of the local militia.[1] In 1775, Antonio Correa de Lemos Leite served as captain major of Parnaíba. The picture of his household in the census indicated that he, a native of the city of São Paulo, was married to Mariana Dias, the great-great-great-great-granddaughter of the founders of Parnaíba.[2] Antonio, Mariana, and seven of their children divided their time between a townhouse and a farm with fifteen slaves. They produced corn, beans, and cane brandy and reared horses on their farm. Two older sons and a son-in-law ventured periodically into the wilderness to trade horses and cattle.[3]

Property set Antonio's family apart from the rest of the men and women of the town. The lands, slaves, commercial ventures, and liquid capital he controlled allowed his family to live very differently than the families of peasants and slaves. The planters of Parnaíba inhabited a separate world, a world much more of their own making than that of the peasants and slaves.

The family life of the planters unfolded in the separate but interrelated worlds of town and country. Families owned farms in rural Parnaíba and townhouses in the town center. On their farms, they lived in simple but solid structures, created from local materials. The most common construction technique used in the eighteenth century was *taipa de pilão*, a process that pressed mud in huge molds to form earthen blocks. When mortared together, these blocks created thick walls. Then, plastered and whitewashed, they provided the cool but dark interiors of the farmhouses. Hewn beams supported roofs shingled with red clay tiles. Each house consisted of several stretches (*lanças*), or separate structures, connected by an open or closed corridor. Some had verandas along one side. Outside the farmhouse could be found a terrace, used for a variety of tasks, the slave huts made from straw or wattle and daub, the sugar house, which housed a small mill (*moenda*) and a still (*alambique*), an outdoor kitchen, and corrals for farm animals. Beyond the farmhouse lay the lands of the farm. By the end of the eighteenth century, much of the forests immediately around the house had already been cleared. What was not planted in cane or other crops was left to regrow or was used as pasture for livestock.

Inside the cool, dark, and damp farmhouse, planter families lived simply, as their forebears had done. The rooms were plain, with only a few pieces of furniture in each. Wooden tables, stools, benches, long chests, wardrobes, and buffets, all of simple construction, were pushed against the walls to maximize space. Home altars provided the only decorative and artistic touches in these austere rooms. Made from wood and painted in bright colors, they held the treasured images of saints, the Virgin, and the Christ. At night, oil lamps, fashioned from metal and tacked into the walls, provided a dim source of light.

While the planters of Parnaíba lived well compared to their slaves or their peasant neighbors, they hardly lived opulently, even by the standards of Brazil. By the end of the eighteenth century, however, their homes began to become more comfortable and took on a more domestic and genteel air. Families acquired beds with mattresses to replace cots woven from sticks and vines. They covered their beds with coverlets sewn from silk, damask, and cotton. They began to use china and pewter plates rather than earthenware, and they ate with forks and spoons rather than with their fingers. A few households added books on law, military rules, or the etiquette of nobles to their small collections of devotional books.

In addition to a farmhouse, every planter family owned a townhouse in Parnaíba's town center, and the richest also owned a house in the city of São Paulo. These houses were two-storied and also constructed from taipa de pilão. Outside, they built a high, long wall around the deep but narrow yard (*quintal*) in which they planted fruit trees and gardens. Families spent time in both houses, but the farmhouse remained their primary residence. Their houses in town provided close access to the church, to the town council, and to religious festivals.

Family life prepared the younger generations for the roles they would one day assume as owners of slaves, managers of large farms, and leaders in the town. Children became intimately familiar with the isolated and agrarian world of the farm as well as the livelier and more public world of the town. From a young age, children learned that they were the masters of slaves on the family farm and that men and women in the town deferred to their fathers and mothers. On the farm, they observed the simple rhythm of the passage of seasons with which family slaves coordinated the planting and harvesting of crops and the milling of sugar. In the town, they participated in the festivals that marked the religious calendar.

Parents reared their sons and daughters differently, according to the roles they would play as adults. A daughter learned to sew, to embroider, and to make lace but not how to read. She lived out of sight (*recolhida*) from the larger community, appearing in public only to attend mass. Protected from the outside world and kept ignorant of the family business, young women were not expected to know much about family affairs. Still, surrounded by family and servants, women managed to keep up with the goings-on in the isolated, but not very private, world of the farm. In the town, hidden from view by the heavily shuttered windows of the townhouse, young women would overhear conversations between servants who left the house to collect water or to do the family laundry on the banks of the river. Outwardly demure and proper, the young women of this class knew more about life in the town and the family affairs than they let on.

How parents reared their daughters can be inferred from a variety of sources, including the inquiries made by the orphan's judge to the guardians of orphaned children. In Brazil, the law considered any child who had lost one parent an orphan, thus such inquiries were a common phenomenon. The surviving parent usually became the child's guardian, and the orphan's judge ensured that the guardian fulfilled his or her obligation to the child and properly educated him or her according to the standards of the day. From the questions posed to Ignacio Diniz Caldeira, for example, we learn that "all of his daughters knew how to sew and all of his sons knew how to read and write."[4] Such a statement suggests that daughters did not, as a matter of course, learn to read and write. Very few women could even sign their names when required to do so in legal documents. Most simply marked a cross, next to which the notary wrote "cross of" so and so.[5] A most unusual document provides another interesting glimpse into the lives of young women. This document survives from the late eighteenth century and pertains to a woman in Parnaíba accused of being a witch. The men who testified against her described how this woman caused the honorable young ladies of the town, who lived recolhidas, to fall into trances, become hysterical, and "speak of things which they could not possibly know" when she entered the church. From these testimonies, it can be inferred that young women lived largely in seclusion except for attending mass. Yet they knew considerably more than men thought they did because, when unnerved by the presence of a suspected witch, they blurted out things they were not supposed to know.[6]

When it came time for a daughter to marry, her parents sought a suitable husband. Since daughters had been raised to respect and defer to their fathers, most of them accepted the men their fathers selected for them to marry. One bit of evidence on how little daughters had to say in whom they married comes from one of the very few divorce cases from Parnaíba which were filed in the ecclesiastical court of São Paulo. The plaintiff, Francisca de Paula de Oliveira, stated that she never wanted to marry her husband and that she "only did it out of obligation and respect for her father." This statement suggests that daughters suppressed their own views and followed the wishes of their parents, particularly their fathers.[7]

With his prospective son-in-law, a father discussed family business matters and the nature of the dowry he would give his daughter on her marriage. The dowry usually included land, slaves, and household necessities the couple would use to set up their own household. Then the parish priest posted the banns. If no impediments to the marriage surfaced, he married the couple in the church according to canon law. After the marriage, the newlyweds often settled close to the bride's natal family. The young wife still remained tied to her family, especially during the early years of the marriage. Her father made sure that her husband treated her well and did not abuse her dowry. For example, in the divorce case cited above, Francisca's father did not hesitate to take her out of her husband's house when he had reason to believe that her husband was mistreating her. Francisca's short-term husband stated in his will that he lived with her for only eight months when his father-in-law came and took his wife "out of his power."[8] It would seem, then, that fathers had considerable authority over their sons-in-law, especially during the early years of marriage.

As the marriage matured, a wife became a more visible person in the town and an important member of her family. By law, she owned half of the community property that her husband, as head of the family, managed with her consent. Her husband could not spend, loan, or alienate her share of the community property without her permission.[9] If she gave birth to children, she raised them much as she had been raised, with the help of her female kin and servants. Women became even more powerful figures in their families if their husbands died before them. Then, as widows, they shouldered the responsibilities once held by their husbands. Widows headed households and managed family properties but always with the support and backing of other male kin.[10]

Women who never married continued to live with their parents. To these women fell the task of caring for elderly parents and relatives. Late in their lives, they, too, might become heads of households and the sole managers of their own property. Such is the story of Anna Caetana de Jesus, who never married and who lived at home all her life. Her father's will mentioned that she had "served" him during his life. After her father died, she continued to care for her mother. In 1798, the census recorded their household—Anna's mother, eighty-two years old, Anna, and a few slaves. After her mother died, Anna ran the family farm on her own. But this was not an easy task for a single woman. In 1816, she lodged a formal petition with a provincial official in São Paulo asking that he intercede because her neighbor had "violently entered her lands because she is a woman and took her lands by brute force with the knowledge of the captain major." What the outcome of the petition was, we do not know, but Anna continued to live on her farm in Parnaíba, for her name later appeared in the census of 1820.[11]

Sons of planters learned how to read and write and to keep

accounts. As young adults, they became members of the militia. At about the same time in their lives, their fathers began to entrust them with serious responsibilities. Many learned how to trade cattle, horses, and mules from ranches in the south of São Paulo to Minas Gerais and Goiás. Men remained minors, however, until they married or reached the age of twenty-five years. Until that time, they were considered family sons (*filho famílias*) or under their fathers' authority (*debaixo do pátrio poder*).[12] Only when men married or were "emancipated" from parental authority by a judge, that is, declared of age, were they recognized as independent adults in the town. Still, absent from home for long periods of time as merchants, they made many decisions about family business matters. When their parents died, men received their share of the family property and might then consider marrying. But since men did not take possession of family property until their parents died, many married late in life, usually much later than women. In 1775, for example, men were, on the average, 10.7 years older than their wives.[13] This meant that men spent longer portions of their lives single and that when they married, they usually selected women several years younger.

As husbands, men represented their households in the town. A man of the planter class would be expected to serve in the militia and to vote in the elections of the town council. One day he might serve as alderman in that body or if he was particularly able, as the orphan's judge. Married men joined religious brotherhoods, such as the Brotherhood of the Most Holy Sacrament, the most important in Parnaíba, which maintained the altars of the church, sponsored festivals, and loaned small sums of money to individuals in the town. As the head of his family, master of his slaves, and a leader in the town, few would challenge the husband's authority or judgment, whatever he did. If a man's wife died before him, he likely as not remarried. If he remained a widower, he continued to manage all family affairs until he died. Powerful in family and community, the married man of the planter class reigned secure until he died.

Thus, one of the most important, and indeed unquestioned, characteristics of planter family life was its patriarchal nature. Individuals of this class grew up in large, inegalitarian households. Women deferred to men; younger men deferred to older men.

Slaves and servants knew their subordinate place in the household. In many ways, the family life of planter families reflected in miniature many of the hierarchies of the larger town.

Dividing their time between the family farm and the house in the town center, individuals of the planter class married, formed families, reared their children, and passed their property on to the next generation. But because of the historic importance of the wilderness in Parnaíba's history, Parnaíba was not the whole sphere of the family's interests. During the seventeenth and eighteenth centuries, the wilderness to the north, west, and south of Parnaíba held the potential for accumulating labor and capital. Families spent considerable time developing investments in the frontier. Men formed partnerships to raise capital and supplies for expeditions into the interior in search of slaves and minerals. The sons and sons-in-law of planter families made their way through the eighteenth-century mining districts selling mules, flour, cornmeal, and cane brandy. Other sons became soldiers, stationed in the south or on frontier military outposts. Still other sons went south to develop the ranches that supplied the cattle and horses planter families peddled in the mining regions.

As the wilderness drew fathers, sons, and sons-in-law away to hunt for Indians, to oversee mining claims, to serve as professional soldiers, or to trade, women remained behind. Women from planter families usually moved into the interior only after towns had been founded, after agricultural estates had been built, or after valuable mining claims had been obtained. Then women, usually as new brides, accompanied men into the interior. This meant that in Parnaíba, women often outnumbered men. Households of planters reflected the presence of women and the absence of men, as the captain major's did in 1775. In that year, his household contained seven women and only three men—himself, his son, and his son-in-law.

Planter families also maintained ties to the colonial empire. For families in Parnaíba, this meant linking themselves, both economically and politically, to the nearest manifestation of colonial power and authority, most often the city of São Paulo.[14] Some families kept houses in the city of São Paulo, where they resided from time to time. Men traveled frequently to São Paulo and to the port of Santos to conduct business. Families also maintained close contacts with religious institutions in the city, such as the Holy House of Mercy (Santa Casa de Misericórdia), religious brotherhoods, or monastic orders. Often wealthy men left bequests to such institutions in their wills.

Planter families sought men from the cities, especially natives of São Paulo or immigrants from Portugal, for their daughters to marry. Some sons-in-law, like Antonio Correa de Lemos Leite, came from well-connected families in the city of São Paulo which could exert influence to obtain for their sons military appointments in smaller towns like Parnaíba. Sons-in-law who came from less wealthy families, such as immigrants from Portugal, were also seen as advantageous additions to the family. For even if they did not bring significant property into the family, they still brought a familiarity with a larger, more urbane and commercial world.[15]

Thus, planter families interacted in the three different spheres of town, kingdom, and wilderness: in Parnaíba itself, in the wilderness to the west, and in São Paulo or other towns and cities to the east. Family customs maintained these interactions as men followed their fathers' footsteps into the interior, as sons-in-law married into families in Parnaíba, and as daughters continued to live in Parnaíba. Each of these spheres contributed to a family's continuing wealth and status in Parnaíba in subsequent generations.

The planters of the late eighteenth century survived as generations of their families had done before them. Like their forebears, they owned slaves, farms, and interacted in the interior. Because they maintained their wealth over generations, the same families were able to dominate the institutions of political and military importance in the town over time. An excellent indication of this is the fact that the captain major, the most important local official in Parnaíba in 1775, had married a direct descendant of the original founders of the town.

How did families of planters maintain their power from generation to generation? The answer to this question has much to do with the ways that planter families planned for their survival in conscious and not-so-conscious ways. It lies in the customs of family life, characteristic of this class, which served to maintain Parnaíba's planters in power over time.

Survival for the planters of Parnaíba was intimately tied to what they did with their property. Ordinary family events such as births, marriages, and deaths all had hidden importance, for each would one day affect the fortunes of all.[16] Such events could never be ignored or left to chance, because they carried too many implications for the family property. Not surprisingly, the planters gradually initiated customs that regulated family life and that, as a consequence, protected the family property. Central to the ability of the planters to maintain themselves as the dominant class was the transmission of property from one generation to the next. Planter families managed to do this in such a way that the family, or at least part of it, remained part of the planter class, in possession of significant property, such as land and slaves.

The division of property in the families of planters carried enormous consequences for every member of the family. Since status and power derived from the ownership of resources, inheritance determined who became powerful in the family and in the town in the next generation. Planter families began to divide their property when their daughters married, a time when parents presented them with dowries. Subsequent divisions occurred after the deaths of each parent, when children inherited the property that belonged to their fathers and mothers. While Portuguese law set the framework for transfers of property at marriage and inheritance, local custom modified the full impact of these laws.[17]

The laws that regulated inheritance in the Portuguese empire rested on the principle that property belonged to a family, not to an individual. Individuals had rights to property during their lifetimes, but their property returned to their families after they died. An individual could not, for example, freely dispose of his or her property as he or she saw fit. Instead, the law required that property be divided by a local orphan's judge between family members according to specific rules. These rules placed the children of the deceased first in line to inherit the property, followed by grandchildren. If the deceased had no children or grandchildren, then parents, or in their absence, grandparents, inherited the property. If the deceased had no children, grandchildren, parents, or grandparents, brothers and sisters came next. If the deceased had no living siblings, then property went to aunts, uncles, nieces, nephews, and cousins. Only when the deceased had no kin related to him or her by descending, ascending, or lateral ties could the surviving spouse inherit the property.[18]

Even if an individual wrote a will, he or she could not dramatically change what happened to the property. An individual could not write a will that disinherited a child, unless that child had committed transgressions that the law recognized as grounds for such an act. These grounds included such things as a daughter losing her virginity before marriage, witchcraft, heresy, incest, or the failure to care for parents in their old age.[19] Writing a will only gave an individual the right to dispose of one-third (the *terça*) of his or her property freely. The rest of the property went directly to the heirs according to the line of succession, as laid out in the law.

The intent of these laws is clear: property came from and reverted to one's blood family. The laws convey a clear sense that the rights of individuals were subordinate to those of the family. The law made certain that families provided for all of their members, which reduced the likelihood that individuals would be abandoned and left destitute. But the law also made sure that one individual could not squander the resources that supported a larger family. As a whole, the legal code gave individuals little control over who inherited their property.

The evolution of Portuguese inheritance law also reflected the preeminent position of the nobility in Portuguese society. Laws of inheritance gave nobles rights that ordinary people did not have. For example, members of the nobility could place some of their property into entailed estates, known as *morgados*, that could not be divided. A morgado protected the family name and status by ensuring that property would pass undivided to the oldest son in each generation.[20] The law clearly set forth the rationale for this:

> The purpose of the grandees and lords and noble persons of our Kingdoms and domains, who create morgados from their property and entail them to pass through their sons and descendants, is to conserve the memory of their name and the increase of their status, houses, and nobleness, and so that the ancient lineage which they come from, and the services which they rendered to the Kings, our predecessors, will always be known.[21]

Portuguese inheritance law did not extend this privilege to the common people, who were not expected to acquire property or to challenge the dominance of the nobility. According to law, commoners had to divide all of their property equally among all their children. This meant that the nobility could use inheritance laws to ensure that one heir inherited the family estate and status. Commoners, however, could not use inheritance laws to maintain their property intact, since the law obligated them to divide it every generation.[22]

Portuguese law permitted different principles to govern marriages, which had the effect of further differentiating the nobles and the commoners. In the usual marriage, the law considered husbands and wives the co-owners of the family property. Half belonged to the husband, and half belonged to the wife. But the law also recognized a second kind of marriage, sealed by a contract of dowry and bride gift. In these marriages, prospective brides and grooms signed contracts that kept their property separate. A bride brought a dowry to the marriage, and a groom gave the bride a bride gift, which was to support her in the event of his death. This exchange of dowry and bride gift took the place of the community property shared by husbands and wives in the ordinary form of marriage. It was probably used extensively by the nobility, who wished to limit the rights of women to property in order to protect the integrity of large estates.[23]

Portuguese inheritance law gave commoners some leeway in the division of their property by allowing the individual to freely allocate one-third of his or her property. The law set aside one-third of whatever an individual owned, and this third could be given to whomsoever an individual wished. But such wishes had to be set out in wills, properly notarized by a government official. Thus, if an individual wrote a will and gave away one-third of his or her property, the legal heirs were entitled only to the remaining two-thirds. Then these two thirds were divided evenly among all the heirs. Each received a *legitima*, or equal share (see fig. 1).[24]

A second way of favoring one child over another worked through the dowry. Commoners could present a daughter with a dowry when she married. The couple used the dowry to establish themselves as an independent household. Then, when the parents died, the couple could either keep the dowry and not receive an inheritance or return the dowry and inherit equally with the other heirs. Since the couple chose whether or not to return the dowry,

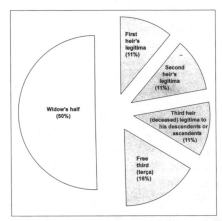

Figure 1. Division of Community Property at the Death of a
Married Man with Three Children

if it was greater than the expected inheritance, they could keep the
dowry and thereby remain in possession of more than their equal
share (legitima) of the family property. If the value of the dowry
was less than the legitima, the couple could trade it in for the larger
inheritance. The law did limit the size of dowries, however, and
stipulated that a dowry could not exceed the value of an heir's
legitima plus the free third (terça) of the parent (see fig. 2).[25]

Portuguese law assigned different rights to children, depending
on the class into which they were born. Children of the nobility
had their rights to the family property spelled out by their sex and
birth order. The oldest living son inherited the entailed estate
(morgado), if the family had one, and only if the family had no
living sons might a daughter inherit it.[26] The younger sons and
daughters of these families could inherit other family property that
was not part of an entailed estate. Natural children had no rights
to the property that belonged to their noble fathers or mothers.[27]

Children of commoners, however, had equal rights to their parents' property. The oldest son had no special privileges that set
him apart from his siblings. Rather, he received just as much of
the family property as each of his younger brothers and sisters.
Natural children did have rights to the family property and could
inherit from their parents along with legitimate children.[28]

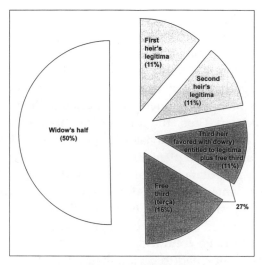

Figure 2. Division of Community Property at the Death of a
Married Man with One Favored Heir

These complicated inheritance laws established clear procedures
for the division of family property. They made it easier for the
nobility to maintain itself as a class apart from the commoners,
because the nobility could limit the division of property. By entail-
ing property, a noble family ensured that its status and prestige
would be preserved in one branch of the family in every generation. The use of marriage contracts, similarly, might allow them to
protect property from division among heirs. Commoners could not
use the law to prevent the division of family property. Except for
dowries and the terça, over which they did have jurisdiction, commoners had to divide their property according to law, or equally
among all their children.

Portuguese marriage and inheritance law derived from Roman
law and from customs that developed in Portugal.[29] The codifica-
tion of Portuguese law in the *Ordenações filipinas* of 1603 applied to
Brazil, even though the realities of life there were often quite different from Portugal. For example, few nobles of great status and
wealth left Portugal for Brazil; instead, lesser nobles, small property holders, merchants, artisans, and the poor—all in search of
social mobility—made their way to the New World. The vast majority of the population in Brazil, then, fell into the category of

"commoners." Even wealthy planters could not claim to be members of the nobility. Moreover, few entailed estates were ever established in Brazil.[30] Similarly, in Brazil, the vast majority of the marriages that occurred took place under rules that applied to commoners. Except for the very rich, few of whom ever lived in a town like Parnaíba, men and women who married in Brazil shared community property.[31] Thus, the laws of inheritance that applied in Brazil called for an equal division of all property. They gave no special privileges to the planters.

Portuguese inheritance law placed the status-conscious planters of towns like Santana de Parnaíba in a quandary. None of these families, with perhaps one or two exceptions, could claim to be noble. None entailed their property in morgados. Very few, if any, ever signed marriage contracts. Many had natural children. According to law, they had to divide their property as the common people of Portugal did, equally among all their children. While the equal division of property among all children was undoubtedly just and humane, it also raised the specter of a shrinking pool of family resources, which would inevitably cause downward social mobility in successive generations.[32] How then, did families of planters in Parnaíba maintain themselves over time?

The families of the planters circumvented the full effect of inheritance law by devising a strategy that encouraged the maintenance of large estates of land and labor. Four common practices lay at the core of this family strategy. First, families took advantage of provisions in the law, such as the use of the marriage dowry or the free third, that allowed them to favor some children over others. This allowed them to grant a larger portion of their property to one or two heirs and discouraged the fragmentation of property. Second, men of the planter class did not automatically allow their natural children to be instituted as heirs, entitled to an equal share of the family property. This effectively limited the number of potential heirs. Third, families took care to ensure that family resources were not finite but expanding. This desire underlay their aggressive pursuit of new resources from the wilderness in each generation. And fourth, families encouraged migration into the frontier in order to limit the number of descendants who would have to be supported by family property in Parnaíba. The presence of a vast frontier, and its use by generation after generation of families, meant that more descendants could be provided for than if a family was limited to simply its resources in Parnaíba. Combined, these practices enabled planter families to retain their social position over time.

Although the law stated that the natural children of a *peão*, or foot soldier (i.e., a commoner), could inherit from their fathers but that the natural children of *cavaleiros* (knights), *escudeiros* (shield bearers), or others who rode on horseback (i.e., nobility) could not, in both the seventeenth and eighteenth centuries, the fathers of natural children in Parnaíba themselves determined if their natural children would inherit equally with their legitimate children. While in the seventeenth century, the decision varied from man to man,[33] by the eighteenth century, few fathers respected the rights of natural children to be named as legal heirs, entitled to an equal share (legitima) of their fathers' property. Salvador Gracia Pontes Lumbria declared in his 1747 will, "I do not have a legitimate son but only a natural son," and countermanded the inheritance laws by declaring his heirs to be both his wife and this son. Moreover, the son had the obligation of remaining with his stepmother. If he left her company, he lost his inheritance altogether. Yet according to law, the natural son should have inherited all of Salvador's property. A wife only inherited in the absence of any blood descendants, ascendants, and lateral kin.[34] Instead of their legal share, natural children in eighteenth-century Parnaíba usually received simple bequests from their fathers' wills. This prevented them from competing with legitimate children for the larger legitimas. Jozeph Pereira Rara named a natural son in his will in 1742 but did not institute him with his legitimate children as an heir, and the son received only a small bequest from Jozeph's free third.[35] Single fathers who did not have other children did name their natural children as their heirs. Father Ignacio de Almeida Lara who had three natural children designated them as his legal heirs.[36] Similarly, Daniel Rocha Franco never married and stated in his will that his natural son was his only heir.[37] Thus, in the eighteenth century, as in the seventeenth century, the custom in Parnaíba was that a man could decide if his natural children would inherit from his estate.

That men of the planter class, particularly those with legitimate children, did not generally allow their natural children to receive equal shares of the family property indicates the existence of a family strategy to modify the dictates of law in the interests of property. These men denied their natural children their legal rights so as to preserve the family property for legitimate children. The fewer children who inherited, the larger the share each would receive.

Planter families did recognize the rights of all children, sons as well as daughters, from legal marriages to inherit family property equally. Yet here, too, customs developed in Parnaíba to favor some children over others in each generation. Families did so to prevent the natural fragmentation of property that would occur if they divided everything equally. One of the most common customs used to favor one heir over another worked through the dowry. Dowries in Parnaíba consisted of a trousseau—linens, bedding, clothes—and productive property such as land, slaves, houses, gold, and silver. A daughter usually received her share of the family property when she married, through the dowry, rather than after her parents died. At marriage, the dowry became part of the community property she shared with her husband and which her husband controlled with her consent. Because a husband managed the community property, was known as the "head of the family" (*cabeça de casal*), and received the dowry directly from his wife's father, he commonly referred to the dowry as his own, even though technically it belonged to his wife. A woman's rights to her dowry were protected by law. For example, her husband was not supposed to loan it or to sell it without her consent.[38]

Beginning in the seventeenth century, planter families of Parnaíba used dowries to attract suitable husbands for their daughters. The eighteenth-century historian, Frei Gaspar Madre de Deus, writing on the early history of São Vicente, summed up the rationale behind this practice:

> The Paulistas [residents of São Paulo] could give their daughters extensive land, Indians, and slaves in their dowries, from which they could live handsomely; for this reason, when they selected husbands for them, they were more concerned with the birth rather than the property of their future sons-in-law; usually they betrothed them [their daughters] to compatriots of kin, or to foreign noblemen; a man in this position, arriving from Europe or other Captaincies in Brazil, could expect a good marriage, even if he was very poor.[39]

The granting of large dowries to prospective sons-in-law evolved into a local custom in São Vicente. In seventeenth-century Parnaíba, the settlement of estates indicates that an heir who had received a dowry had the right to return the dowry and inherit, or keep the full dowry, regardless of how large. Parents used considerable latitude in favoring daughters and sons-in-law, and there was little that less-favored sons and daughters could do about it. This practice counteracted the true intent of the law, which limited the size of a dowry to an heir's equal shares (legitimas) of the family property plus the free thirds (terças) of the parents.[40] Muriel Nazzari's work on dowries granted in the city of São Paulo also shows that the dowries granted in the city commonly exceeded a daughter's equal share of the family property.[41]

The inventories and wills of planter families in seventeenth-century Parnaíba reveal that there, as in the city of São Paulo and indeed in many inheritance systems,[42] the dowry served as an important means of transferring property to the younger generations. At inheritance, the seventeenth-century orphan's judges did not adjust the size of dowries to take into account the rights of the other, less-favored, heirs. When Izabel da Cunha's estate was settled in 1650, the orphan's judge ordered that "Claudio Furquim be summoned to see if he wished to return the dowry to inherit from this estate with the other heirs," but "he, the said Claudio Furquim, said that he did not want the inheritance."[43] Claudio simply elected to keep the dowry, and the judge considered it to be his inheritance, even though, according to the law, the orphan's judge was supposed to make sure that its value did not exceed the value of one equal share plus Izabel's third. If it did, by law, Claudio would have to return the excess.

Seventeenth-century inventories also make clear that families saw the dowry as essential for their family's survival. Few sons questioned the "fairness" of the large dowries paid to their brothers-in-law. Rather, brothers made sure that their sisters received dowries, even if it meant relinquishing their own inheritances. This attitude can be seen in the settlement of Izabel Mendes's estate: her sons forfeited their inheritances to provide dowries for their sisters. This inventory stated that "the sons gave up their share, which by law came to them in the property and slaves, and which by law they inherited, to marry their sisters, and as all were satisfied, they agreed never to go against the intent of this agreement and accepted the division as complete and settled from this day and forever."[44] Thus, five men agreed to give up their own inheritances so that two women could have marriage dowries.

While the orphan's judges of the seventeenth century had the obligation of enforcing the laws regarding inheritance, they did not interfere in the actual distribution of family property among heirs. Rather, they oversaw the appraisal of the family property and made sure that outstanding debts would be paid. Then, as long as the widowed spouse obligated himself or herself to pay the debts, the judges turned over the property to the widowed spouse and did not supervise the division of property among the children. This gave the widowed spouse considerable freedom in distributing the family property among the children. As a result, when individuals wrote their own wills, complaints often surfaced over the fact that they had not yet received their inheritances.[45] The fact that orphan's judges did not appear to have been powerful actors in the inheritance process thus worked to the advantage of families who wished to favor certain heirs over others.

In the eighteenth century, however, the rights of the endowed heirs began to diminish, and orphan's judges became powerful individuals, intimately involved in the distribution of property. Judges selected the property for each legitima and required sons-in-law to return part of their dowries if they exceeded their fair share. Orphan's judges finally enforced the upper limit on the size of the dowry, too, by making sure that it did not exceed the value of a legitima plus the free third. A visiting judge left clear instructions for orphan's judges in Parnaíba: judges could only allow one dowry per family to be greater than an equal inheritance plus the free third. Thus, the endowed heir was entitled to keep his dowry as long as it did not exceed the value of his wife's equal share of the family property *plus* the thirds of both parents. If a dowry exceeded this formula, the son-in-law had to return the excess. This modification protected the other heirs from the rights of endowed sons-in-law by placing a ceiling on how much of the estate could be granted in dowries. But it nevertheless protected the rights of parents to favor at least one heir.[46]

These controls diminished but did not eradicate the long-standing custom of granting large dowries in Parnaíba. Planter families still favored sons-in-law, for the orphan's judges allowed one dowry to be as large as a daughter's two equal shares (one from each parent) plus the free thirds of each parent. The favoring of sons-in-law with large dowries can be seen in the family of Mariana Pais, a great-great-granddaughter of the founders of Parnaíba. Her son and second husband had promised exorbitant dowries to the fiancés of her daughters. These dowries greatly exceeded the equal shares of the family property which the daughters would eventually receive when their father and mother died. The dowries themselves were never fully paid. Yet even so, the sons-in-law received an extensive amount of property when they married and only repaid the excess many years later, when Mariana Pais died.

The division of Mariana Pais's estate shows that dowries still provided the means for favoring some heirs over others in the eighteenth century. By reconstructing her estate, we find that she promised Andre Pinto da Fonseca Coutinho a dowry of 32 pounds of gold when he married her daughter. This son-in-law actually received 25 pounds of gold, still a hefty sum. She promised a second prospective bridegroom, Pedro Vas de Campos, 4,800,000 reis in gold plus his bride-to-be's inheritance from her father (400,000 reis) as his marriage dowry. Another son-in-law, Caetano Alves Rodrigues, was to receive a dowry of 4,800,000 reis, fifteen slaves, and the family estate in Parnaíba. When Mariana died in 1740, Andre Pinto da Fonseca Coutinho and his wife, Antonia, who received the first dowry, told the orphan's judge, "We are not obliged to return the dowry because it was the first dowry paid." The orphan's judge ruled that as the first endowed couple, they were entitled to Mariana's third but that they had to repay the estate the amount of the dowry above and beyond the value of Antonia's legitima plus Mariana's third. Pedro Vas de Campos and Caetano Alves Rodrigues both claimed that they had not received the full amounts of their dowries. Since what they had received exceeded the value of their wives' equal shares of Mariana's estate, the judge ruled that they must return the excess. When the judge constructed the inheritances for each heir, he stipulated that those heirs who did not receive dowries, or whose dowries did not amount to their full inheritance, receive payments from the three sons-in-law who had been granted large dowries. On paper, then, the less-favored heirs were compensated "from the hands of" the favored heirs (see table 7). But the documents do not tell us when, if ever, such transactions took place. If left unpaid, such debts would maintain a de facto inequality between the heirs, even though on paper all had received equal inheritances.[47]

Throughout the eighteenth century, planter families favored daughters and sons-in-law by granting them dowries that exceeded their daughters' true share of the family property. These inequities remained in place until the deaths of the parents, when the sons-in-law had to return what they had received in excess. This effectively gave a favored daughter and her husband access to family property that other brothers and younger sisters did not have for many years. It led to a gradual separation between those whom the parents had favored and those whom they had not. Over time, inequality between the siblings of the same generation became an established fact, a fact that could not be altered even by the return of part of a large dowry at the death of each parent.

Since on paper, all heirs received equal inheritances, this inequality between siblings can be seen only by carefully reconstructing what happened to family property over time. Two very different sources, the inventories of family estates and town censuses, both provide a record of family property. The inventories describe in detail what the family owned and what each child inherited. The censuses list the slaves owned by those heirs who remained in Parnaíba. Thus, the inventory and the census tell two stories that, when linked, provide a full account of the disposition of family property.

Inventories of estates of men and women from the planter class in the eighteenth century provide detailed lists of the kinds of property Parnaíba's planters owned. These inventories make clear that following the transition from Indian to African slavery, African slaves were the most valuable assets families owned. Slaves commonly accounted for more than 50 percent of the value of an eighteenth-century estate, far eclipsing the value of land. On the average, land accounted for 10 percent of a planter family's assets, while other property, such as houses, household furnishings, livestock, gold, silver, and so on, accounted for 30 percent (see

Table 7. Division of Mariana Pais's Estate, 1740

Heirs	Dowry		Inheritance	Excess
Andre and Antonia	3,840,000		378,178[a]	991,622
Caetano and Francisca	7,500,000		0	5,029,800
Pedro and Escolastica	3,835,240		0	1,365,040
Barbara	1,910,000		560,200[b]	–
Maria	1,920,000		550,200[c]	–
Maximiano	–		2,470,200[d]	–
Bento	877,900	(debt)	1,557,700[e]	–
Francisco	140,000	(gift)	2,330,200[f]	–

Source: Inv. Mariana Pais, 1740.
[a] 100% from Mariana's third.
[b] 76% from the "hands" of her brothers-in-law.
[c] 100% from the "hands" of her brothers-in-law.
[d] 100% from the "hands" of his brothers-in-law.
[e] 98% from the "hands" of his brothers-in-law.
[f] 69% from the "hands" of his brothers-in-law.

table 8).[48] For the largest slave owners, land accounted for even less.

The inheritance of slaves clearly affected the future lives of those heirs who received them. The distribution of slaves also provides evidence that historians can use to determine how equally the planters divided their property among their children.

It is possible to reconstruct the ownership of slaves among members of two generations of several planter families who lived in Parnaíba. The estates of these families were divided among the children after the parents died, as required by law. Later censuses, which recorded the households of many of the children who remained in Parnaíba, reveal how many slaves those heirs owned. By comparing how many slaves each of the children owned, it is possible to evaluate the extent to which families favored some of their children over others.

Manoel Rodrigues Fam's family serves as an illustrative case study of how the granting of a large dowry to one daughter differentiated her from her brothers and sisters. When Manoel married his daughter, Maria, he carefully selected a son-in-law and presented him with a handsome dowry. Because of this dowry, Maria fared better than any other of his children. When Manoel

Table 8. Composition of Planter Family Estates,
Eighteenth Century

Property	Small[a] N = 127	Large[b] N = 67	Largest[c] N = 5
Slaves	59%	56%	43%
Land	10%	10%	1%
Other[d]	31%	34%	56%
Total	100%	100%	100%

Source: Inventories from eighteenth-century Parnaíba.
[a] 1–9 slaves.
[b] 10 or more slaves.
[c] 50 or more slaves.
[d] Includes houses, animals, tools, household furnishings, clothing, credits (outstanding loans), gold, and silver.

died in 1757, his estate consisted of forty-five slaves, various tracts of land in Parnaíba, his farm, and townhouses. In his will, he stated that he gave his son-in-law three slaves, 1,000,000 reis, a riding horse, and household items in Maria's dowry. At the time of his death, the value of this dowry represented 8 percent of the community property shared by Manoel and his wife. It was three times larger than the dowry Manoel set aside for his second daughter. When Manoel died, Maria presented her dowry to the orphan's judge, as required by law, and half of it was considered to be her paternal inheritance. Since Maria's half dowry exceeded the equal share that each heir was to receive, Maria should have repaid the remainder to the estate. But as the first endowed daughter, part of her father's free third automatically covered the shortfall.

The census of 1775, conducted eighteen years after Manoel Rodrigues Fam died, reveals considerable inequality among the heirs of his estate. In 1775, Manoel's widow and eight of his children lived in Parnaíba. Manoel's widow still owned her share of the community property, which in 1775 consisted of twenty-six slaves as well as other property. Of the children who remained in Parnaíba, Maria and her second husband, Ignacio Joze da Silva, owned the most slaves, fourteen, while her brother Joze had seven, Manoel six, Baltazar three, Ignacio two, João one, and Pedro and Anna none.[49]

When Maria's mother died in 1779, the inequality among the brothers and sisters of this family became even more explicit.

Maria's mother's estate totaled only 3,006,522 reis. Of this amount, Maria's half dowry accounted for 21 percent. The equal share for each heir of the estate reached only 185,167 reis, but Maria's half dowry alone amounted to 625,080 reis. All of Maria's mother's third went to cover Maria's dowry, but it was not enough. Only then did the judge order that Maria return the excess to the estate.[50]

By reconstructing the process of inheritance after Manoel died in 1757 and after his wife died in 1779, the evidence unquestionably shows that Maria's dowry proved larger than the inheritances received by any other heir. Maria's dowry, calculated at 1,254,160 reis in 1757, exceeded by 515,084 reis the paternal and maternal inheritances that each of her brothers and sisters received. Eventually, the orphan's judge took back some of the dowry, but only in 1779, some thirty years after Maria received the dowry. Even then, that amount came to only 10 percent of the original dowry. Thus, when Maria and her husband married, they immediately came to possess a large amount of capital. In contrast, Maria's brothers received smaller inheritances much later and in stages, after each of their parents died. Such facts made Maria and her descendants the favored heirs of Lieutenant Manoel Rodrigues Fam.

Inequality in the division of family property sometimes relegated the less-favored heirs to extremely dependent positions in the town. Several of Miguel Bicudo de Brito's descendants became slaveless farmers one or two generations later, while others remained part of the planter class. Miguel Bicudo de Brito and his wife, Anna, had thirteen children when Miguel died in 1746. At that time, the property consisted of a farm and twenty-three slaves. In the census of 1775, twenty-six years after Miguel Bicudo de Brito's death, substantial inequality existed among his heirs. One daughter and her husband owned more slaves than any other heir, and some heirs owned none at all. Escolastica and her husband, João Martins da Cruz, owned twenty-one slaves, while her sister, Gertrudes, owned eleven, Izabel seven, Rita two, and Francisco none. Escolastica's niece owned one slave, and the children of her oldest sister owned no slaves. Three heirs had left Parnaíba, one had died, and two others may also have left or died, for they do not appear in the census. In this large family, Escolastica, the tenth child, and her husband inherited the place in the town held by her parents. Her husband became a well-known figure in Parnaíba and served as an alderman on the town council and as the influential orphan's judge. As time passed, other heirs, although they had received equal shares at inheritance, had less property and less status in the town.[51]

The inequality among siblings, such as that among the children of Manoel Rodrigues Fam or Miguel Bicudo de Brito, usually resulted from the choices made by parents when they granted a large dowry to one daughter. But in some families, siblings consented to an unequal division of property. For example, in the division of Antonio Francisco de Andrade's estate, the heirs agreed to stop the inventory and accept a *composição amigável*, an amicable settlement. In essence, this meant that the heirs agreed to "settle out of court" and to renounce their right to an equal division of the family property. This estate, inventoried in 1780, included ninety-one slaves, several large cattle ranches, and a sugar plantation in Parnaíba. The heirs agreed to desist from the inventory in 1784. In later censuses, five children remained in Parnaíba and two had left for the western town of Campinas. Of those five in Parnaíba, two owned substantially more slaves than the others. Senhorinha and her husband owned thirty slaves, and Francisco, who lived in the western parish of São Roque, owned twenty-two; while Antonio, the oldest son, had seven, Mariana had eight, and Anna had six. Sometime after 1798, the oldest son (Antonio) moved to Campinas where he appeared in the census of 1816 with six slaves, while his younger brother, who had moved there before him, owned forty-one in the same year. In this family, three children owned substantially more slaves than the others. In Parnaíba, Senhorinha and Francisco had many more slaves than their siblings. In Campinas, João had become a leader, but his older brother had not done so well. By agreeing to desist from the inventory and to accept a composição amigável, the other heirs gave up their legal right to equal inheritances. This prevented the property from being divided according to law. While we do not know how the property was divided in this family, because it was not recorded in the inventory, all the heirs gave their tacit approval to the division of family property that did take place. The results of that division are visible in subsequent censuses.[52]

In other families, the selling of shares between family members allowed one heir to emerge as the owner of the family farm in Parnaíba. While each heir generally received an equal share of the farm, some chose to sell or to trade their share with another heir. Through such exchanges, one heir usually emerged as the clear owner. Then that heir, likely as not, became the family leader in Parnaíba. Such a pattern occurred after Cosme Ferreira de Meirelles died in 1760. At that time, his estate consisted of a farm with ten slaves, townhouses, household furnishings, gold, and silver. His widow received one-half of the farm and one-half of the other property as her share of the community property, while his children each received an equal share of the other half, except for the two oldest children whose previous gifts (a dowry to the daughter and a patrimony for the son to enter the priesthood) constituted their entire inheritance. After this division, some of the heirs continued to live on the farm, and one, Anna Maria, married and lived in a separate household with her husband and children. In 1790, Cosme's widow sold her share of the farm, which then consisted of half of the original farm plus two shares she had purchased from two of her daughters, to Anna Maria's husband, Joze Pedrozo Navarro. This act cemented Joze's and Anna's position on the family farm. Thirty years after Cosme's death, they owned five-sevenths of the original farm, ten slaves, another farm, two sugar mills, forty-two horses, and seventeen head of cattle. When Joze died four years later, his inventory stated that his sister and brother-in-law still owned part of the farm, but that amount came to a paltry 21,428 reis. In this family, the selling of shares in the family farm allowed one heir to inherit the position of the parents. It also prevented the division of their farm.[53]

The reconstruction of the history of family property in Parnaíba tells us what happened to descendants of planter families who remained there. Yet since families in Parnaíba consciously expanded their resources by sending their sons out into the interior, the possibility exists that sons who migrated managed to remain part of the planter class but in a western town. Such was the case with Antonio Francisco de Andrade's son, João, who moved to Campinas where he owned forty-one slaves, more slaves than any of his siblings owned in Parnaíba. The constant movement of sons out of Parnaíba does suggest that sons saw the frontier as a potential means for social advancement. Like their fathers who moved into Parnaíba from someplace else, sons also left Parnaíba to seek marriage, their fortunes, and a new life.

As a family custom, deeply ingrained in planter families since the earliest days of settlement, the migration of sons helped to solve the inevitable decline in a family's property base as it became subdivided among more and more descendants each generation. The tradition of migration into the interior, which began with the bandeiras and continued with the gold rush, remained as much a part of life in Parnaíba in the late eighteenth century as it had been in the seventeenth. Its prevalence can be seen in the unequal sex ratio of 84 men to 100 women among the planters of Parnaíba in 1775.[54]

The migration of men appeared in family after family and persisted generation after generation. The cumulative effect of such a deeply ingrained pattern was to populate the towns and regions to the west and to re-create there the social structure characteristic of Parnaíba. The level of migration, even during Parnaíba's early days as a town, can be seen in the oldest family of Parnaíba, that of its founders, Manoel Fernandes Ramos and Suzana Dias. In only three generations, more of their descendants lived to the west of Parnaíba than in Parnaíba. Of their known children, half remained in Parnaíba. Of their twenty-six known grandchildren, eleven still lived in Parnaíba, while ten lived farther west, and five others lived to the east of Parnaíba. More than half of their forty-five known great-grandchildren lived to the west of Parnaíba, in western São Paulo, Minas Gerais, and Goiás. Moreover, most of the descendants living in Parnaíba were women, not men. Only five great-grandsons of Suzana Dias and Manoel Fernandes Ramos continued to live in Parnaíba, compared to ten great-granddaughters (see table 9). Such settlement patterns emerged as men interacted in the interior and later settled there with their wives. This constant drain of men and women to the west meant that family resources in Parnaíba would only have to support a portion of the descendants.

The migration patterns of the eighteenth-century descendants of Suzana Dias and Manoel Fernandes Ramos illustrate the same phenomenon. Their descendants continued to leave Parnaíba for the frontier, thus reducing pressure on finite resources in Par-

Table 9. Settlement Patterns of the Descendants of
the Original Founders of Parnaíba

| | Generations | | | | | |
| | First | | Second | | Third | |
	N	%	N	%	N	%
Parnaíba	4	50	11	42	15	33
West	2	25	10	38	25	56
East	2	25	5	19	5	11
Unknown	(2)		(10)		(20)	
Total	8	100	26	99	45	100

Source: Luis Gonzaga da Silva Leme, *Genealogia Paulistana* 7: 224–258.

naíba, such as land. One of these descendants was Mariana Pais, Suzana's great-great-granddaughter, who lived in Parnaíba and had nine children. Of them, only four remained in Parnaíba. These four had thirteen children who were born in Parnaíba, only three of whom remained there. The rest of Mariana's grandchildren left the town. The majority moved west. Thus, many of Mariana's children left Parnaíba, primarily for Minas Gerais and Goiás, as did her grandchildren, who moved to the towns of western São Paulo (see table 10).

Clearly, the planters attached as much importance to the wilderness as to their home base in Parnaíba. Fathers sent their sons out into the frontier to plan for the future; they recruited their sons-in-law to protect what the family already had. This attitude can be seen in the ways they viewed their sons and daughters. They saw their sons as independent and resourceful, able to take care of themselves, and their daughters as vulnerable, needing protection. As Bento Pais de Oliveira put it, "I have seven children . . . and as my sons have the natural ability to take care of themselves and even though the love I have for all of my children is the same, piety and compassion dictate that I think more of my daughters, and thus I institute them as the heirs of the remainder of my third." [55]

This family custom of sending sons into the wilderness served other functions as well: it reduced potential conflict between fathers and sons and between sons and sons-in-law. Anthropologists note that in patriarchal families, fathers are often loathe to yield control over the family property to their sons; yet sons, espe-

Table 10. Settlement Patterns of the Descendants of
Mariana Pais, Great-Great-Granddaughter of
the Original Founders of Parnaíba

	Generations					
	First		Second		Third	
	N	%	N	%	N	%
Parnaíba	3	43	4	14	15	22
West	4	57	24	83	52	76
East	0	0	1	3	1	1
Unknown	(1)		(4)		(26)	
Total	7	100	29	100	68	99

Source: Luis Gonzaga da Silva Leme, *Genealogia Paulistana* 4: 331–379.

cially the older sons, chafe under the authority of their fathers.
Such conflicts can be resolved by the migration of older sons or by
inheritance patterns that favor the youngest son, for by the time
a younger son is old enough to take over the family business, the
father is ready to retire.[56] In the case of Parnaíba, the son-in-law
played this role. Recruited by his father-in-law, he became a junior
partner, cognizant that his future depended on his father-in-law.
In contrast, sons could be active and independent on the frontier.[57]

Sons who resented their role in this family strategy had few
other choices. Raised in patriarchal families, young men deferred
to their fathers. Sons had few options as long as their fathers were
alive. Possibly, it was conflict between father and son that led
Manoel Rodrigues Fam's son, Antonio, to leave home without permission, taking some of his father's slaves and best horses with
him.[58] Only after fathers died did sons inherit any of the family
property, for fathers would continue to be the heads of families
even if their wives died before them. Thus, as long as their fathers
lived, sons could not establish themselves as independent prop-
erty-owning individuals in Parnaíba. In such a setting, they undoubtedly saw migration or marriage into a family in the interior
as a favored son-in-law as a viable, if not attractive, alternative.

Few sons managed to wrest control over the home base in Parnaíba from their brothers-in-law, and those who did could only do
so after their fathers died. One of the very few examples of this
inversion of the common family strategy occurred in the family of

Baltazar Rodrigues Fam, brother of Manoel. Baltazar and Izabel da Rocha do Canto's fourth son, Policarpo Joaquim de Oliveira, managed to become the leader of his family in the next generation but only after his father died. He did so by convincing his mother, who received half of the family farm as part of her share of the community property, to sell it to him for less than its assessed value. Such an act, completely legal, meant that he, not his brothers or brothers-in-law, would own the farm. In 1775, Policarpo owned fifteen slaves, while his sister and brother-in- law owned ten. Later, he rented the Jesuit estate of Araçariguama (confiscated by the crown following the expulsion of the order in 1759), which gave him access to a much larger slave labor force. By the end of the eighteenth century, he had consolidated a great deal of land by intimidating his neighbors, and as the colonel of the provincial militia, he was one of the most powerful men in Parnaíba.

Policarpo Joaquim de Oliveira made himself the favored heir by convincing his mother to turn over significant portions of the family property to him in much the same way that fathers negotiated with prospective sons-in-law. He did not question the underlying inequality of family strategies; rather, he manipulated them to his own advantage. Because of his ruthless and despotic behavior in Parnaíba, Policarpo became an unpopular figure. The governor of São Paulo began an unprecedented investigation into his behavior in 1779, following the complaints of many citizens. In the investigation, residents of Parnaíba testified to his abusive, sadistic, and immoral behavior.[59] Was Policarpo singled out in this way because the townspeople perceived him as different from the sons of the planters who made their way west? Or was Policarpo simply acting out the violent underside of a highly stratified and patriarchal social order? We shall never know for sure. His eventful life story, however, should not obscure the fact that many sons accepted the favoring of sons-in-law and the benefits to be gained from leaving Parnaíba and settling in the frontier.

The role of women in planter families poses some interesting questions about the influence that women had over property. Women had legal rights and were favored in key ways. Wives had to cosign property transactions. Widows became active managers of the family property after their husbands died. Entitled to an equal inheritance and to half of the community property in marriage, women, moreover, often received a lion's share of the family property in their dowries. Land tended to be passed through a female line, a dramatic departure from the European tradition of patrilineal devolution, such that women, not men, lived in the homes and on the lands of their forebears. Thus, it would seem that women inherited a strong position in family and town life.[60]

Yet women wielded no actual political power in the town. They could not serve on the town council or in the militia. The law did not allow them to use their property to guarantee the loans of others, a common business practice in colonial Brazil.[61] While some did join religious brotherhoods and sponsored religious festivals, their influence remained confined largely to the home. Even in the home, it is not clear how much authority women had. How much control did women have over the selection of husbands for their daughters? Or over the management of the community property? The position of women in the family may have been more symbolic than real. At specific times in their lives, such as at marriage, major property transactions took place which affected not only them but the entire family. Similarly, as widows, they inherited tremendous responsibilities. Clearly, women were crucial to the reproduction of the social order in Parnaíba. But that did not mean that a woman could exercise power as an individual. Rather, women played a key role in the family strategy: that of serving as the conduit for the mantle of power and authority as it passed from generation to generation of men.

The family strategies developed by Parnaíba's planters were environmental adaptations that, over time, left their mark on that society as well. Accepted attitudes toward men and women, marriage, inheritance, migration, and sons-in-law affected not just individuals but generations of descendants in Parnaíba and the towns of the wilderness as well. Inequality among siblings can be seen in virtually every propertied family in eighteenth-century Parnaíba, despite the fact that at inheritance each heir received an equal share of the family property. The favoring of one child with a greater share of the family property encouraged some of the less-favored children to leave Parnaíba and seek their fortunes elsewhere. It condemned those who remained to a dependent and marginal existence.

Planter families groomed their sons-in-law to take over the

leadership of the family in Parnaíba. In most families, it is clear that sons-in-law were in a much stronger position than sons to inherit the management of the home base in the next generation. Land in Parnaíba tended to be passed through daughters, which allowed sons-in-law to take over after their fathers-in-law died. Antonio Correa de Lemos Leite, captain major of Parnaíba in the late eighteenth century, for example, was the quintessential son-in-law. Born in the city of São Paulo, he had married into the oldest family in Parnaíba and had become the leader of that family. Sons, meanwhile, tended to leave Parnaíba, at first temporarily as young men working for their fathers and later permanently when they married and settled in the interior, as Antonio's own sons did. Those sons who did not migrate, as well as daughters who did not make advantageous marriages, became part of the less wealthy and more dependent subgroup of poor planters. Some were reduced to being slaveless peasants in one generation.

The family strategies used by the planters to protect their resources and social position in subsequent generations preserved the basic contours of Parnaíba's class structure. The censuses from the late eighteenth century show that the number of planter families with large slave labor forces remained small from 1775 to 1820. The number of planters with ten or more slaves also stayed virtually constant. Only the number of poor planters, those with less than ten slaves, increased from 1775 to 1820. This fact suggests that the inheritance patterns of the planters preserved family resources in the hands of a few and gradually created a dependent subgroup of poor planters (see table 11).

Other historians, such as Maria Thereza Schorer Petrone, have noted the proliferation of poor planters in Brazilian rural society but tend to see this phenomenon as an example of the inherent weakness of a cash-crop economy.[62] While the fluctuations in the cash-crop economy and the high capital costs of slaves undoubtedly had a negative effect on many families, the more likely possibility is that the increase in poor planters was the result of conscious choices made by families to disinherit some descendants in order to provide for others. As Stuart Schwartz indicates, many of the small planters (*lavradores*) of the northeast were related to the large mill owners.[63] Thus, the family strategies of the planter elite throughout Brazil probably contributed to the formation of a

118   *Families of Planters*

Table 11. The Planters of Parnaíba

Households	1775		1820	
	N	%	N	%
Poor planters (1–9 slaves)	150	81	232	84
Large planters (10+ slaves)	34	18	41	15
Largest planters (50+ slaves)	2	1	3	1
Total	186	100	276	100

Source: 1775 and 1820 censuses, Parnaíba.

substratum of the planter class—those with slaves and land but without great wealth.

The planter families of Parnaíba counteracted the laws calling for equal inheritances for all children. They provided for all of their children, yet reserved a significant portion of family resources for favored heirs. As table 11 illustrates, these strategies kept intact the basic social structure of Parnaíba during the late eighteenth and early nineteenth centuries. The censuses from this period reveal almost no change in the make-up of the planter class. A more equal division of family estates would have tended to level the differences between the small and large planters. Instead, the favoring of a few heirs, the migration of others, and the downward mobility of some in each generation caused the composition of the planter class to remain virtually unchanged over a forty-five-year period.

At the end of the eighteenth century, Parnaíba's captain major, Antonio Correa de Lemos Leite, who had come from São Paulo to marry the great-great-great-great-granddaughter of the founders of Parnaíba, died. After his death, his heirs squabbled among themselves over the fact that Antonio had freed several slaves, an action that irritated them because it diminished their own inheritances. But the heirs did not quibble over the fact that Antonio's son-in-law, married to the great-great-great-great-great-granddaughter of Parnaíba's founders, seemed destined to be the one who would inherit the family farm and Antonio's position in the town. Perhaps it seemed to them to be ordinary and logical; perhaps it seemed simply fated to be so. But for whatever reason, after

Antonio's death, his son-in-law, Joze de Medeiros de Souza, became the family leader. He served as the executor of Antonio's estate. Because of the dowry he received, he immediately came to directly own one-third of the family farm. Twenty years after Antonio's death, a document registered with the town clerk referred to Joze's farm as "the one which formerly belonged to Antonio Correa de Lemos Leite." Joze became the sergeant major of the provincial militia, its highest ranking officer. He was known in Parnaíba as a sugar planter and mill owner (*senhor de engenho*). Meanwhile, none of Antonio's sons remained in Parnaíba. Several of his daughters had left the town as well, to settle in Campinas and nearby Jundiaí. Anna Esmeria still lived in Parnaíba, but she and her husband owned only one slave. And so history repeated itself in this family. The next son-in-law took charge in Parnaíba, sons moved on, and the rest got used to their "reduced circumstances." Family resources had been distributed to the next generation, and the family's position as part of the planter class remained intact.[64] The members of Antonio's family may have acted unconsciously and may not have seen the outcome of their actions. But whether intended or not, events in this family successfully reproduced the basic contours of the planter family strategy in yet another generation of descendants in Santana de Parnaíba.

Seventeenth-century Chapel of Our Lady of Conception, Vuturuna Estate, Santana de Parnaíba. Photograph by the author.

Seventeenth-century wattle-and-daub church from Areias, São Paulo. Watercolor by Thomas Ender, early nineteenth century. From Gilberto Ferrez, *O Brasil de Thomas Ender 1817* (Rio de Janeiro: Fundação João Moreira Salles, 1976), 258. Permission to reproduce kindly granted by Kupferstichkabinett der Akademie der bildenden Künste, Wien.

Indians captured from the *sertão*. Lithograph by Jean Baptiste Debret, early
nineteenth century. From *Voyage pittoresque et historique au Brésil:*
Ou séjour d'un artiste français au Brésil, depuis 1816 jusqu'en 1831 inclusivement.
Facsimile ed. of original by Firmin Didot frères, Paris, 1834 (Rio de Janeiro:
Distribuidora Record, 1965), pt. 1, pl. 20.

Making war on tribal Indians. Debret, early nineteenth century.
From *Voyage*, pt. 1, pl. 21.

Guaraní Indian women on their way to mass. Debret, early nineteenth century.
From *Voyage*, pt. 1, pl. 24.

Sparse interior of a wealthy family home, city of São Paulo. Ender, early nine-teenth century. From *O Brasil*, 325. Permission to reproduce kindly granted by Kupferstichkabinett der Akademie der bildenden Künste, Wien.

Eighteenth-century *taipa de pilão* houses of Santana de Parnaíba.
Photograph by the author.

Burning the virgin forest. Mid-nineteenth-century São Paulo.
Lithograph by E. Riou. From F. Biard, *Deux années au Brésil. Ouvrage de* 180
vignettes dessinées par E. Riou d'aprés les croquis de M. Biard
(Paris: Librarie de L. Hachette et. Cie., 1862), 205.

Poor women: spinners and seamstresses. Ender, early nineteenth century. From *O Brasil*, 278. Permission to reproduce kindly granted by Kupferstichkabinett der Akademie der bildenden Künste, Wien.

A slave marriage in a wealthy household. Debret, early nineteenth century.
From *Voyage*, pt. 3, pl. 15.

Slaves punished in plantation stocks. Debret, early nineteenth century.
From *Voyage*, pt. 2, pl. 45.

5

Families of Peasants

In the census of 1767, when Antonio Correa de Lemos Leite headed the lists as the captain major of Parnaíba, Bento Cardozo Correa's household appeared in the third militia company. The same age as Antonio (42), Bento lived with his wife, Maria, (39), and five children, ranging in age from eighteen to four. The census transcriber noted that Antonio lived "by farming and mining" and that he "owned 400,000 reis," while Bento who also lived from farming "owned nothing."[1] Apart from the fact that Antonio and his wife had eight children and Bento and his wife had only five, the two families appear to be very similar. Both were large nuclear families that lived predominantly from farming.

Yet the 1767 census did not record information on slave ownership. Because it did not, it obscures the fundamental class difference between the families of Antonio and Bento. From the 1775 census, however, we learn that Antonio owned fifteen slaves, while Bento owned none. Antonio thus was assured of a sizable labor force that he could use to produce not only the food that his family needed to survive but cash crops such as sugar. Bento and Maria relied only on the members of their own family for labor. Changes in the composition of their family, therefore, would affect how much food they needed and how much they could produce. Thus, while the structure of Bento's and Antonio's families seemed similar in the 1767 census, in fact their lives were very different. Families of slaveless farmers, like Bento's, were part of a rural peasantry, while families of slave owners, like Antonio's, formed the wealthy planter class. This distinction became ever more pronounced as commercial agriculture became the mainstay of São Paulo's economy in the second half of the eighteenth century.

When commercial agriculture began to spread into the older

towns of São Paulo, this new economic orientation, reinforced by new royal policies, transfigured the traditional life-style of the peasantry.[2] In Parnaíba, peasants found themselves under increasing pressure to yield their farmlands to the sugar planters. Simultaneously, the competition for nearby frontier lands increased, forcing them to seek lands ever farther west. A crisis was at hand by the end of the eighteenth century which had dramatic effects on family life. Caught between the vice of an expanding commercial agricultural economy and a receding frontier, families of peasants found it increasingly difficult to survive in the town.

The population of the peasantry, moreover, continued to grow in Parnaíba, fueled by natural increase and in-migration. Faced with limited opportunities for maintaining their traditional life-style, many moved away, to the frontier far to the west where they reestablished themselves in the wilderness and to the growing town centers, especially the city of São Paulo. Those who remained in the town traded their traditional life-style for a new and more sedentary way of life. Some became artisans, laborers, or muleteers and gradually left the rural areas for the town center. Those who continued to farm planted on smaller, finite plots of land that supported reduced households. Thus, as the once wilderness town of Santana de Parnaíba became more tied to the kingdom in the second half of the eighteenth century, families of the elite embraced and profited from these economic changes, but peasants did not. Far from benefiting from the economic growth that took place around them, peasant families found themselves increasingly at risk and vulnerable in the town.

The traditional life-style of the peasantry in the eighteenth century relied on the presence of the wilderness and the availability of free land. Their lives reflected the synthesis of Indian and Portuguese lifeways, characteristic of the early years of colonization in São Vicente. Even during the eighteenth century, the lives of peasants still resembled those of the original settlers of São Vicente one hundred years before. They lived on small family farms, dispersed through the forest, and owned little besides the tools they needed to farm, produce food, and provide shelter.

The yearly agricultural cycle that dictated the lives of the peasants revolved around the work required to clear and burn fields, to plant and harvest crops, and to process food. The most difficult and dangerous work was clearing land. The Morgado de Mateus described the technique used throughout São Paulo:

> The fields are prepared very easily; it is no more than just cutting all the trees on a hillside on one side and first felling the trees on the top of the hill. These, falling, take before them the nearby trees one after another until everything is leveled. Dry in a few days, they burn it and later plant in the ashes.[3]

Nothing more is needed, the Morgado wrote, until the harvest, an easy time, when the farmers "pick what they need and nothing is left over."[4]

Peasants had learned this method, known as "slash-burn" or "swidden" farming, from Indians. It took advantage of the fertility of forest soils, rich in organic matter, and the carbon from the burned wood. After a few years, however, rains had washed the organic matter away, and the land produced less. Again, peasants learned from the Indians: they moved on to new places in the forest where they cleared new fields. This practice was known as "moving farms" (*sitios volantes*) because farmers moved their fields every few years, rather than continually cultivating and rotating the same plots of land in the European way.[5]

In São Paulo, as in all Brazil, farmers cultivated almost entirely by hand, unlike peasant farmers in Europe who used domesticated farm animals and the plow to increase their yields.[6] Yet Brazilian peasant farmers did not farm solely according to native American ways, for they devised their own hybrid techniques that combined European and native American methods. Tools, made from iron,[7] such as axes, machetes, hoes, billhooks, and knives, were of European origin, while the use of forest hillsides and fire and the abandoning of fields were of American origin.

The temperate climate of the Piratininga plateau, the abundant forest, and the farming techniques devised by peasants all allowed a variety of crops to be cultivated with a minimal amount of work. Families planted corn, the staple of their diet, in the spring—in August, September, and October—and harvested it six to seven months later. Other crops such as rice, manioc, cotton, and peanuts were also planted from August to October and harvested from February to May. Beans could be planted and picked twice yearly;

the first planting occurred from January to March, with a harvest in April, May, or June; the second planting in August, with a harvest in November and January. Sugarcane, usually planted from November to April, could be cut a year and a half after planting.[8]

The staples of the family diet came from American crops: corn, beans, and manioc. The Tupi Indians had cultivated these basic foodstuffs in São Paulo long before the Europeans arrived and taught the first settlers how to raise and prepare these foods unknown in Europe. Each of these staples yielded a high ratio of food per hectare planted. A nineteenth-century statistician, Daniel Pedro Müller, estimated that the ratio of seed to harvest was 1 to 100 for corn, 1 to 20 for beans, and 1 to 50 for rice in São Paulo in the early nineteenth century.[9] In Parnaíba, references to yields in the 1798 census suggest that they were considerably lower than those calculated by Müller. Corn gave a ratio of 1 to 39, beans 1 to 11, and rice 1 to 18.[10] Still, considering that the highest average yields in Europe for cereals (wheat, rye, barley, and oats) at the same period of time were 1 to 10.6, farmers in São Paulo harvested more per seed planted than their European counterparts.[11] The farmers of São Paulo may not have been as sophisticated, but the foods they subsisted on, all native to the Americas, were far more easily and efficiently grown than those of Europe.[12] Ironically, peasants in São Paulo did not have to work nearly as hard to feed their families as Portuguese farmers did. Perhaps this is one reason that the "laziness" of farmers in São Paulo constantly amazed the Morgado de Mateus.[13]

Once a crop had been planted and harvested, families devised simple methods to process and store their basic staples. Simple hand-hewn mills and presses adorned the terraces of beaten earth that surrounded their small wattle and daub huts. Here they made flour from corn and manioc. To make cornmeal, women used a wooden mortar and pestle or a water-powered corn pounder (*monjolo*). Of the two, the wooden mortar and pestle required the most work, for the dried corn kernels had to be beaten by hand until they became a coarse meal. The monjolo, a European innovation, used simple mechanics to replace the back-breaking work of pounding corn.[14] Resembling an enormous seesaw, the monjolo consisted of a huge wooden beam, hollowed out at one end to form a trough, with a wooden head on the bottom of the beam at the other end. Balanced on a fulcrum, the head was heavier than the trough and rested in a bin of corn. But when water filled the trough, making that end heavier, the head rose until the trough hit the ground. Then the water spilled out and caused the head to crash down into the wooden bin filled with corn kernels. Over and over again, the head rose and fell as water filled the trough and spilled out on the ground. Creaking, groaning, and thudding all the while, the monjolo eventually produced cornmeal with a minimum amount of human effort.

Manioc had an extremely high caloric yield per hectare and kept for long periods.[15] Because it was inexpensive and resilient, families relied on it as one of their major sources of carbohydrates. Tupi Indians taught early settlers how to cultivate and prepare manioc. Jesuit Father Anchieta described how the Indians fixed manioc in several of his letters. "[I]f eaten raw, roasted, or cooked, it kills," he wrote, "it is necessary to soak it in water until almost rotten; then rotten as it is, they convert it into flour which can be eaten by toasting it in large pottery vessels."[16] Families of peasants modified the original Indian technique with European additions, such that the transformation of the raw poisonous manioc into edible and long-lasting flour became an easier process. Like yams or potatoes, manioc grew as a tuber in the ground. It required minimal cultivation until ripe, when women simply dug it up. Then they took it to their terrace or to that of a neighbor who owned a manioc wheel and a press. There women peeled the manioc, while men grated it using a hand-turned wheel. One person cranked a large wheel, attached by a belt to a smaller wheel, while another fed the peeled manioc into a series of rapidly turning teeth that chipped away at the white tubers. The grated manioc fell into wooden basins, and when enough had collected, they placed it into a press attached to a heavy beam, which pushed the poisonous milk down to the bottom of a basin and out holes in the bottom. Finally, they toasted the manioc over an open hearth to produce manioc flour.

Corn, beans, and manioc occupied most of the time and acreage planted by peasant farmers, but other crops, such as rice, cotton, and sugarcane, were also grown. The rice cultivated by peasants was dry, grown without irrigation. After it had been harvested, women removed the outer shell by pounding it in a mortar and pestle. Then they winnowed the rice by throwing it up and down in a wide flat basket until the wind had blown away the lighter chaff.

A few families planted sugarcane and distilled their own cane brandy using primitive methods characteristic of the early years of sugar production in Brazil. Small amounts of cane brandy, for household consumption, work parties, exchange, and sale, could be produced without extensive capital investment. After men cut the cane with long knives or machetes, they took it to be crushed in a small mill. Then they boiled the juice in large copper vats. When the juice was poured from these vats into molds to crystallize, molasses dripped out of the bottom of the molds. From the molasses, they distilled cane brandy using a copper still.

In addition to cultivating these foods, the peasantry supplemented their diet with hunting and fishing in the forests near the town. They kept domestic animals, especially pigs, as a source of meat and fat. Cotton, which many families grew, was spun into thread by women and then woven into cloth or used to make hammocks to sleep in. Men and women collected clay from the streambeds which they fashioned into ceramic pots, plates, jars, and jugs.

Peasant families depended on free land from the wilderness for their survival. Most exercised squatters' rights by virtue of unchallenged occupation. In a sense, their views of landownership were closer to the Indian practice of owning the fruits of the land but not the land itself.[17] Those who wished to own land as private property in the European sense had to secure a legal land title, which required receiving land through an inheritance conducted by the local judge, or purchasing land and registering the land sale with the town notary, or receiving a royal land grant from the crown. All of these processes discriminated against the families of peasants, who lived on the fringes of colonial society. Few had the contacts or the resources needed to obtain legal titles to land. Not surprisingly, peasants only sporadically held legal title to their land.

In the seventeenth and even eighteenth centuries, the presence of the wilderness, however, meant that land was not yet a scarce resource in São Paulo. Not having legal title did not prevent families from farming unclaimed land. The laws of Portugal inadvertently protected their rights. Lands granted as sesmarias, for example, were given "without loss to a third party or to the rights which someone may have to them."[18] This provision extended to those who "owned" land by virtue of their "occupation" of it. When Anna Maria Xavier Pinto da Silva requested a land grant for a region of thick forest between Parnaíba and the neighboring town of Jundiaí, her petition was at first denied because nine families were living on the lands. These families, although very poor, still paid the tithe to the church each year. When the crown finally did award her the land grant, it upheld the rights of these nine families to their plots.[19] Thus, as long as land was plentiful, peasant families had little trouble finding room to plant their fields.

In the traditional peasant life-style, individuals could not survive without their families. Together, members of a family worked to grow the food that all needed to survive. Whereas the ownership and allocation of property played a major role in binding the families of the elite together, a never-ending cycle of work tied the families of peasants together. Each member of a household contributed to the household economy, and the labor of all made it possible for the family to survive as a group.

Unlike the families of the planters, equality among individuals characterized the family lives of peasants. They lived in households rarely differentiated by race, since members of the household generally came from the same family. Both men and women worked in the fields and in the preparation of food, such that husbands and wives and brothers and sisters performed similar tasks and held equivalent responsibilities.[20] Since few learned to read and write, both males and females were illiterate, and none served in community institutions.

Even children played important roles in these families. They worked with their parents from a young age and greatly increased the labor capacity of the household.[21] For this reason, women bore many children, and families had little incentive to limit the size of their families. For the same reason, families discouraged their children from marrying at an early age. Children remained at home, working for their parents until they married, usually in their twenties. Only then did they form their own households.

Peasant families extended their work force by taking in servants or retainers. Families, especially the better off, often had dependents (*agregados*) living with them. These might be kin, orphans, or poor people who worked in the fields, in the preparation of food, and as domestic servants in exchange for food and lodging. Families might seek servants at specific times in their lives, such as when their children were young or after they had left home. In this way, they could expand the productive base of the household.[22]

At times of harvest, or during the preparation of the fields, peasants relied on their neighbors. Work parties, or *ajuntamentos*, were an important means of expanding a family's labor force. José Arouche de Toledo Rendon described this practice in 1788:

> He who wishes to establish his farm or clearing in the woods calls all his neighbors for a certain day in which, after eating a lot and drinking more, they take up their axes and billhooks, more animated by the spirits than by the love of work. When that event is over, they get together for others, and this becomes the only time when they work.[23]

These work parties were reciprocal, in that those who benefited from the parties were expected to return the favor at a later date.[24]

The ajuntamentos themselves may have been of Indian origin. The Jesuit, José de Anchieta, observed the custom in sixteenth-century São Vicente:

> Whenever he [an Indian man] decided that his *roça* [field] required attention, his wives made a great quantity of wine. . . . With a fresh supply of brew on hand, neighbors were invited to bring their sticks and to work on the land, sometimes all day and occasionally into the night. As compensation, they gathered at the hut of the owner of the roça and finished the wine made from manioc roots.[25]

This account holds much in common not only with José Arouche de Toledo Rendon's description but with a portrait drawn by Lia Freitas Garcia Fukui of a workday in 1964:

> At a prayer day at the chapel, the head of the family invited all the residents of the neighborhood to his farm to work. On the set day, ten people—family, neighbors, and friends—responded to his request. They began the work in the morning, breaking only for lunch, and, at the end of the day when dinner was served, the walls of the house were finished. Drink was served abundantly throughout the day.[26]

The family life of peasants left even less room for privacy or for individual self-expression than among planter families. These families lived in small huts, constructed from woven sticks and mud or simply straw. Everyone slept in close proximity, in hammocks, on mats on the floor, or in cots made from woven vines. What few possessions families owned, such as cooking utensils, furniture, clothes, and tools, were usually of such limited value that combined, they did not reach the minimum amount of property needed to justify a property inventory when someone died. Thus, formal inheritance, a crucial event to families of planters because of the property transfers involved, concerned peasants less. Since families had little to divide among their children, they did not devise elaborate strategies to modify the impact of inheritance law.

The censuses initiated by the Morgado de Mateus provide historians with an excellent source for reconstructing the lives of peasant families at the end of the eighteenth century. By comparing the first census, undertaken in 1775, to record information on slave ownership and landownership to one forty-five years later, in 1820, it is possible to see peasants at two distinct moments in time. In 1775, a sugar economy had taken root in Parnaíba, but the traditional life-style of peasants was still in evidence even as sugar was beginning to change the lives of all farmers, both those who began to plant cane and those who continued as subsistence farmers. By 1820, the sugar economy had radically altered the agrarian spaces of the town and the lives of the peasant farmers.

To live in Parnaíba in 1775 meant to accept the world of the captain major, to serve in the local militia, to have one's house enumerated in the census, and to be subject to provincial levies for men and food. Each of the households in Parnaíba in 1775 had its agricultural production, as well as its agricultural property, calculated for the year. Bento Cardozo Correa, for example, "owned a small farm, six horses, and one sow, and harvested 25 *alqueires* (907 liters) of corn and 2 (73 liters) of beans." His health and the general fitness of his sons also merited evaluation. Bento, the census taker noted, "had been sick with a serious illness for seven months," his son Antonio "was overcome with plague,"[27] and his son Francisco "had a thickness in his neck."[28] The censuses gave royal governors important information on every household in the town, information that could be used to call up recruits, requisition food and supplies, recruit families for settlement projects, and estimate tax revenues.

Despite these changes, the 1775 census portrays many of the traditional strategies used by peasant families for survival. Families continued to live as they always had, as subsistence farmers. The majority of them lived in the outlying areas of the town, beyond the reach of local institutions. These were the moving farms (sitios volantes) so disliked by the Morgado de Mateus. For these men, women, and children, survival depended on planting freely on unclaimed lands. They relied on their families for labor in their fields, and they avoided the agents and institutions of social control as much as possible. But the census also portrays a second group of peasant farmers who lived more sedentary lives. These peasant farmers owned small farms and saw their survival differently. They integrated themselves into the community and linked themselves to the more powerful families of the town. They sought to limit the division of their lands between their heirs.

According to the 1775 census, 39 percent of the slaveless farmers in Parnaíba planted "by favor" (a favor) (see table 12).[29] Planting "by favor" appears to have meant planting freely wherever families found available land. The few references to the term suggest that these farmers planted either on vacant or unclaimed lands or with the permission of the actual owner. When families had permission to plant on the lands of others, such permission may have involved an exchange of some kind, either in rent or harvest. But the meaning of "by favor" suggests that these families received land freely, because it was abundant, and because no one minded their presence. While evidence is scant, such an interpretation is confirmed by a document left by João Ribeiro Fernandes, Paulo Pereira, Antonia Pais de Oliveira, and Matheus Rodrigues with the town council in 1784. On April 17, the four appeared at the town council to register their relationship. João stated to the notary that "it was his wish . . . that Paulo Pereira remain situated on his fields and that he retain a grove of trees . . . without the obligation of paying anything, which was accepted by Paulo Pereira."[30] João continued that it was also his wish that Matheus Rodrigues remain with his fields "without paying anything" and that, likewise, Antonia Pais de Oliveira stay without obligation, except that she con

Table 12. Land Use Patterns of the Peasantry, 1775

Households	N	%
By favor	194	39
Landowners	163	32
Tenant farmers	60	12
Landless	86	17
Total	503	100

Source: 1775 census, Parnaíba.

struct a fence. This agreement, signed "to avoid any contention" between the four families, on the surface seems to reflect *a favor* relationships between João and the three others. Searching for these households in the 1775 census, we find that João Ribeiro Fernandes lived in the parish of São Roque where he owned a farm, planted corn, and raised cattle, pigs, and horses. Matheus Rodrigues and his wife and five children lived in the same neighborhood and planted by favor.[31] The households of Antonia and Paulo do not appear in the census, but from the households of João and Matheus, the relationship described in the document signed at the town council becomes clear. Matheus planted by favor, on lands that João claimed as his own.

From the point of view of the peasant farmer, undisputed cultivation of land implied ownership, irrespective of legal claim. Thus, the family that planted the same lands by favor over many years came to view those lands as their own. For example, the census of 1775 noted that João Leite de Lima, his wife, and four children planted by favor. Fifteen years later, a bill of sale appeared in the town's notary books. In the bill of sale, the farm consisted of almost half a league of land, two fields of corn, a field of cotton, fruit and pine trees, a wattle and daub house thatched with straw, and a pen for pigs. João and his wife claimed that the farm had belonged to their parents and grandparents and that they had been in "possession" of it for over sixty years. Over time, then, unchallenged occupation became the grounds for legal ownership of land.[32]

Because the meaning of the term "by favor" is impossible to define clearly in the 1775 census, it is difficult to know exactly what kinds of relationships the majority of peasant families had to land.

Given the clarity of other relationships, however, it is possible to say what by favor was not. Since the census clearly stated when farmers owned land, it did not refer to actual ownership. Nor did it mean renting land, for those families were known as renters (*foreiros*). By the same token, by favor did not mean tenancy, since those who lived as tenants in the European sense were called retainers (agregados) or Indian wards (administrados). Nor did it mean that the households did not farm, since nearly all who lived by favor produced agricultural crops. Thus, based on the few clues gleaned from other sources and from what by favor was clearly not, by favor appears to have meant planting freely on unclaimed lands or on private lands, with the permission of the owner.

A second meaning of by favor that appears in documents suggests a different kind of land tenure. Families who owned land sometimes granted permission to others, usually their immediate kin, to plant on their land. According to the census, João Rodrigues, his wife, and two children lived "by favor of his parents." Unlike families who lived simply by favor, João and his family depended on their family for land. Rather than searching for free frontier land, they planted on lands that had already been claimed.[33] This meaning of "by favor" depicted a very different kind of land use—one where families shared land. Thus, I have included it in the category of landownership in table 12.

The 163 households of peasant farmers who owned land in 1775, or lived by favor on the lands of immediate kin, or planted on lands owned jointly with others, or rented land had the most stable access to land. While they may have obtained land through squatters' rights, when they bequeathed those lands to their children by a legally recognized will or property inventory, they established a legal claim to the lands that would be accepted by the local judges.[34] This served as an important strategy used by the more established of the peasantry to legalize their land claims.

Families used a variety of strategies to create and maintain small farms. Some joined parcels of land to form one viable farm. Francisco Xavier de Oliveira and his wife, for example, created their farm by combining a piece of land they inherited with some land they bought from a nephew.[35] Another strategy worked to prevent the division of land through inheritance. Rather than dividing the family lands, the eight children of Anna Leme do Prado decided to live together and share the property.[36] Some families rented land from local institutions, such as the church, the town council, or the Indian community of Baruerí. Rented lands often remained in the family for several generations and represented stable access to land. The local institutions that owned the lands collected a nominal rent each year, and tenants could sell their rights to the land and bequeath them to their heirs.[37]

In 1775, sixty families lived as tenant farmers on the religious estates of the town. These peasants did have obligations to their landlords. The confiscated Jesuit property of Araçariguama had thirty-nine households attached to it in 1775, the people of which the census takers labeled as "freed" (*forros e libertos*). These were former Indian wards and free slaves. Traditionally, they had worked three days a week for the Jesuits in return for their land and cottages.[38] Those who rented the Jesuit estate from the crown after 1759 may have also expected the same from the tenants on the estate. The Monastery of São Bento, a small Benedictine estate in Parnaíba, had eight tenant households labeled as agregados in 1775. According to the census, these tenants were both mulattoes and Indians. On the estate of the Chapel of St. Antonio in the parish of São Roque, the census listed thirteen tenant households and called them "Indian wards" (administrados), even though the relationship of administração had been formally abolished in 1750. On each of these estates, it is likely that the tenants, who were formerly Indian wards, continued to live on these estates after the abolition of administração and exchanged their labor or part of their harvest for the right to plant.[39]

The majority of the peasants lived in nuclear families in 1775. Nuclear families, composed of a married couple and their children, proved to be critical to the survival of peasant farms, for they provided peasants with the best ratio of laborers to land. By plotting the ages of heads of households in the census with the types of households they headed, it is possible to see a common peasant family cycle in which the nuclear family dominated.[40] That cycle began when a couple married and set up their own household. It continued as the couple had children and formed a nuclear family. This household structure endured until heads of households reached middle age, when single-parent and complex households began to appear as spouses died or as families became extended, such as with dependent kin. Widows headed many of the single-parent households, while married men and widowers tended to head the complex households. As children married, the cycle began again.

The contours of this common family cycle can be seen in the family of Bento Cardozo Correa. In 1767, at the age of 42, he lived with his wife and five children in a nuclear family. The census of 1775 reveals that the household was still a nuclear family, the only difference being the birth of two more children, Joze and Bento. In 1798, twenty-three years later, the household had changed. Maria had died, and Bento, now an old man of 77 years, lived with three of his children: Francisco, 35, Joanna, 40, and Roza, 37.[41]

The census of 1775 provides a snapshot of this cycle for the whole population, and as figure 3 illustrates, the majority of the heads of households in their twenties, thirties, and forties presided over nuclear families. Single-parent and complex households, however, appear increasingly in the older age groups as nuclear families evolved into single-parent households or extended families. Land was still plentiful in the town in 1775. Thus, the complex family structures often found among European peasants to regulate the use and transfer of land among family members did not emerge in Parnaíba. In Europe, these complex family structures included households created by the co-residence of married children with their parents, households formed by married brothers and sisters, and extended families composed of nuclear families with the addition of grandchildren, grandparents, or other kin. Complex households of this kind often formed in Europe because of scarcity of land. Such households rarely appeared in Parnaíba because it was easier for the younger generations to find land of their own in the wilderness.[42]

The census of 1775 shows how crucial children were to the survival of the families of peasants. Nuclear families had, on the average, 3.3 children living at home in 1775. Women gave birth to many children, not all of whom, however, lived at home at the same time. High birthrates ensured the household of a constant source of labor. For example, in 1767, Antonio Leal das Neves and his wife, Luzia Pinta, had five children living with them. In 1775, they also had five children living with them but not the same ones. Anna, eight years old in 1767, did not appear in the 1775 census,

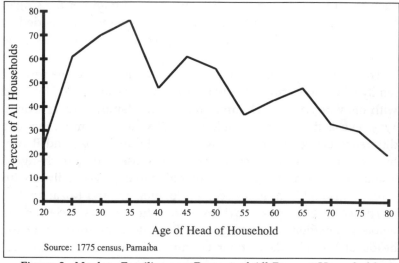

Figure 3. Nuclear Families as a Percent of All Peasant Households
Across the Family Cycle, 1775

when she would have been fourteen years old. Perhaps she had married or left home to work as a servant for another family. Meanwhile, young Ignacio had been born. In 1798, Antonio and Luzia lived with three children, two of whom did not appear in the earlier census. Thus, while Antonio and Luzia had at least eight children, the census of any given year would never list all of them. Similarly, Domingos de Souza and his wife, Maria de Conceição, had at least eleven children, though the censuses of 1767, 1775, and 1798 listed only six, five, and three children, respectively.[43]

The nuclear family provided peasants with a stable family structure over time, but the members of a nuclear family always changed. From the parents' point of view, this proved advantageous, for it meant that as older children married or left home, younger children could take their places in the fields. A woman's childbearing years were long ones, which accounted for the endurance of the nuclear family in the family cycle. The constant replenishment of the pool of children who served as workers for the family provided long-term stability for peasant families.

Nuclear families persisted not just for demographic reasons but because they provided peasants with a viable household structure capable of meeting the needs of the family. They were successful working units and yielded a larger surplus than households composed of one adult and children, extended families, or families with no children (see fig. 4). Not surprisingly, children are positively associated with the total value of household agricultural production (Pearson's correlation coefficient: $r = 0.24$). Not only did nuclear families produce more than other household structures but production rose and fell during the life cycle of a nuclear family. The value of agricultural production increased from an average of 6,700 reis when heads of households were in their early twenties to 7,700 reis when they were in their early thirties and peaked at 11,000 reis when they reached their late forties. Then the average value of agricultural production per household began to decline slowly (see fig. 5).

As the 1775 census makes clear, families compensated for changes in family structure that might affect agricultural production by taking in extra laborers or retainers. Their presence expanded the labor pool of the family. In 1775, 104 households had live-in retainers. In Antonio Joze da Silva's household lived his wife, Izabel, five children ranging in age from fifteen years to six months, and a young mulatta named Antonia, listed by the census taker as an agregada. Antonia's role in the family can only be inferred, but it seems likely that she worked for them as a live-in servant. Since the household had cattle, pigs, and horses in addition to planting corn and rice, her labor, whether in the fields or in the house, greatly extended its productive capacity.[44] Like children, agregados also have a positive association with the total value of agricultural production of nuclear families in 1775 (Pearson's correlation coefficient: $r = 0.29$).

The 1775 census portrays the mobility of peasant families and the ease with which they packed up their belongings and left town. Moving to the frontier was as common as it was easy. Peasants crossed the boundaries between parishes and towns looking for available land. Sometimes they simply moved their fields; at other times, they picked up everything and left. In 1775, the captain major of Parnaíba noted that fifty-four families, 8 percent, had left the town that year. Most of those who left were peasant families such as Salvador Ricardo, his wife, and their six children who moved to the neighboring town of Jundiaí. Estevão Pais, his wife, and their seven children moved farther west to Piracicaba. Other

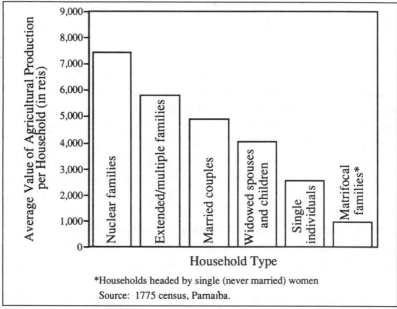

Figure 4. Peasant Agricultural Production by Household Type, 1775

families likewise moved west to the towns of Itú, Sorocaba, Mogi Mirim, and Lages. Some families simply moved from the more developed parish of Santana to the less settled parishes of Araçariguama and São Roque. Single men migrated to the city of São Paulo, to Minas Gerais, or to western towns. One hundred one men left in 1775, 6 percent of all men in the town. Quite a few peasants simply vanished, the captain major remarking, "No one knows where."[45]

Peasants moved for a variety of reasons, one of the most important being to find land. But peasant families also moved to avoid military conscription and forced labor obligations. According to militia captain João Martins da Cruz, Fernando de Morais and his family left Parnaíba in 1775 to avoid being sent to Iguatemí, a colonization project of the Morgado de Mateus on the far western frontier.[46] Ignacio Rodrigues and Luis Gomes and their respective families left Parnaíba for the same reason. Those that remained in Parnaíba were liable for induction into the regular forces stationed in Santos; in 1775, for example, seventy-seven men were sent to Santos from the town.[47] Families in Parnaíba were requisitioned

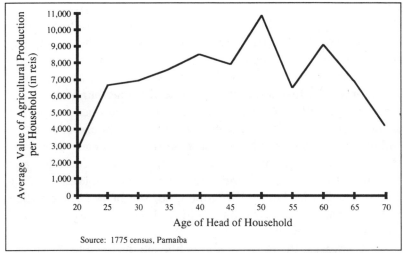

Figure 5. Agricultural Production of Peasant Nuclear Families Across
the Family Cycle, 1775

for food and supplies used to support the Santos garrison or the troops and colonists stationed on frontier outposts.[48] Sons might also be sent to work on rebuilding the road between Santos and the city of São Paulo. For many peasant families, then, moving was an effective strategy that freed them from numerous obligations and allowed them to continue a frontier existence that was increasingly under fire in the older towns such as Parnaíba.

Peasant families who left Parnaíba took with them their traditional strategies for survival. They searched out unclaimed lands on the edges of towns or in the wilderness. There they continued to live in nuclear families and paid little attention to the agents and institutions of local government.

The families who remained in Parnaíba, however, perceived the changes there. Because the wilderness had virtually disappeared from the town, families could no longer count on free land for their children. The handful of wills and property inventories that describe the property of the eighteenth-century peasant families show that when peasants did own land, they sought to limit its division among their heirs. Francisco de Oliveira Gago owned a small farm, one slave, livestock, and farm tools. When he died in 1755, his property remained relatively intact (except for the slave, who died or was sold), under the administration of his wife. After she died in 1771, the children decided not to undergo a formal process of inheritance, which would had divided the property equally among them. They argued that an inventory and division of property conducted by the orphan's judge would consume too much of the property. Instead, they wished to live together and use the family property to their mutual benefit. The seven heirs appeared in the 1775 census living together in the same household. None had married, even though the eldest, Anna, was already fifty years old. Together, they farmed the land and grew corn, rice, and peanuts.[49] By sharing the land, then, this family avoided dividing it as mandated by law. But by doing so, the heirs gave up their rights as individuals and thus would find it difficult to marry and form their own families.

In other cases, the orphan's judge himself declined to divide the property, citing the fact that the value of the property in question was less than the cost of a legal division of that property. Indeed, almost half of the estates of peasants brought to the orphan's judge (10 of 26) were never completed. Whether by petition by heirs, or the desire of the judge not to let the entire estate disappear in court costs, or excessive outstanding debts, these estates were never divided as required by law. This fact reinforces the point that peasants owned little property and allocated it to their heirs outside of the formal process of inheritance.

The families that remained in Parnaíba sought the patronage and protection of the propertied class. These ties gave families powerful patrons who might defend them before community institutions. While such ties implicitly recognized a dependence on or a subordination to planter families, they did confer on poor families certain advantages. The most common way of nurturing such ties worked through godparentage. At birth, parents selected a godfather and godmother for their infant. If parents selected godparents from among the planters, they linked their children to the ruling class. Between 1774 and 1776, the priest baptized seventy babies in the parish church of Santana. Nearly all of the babies for whom it is possible to identify the social status of parents and godparents had godparents who were planters. Only 17 percent of the babies had peasant godparents compared to 83 percent who had planter godparents (see table 13). Moreover, it was quite common

Table 13. Godparents of Peasant Children

	1774–1776		1819–1821	
	N	%	N	%
Wealthy planters	37	53	18	20
Poor planters	21	30	33	38
Peasants	12	17	37	42
Total	70	100	88	100

Source: Baptismal Records, Parish of Santana.

to reinforce the godparent bond by asking members from the same family (a husband and wife, or a brother and sister) to serve as godparents. In this way, peasants doubly bonded their child to a powerful planter family.[50]

Godparents served as powerful patrons for poor families in the community. Sometimes this extended to defending their godchildren before local institutions. For example, when Mauricio da Rocha Campos filed suit against Francisco Joze de Paula, a mulatto soldier accused of kidnapping his daughter Roza from his house, Roza's godfather came to her aid. Mauricio accused Francisco of entering his house and forcing Roza to accompany him to the city of São Paulo, where he kept her against her will. Roza's godfather, an established sugar planter, testified before the local judge that Mauricio's house had always been "respectable" and "upright." Roza's godfather's brother-in-law also testified that Francisco was a person of low status, not Roza's social equal. Such statements undoubtedly strengthened Mauricio's case, but the judge decided that it had not been proven that Francisco had taken the girl against her will.[51]

The gradual growth of a cash-crop economy based on sugar spelled the end to the independent existence of peasant families in São Paulo. When the mining regions began to decline at mid-century, planters began to recapitalize their farms in Parnaíba to produce a cash crop for export. As the sugar economy became profitable and spread, peasant families who did not have legal title to land began to find themselves expelled from the lands on which they had traditionally planted. Others who did have papers that proved their ownership of land found themselves under increasing pressure to sell their lands to sugar planters.

Royal policy reinforced the expansion of cash-crop agriculture in a number of ways, all of which worked against peasants. In the latter half of the eighteenth century, officials such as the Morgado de Mateus challenged the traditional life-style of peasants because they saw it as a hindrance to the development of a commercial agricultural economy in São Paulo. The Morgado de Mateus feared that farmers who lived in the nebulous zone between the towns and the wilderness would revert to Indian ways. "Men behind the virgin forest," he wrote, "gradually distance themselves from civil society, and those who were already civilized slowly forget the doctrines which they have learned and begin to assimilate again the savage ways which they had left behind."[52] To the Morgado, such men and women were an undesirable element because of their "laziness" and potential for reversion to "savage" ways and because they did not participate in the market economy. They produced little beyond the needs of their households and did not contribute to the economic development of the province.

As part of his plan to develop São Paulo, the Morgado de Mateus took steps to reinforce the power of local planter elites in order to obtain more rigorous social and political control over the peasantry. Central to this was the creation of militia companies under the command of men from planter families.[53] Peasants served in these militias as soldiers under officers, all of whom were drawn from the families of the planters. While the planters of Parnaíba initially resisted the growing influence of the crown in the province, as commercial agriculture became firmly established, they embraced the new royal presence and used it to bolster their local hegemony and to limit the rights of peasants to land. The policies of the royal governors benefited the population of São Paulo unequally, for they worked to the advantage of the planters who planted crops for export.

One of the first steps taken by the Morgado was to bring frontiersmen under the authority of the local militia captains. The Morgado ordered the militia captains to prepare a detailed list of those in their district with "the names of the heads of each household, their age, the names of their wives, the value of their property, and each of their children distinguished by their names and ages."[54] Such lists gave both the captain major and the governor important information on the population and wealth of each town which could be used for military recruitment and taxation. Later that same year (1765), the Morgado ordered all residents of the province to register their titles to land with the governor's office. He did this because, in his view, "The inhabitants of this captaincy are situated in many places cultivating tracts which by no title belong to them . . . from which originates continuous discord, lawsuits, and sometimes homicides."[55]

One year later, in 1766, the king, in response to requests sent to him by the Morgado, decreed an end to the practice of moving farms and planting in the virgin forest. He ordered that

> all men who can be found in the wilderness as vagabonds or on moving farms, are now obliged to select appropriate places to live together in civil settlements which have at least 50 households or more, with a judge, aldermen, and a procurator, dividing among themselves with just division the adjacent lands.[56]

The king went on to state that those who refused to appear and submit themselves to a permanent residence in civil society "should be treated like highway robbers and public enemies, and as such punished with the severity of the law."[57] This law, like the recently ordered censuses, reflected a new ideal projected for São Paulo: that of a settled, sedentary province where families lived in recognized towns under the authority of the planter elite, who, in turn, served the royal governor.

These royal policies did not immediately affect the life-style of peasants in São Paulo. As is clear in the 1775 census, families continued to live by favor and freely moved into and out of towns like Parnaíba. Yet gradually, the policies inaugurated by the Morgado de Mateus and reinforced by his successors did alter the character of rural life in Santana de Parnaíba.

Between 1775 and 1820, economic and political change in Parnaíba dramatically modified the space in which peasants lived, as well as the character of their lives. In 1775, the entire town of Parnaíba produced only 676 liters of cane brandy worth 352,806 reis. By 1798, the town produced twice the amount of brandy, as well as 70,000 kilos of sugar and other sugar products. Combined, the total income from sugar cultivation amounted to 7,247,981 reis.

Peasants were not unaware of the larger changes taking place. They perceived their increasing vulnerability in the face of those who, allied with the royal governor, had increased their power and

authority in the community. To peasants, one individual symbolized their growing powerlessness: Colonel Policarpo Joaquim
de Oliveira. Policarpo became an officer in the militia created by
the Morgado de Mateus and used his newfound authority to increase his personal power and wealth. He imprisoned the mothers
and sisters of those who refused enlistment in the new militia.[58]
He forced the poor of Parnaíba to build a terrace on his farm and
a road from his canefields to his mill. Those who did the work,
often in chains, received no pay and labored under the guard of
soldiers. João Leite Pais, one of these men, recounted, "With absolute power the Lieutenant Colonel imprisoned me in his house,
in irons and stocks, making me work as if I were his slave or one
of those, who because of their crimes, are sentenced by Your
Majesty's judges to the galleys; I went on this way for four
months."[59] Moreover, João's wife was also imprisoned, forced to
work and to suffer hunger and cruel punishments, as was his
daughter, whom Policarpo forced to spin cotton day and night.
João exclaimed how, with tears in his eyes, he cried to God for justice but that "in that time, during the governorship of Dom Luis
[Antonio de Souza, the Morgado de Mateus] there was no justice
for this man."[60]

As the sugar economy spread, the rate of conflict over land
surged. The books kept by the notary reveal that the peasantry
began to sell their lands for small sums to expanding sugar planters.[61] Policarpo Joaquim de Oliveira acquired many of these farms.
Antonio Ribeiro de Barros sold his farm to Policarpo for 38,000 reis
in 1789. While this may have seemed like an enormous sum to
Antonio, to Policarpo, it was not. Property inventories provide a
rough measure of the relative worth of 38,000 reis to planters and
to peasants: 38,000 reis represented 6 percent of the assets of Antonio Correa de Lemos Leite and his wife, who were planters and
contemporaries of Policarpo Joaquim de Oliveira, but this sum represented 99.9 percent of the assets of Bernardo Pereira de Azevedo
and his wife, peasants like Antonio Ribeiro de Barros.[62]

Many peasants lost their lands through intimidation. The town
council of Parnaíba reported in 1801 that by "absolute power"
Policarpo had taken over farms and lands of people "who because
of the fear they had for him, gave him the lands which they
owned."[63] Some peasants became his tenants, paying rent to farm

what had once been theirs. Those who resisted, Policarpo accused of wrongdoing and threatened with imprisonment. In one district, thirty or forty residents lost their lands when Policarpo had the area declared unclaimed and then petitioned the crown for it in a royal land grant, which the crown duly awarded. "By these means," the town council wrote, "he has taken over not only the lands of the residents but whole rural neighborhoods."[64]

By 1820, Parnaíba was a different town, and the lives of peasants had taken on a very different character. Forty-five years had brought many changes. The population had expanded from 4,676 persons in 1775 to 7,090 in 1820. The peasantry had increased by 57 percent, from 2,444 individuals in 1775 to 3,842 in 1820. The town center had grown and now supported a much larger group of artisans, laborers, muledrivers, and domestic servants. Thirty-three percent of all households without slaves lived in the town center or in the centers of the rapidly growing parishes of São Roque and Araçariguama. Rural households of peasants, down from 84 percent of all slaveless households in 1775 to 67 percent in 1820, continued to produce sugar, cotton, corn, beans, manioc, rice, beef, and pork.

The expansion of the sugar economy between 1775 and 1820 had pushed many families off of the land and into the town center. This movement accounts for the declining percentage of households in the rural areas and the increasing number of artisans and day laborers in the town center. Guilherme Luis Pais, for example, appeared in the 1775 census as a farmer who harvested corn, beans, and peanuts and raised horses, cows, and pigs. Soon thereafter, he sold his land and moved into the town, where he worked as a weaver.[65]

Many families made the transition from farming to artisan trades. Bento Cardozo Correa, who in 1775 had owned a small farm with horses and pigs, had lost or given up his farm by 1798. The 1798 census, taken when he was 77 years old, showed that he lived in the town center with his two daughters and son. His daughters supported the family "by spinning and weaving cotton cloth" from which "they earn 8,000 reis per year."[66] Antonio Joze da Silva underwent a similar transition. A farmer with cattle in 1775, he had become an artisan, cutting and tanning hides, by 1798.

One of the few households that spanned the years between the 1775 census and the 1820 census, that of Alexandre Joze and Anna Maria da Trinidade, illustrates many of the changes that came into the lives of peasants in this forty-five-year period. In 1775, Alexandre and Anna Maria had three children and lived on rented lands where they planted corn and beans. In 1798, with four children living at home, they planted corn and hired out their canoe to ferry passengers across the river. In 1820, the family had five children and one grandchild at home, but they no longer farmed. Instead, the census stated that they "lived by their wits" (*vivem de suas agencias*), a ubiquitous term in the census which meant that they lived from a variety of jobs, as best they could.[67]

As peasants moved from the rural districts to the town center, their lives changed correspondingly. The majority of the inhabitants of the town worked as artisans. These households, headed by men and women, worked as tailors, shoemakers, spinners, seamstresses, tilemakers, carpenters, blacksmiths, and potters. They produced simple items for local patrons or services for local families. Most worked out of their homes and kept gardens behind their makeshift huts where they grew corn and beans. Others who lived in the town owned small stores and taverns or worked as muleteers. The members of households that supported themselves by "living by their wits" may have been servants, laborers, or odd jobbers who worked from job to job as best they could. The poor, mostly women, children, the sick, and the infirm, pleaded for alms outside the parish churches and walked from house to house, begging for food.

Women headed the majority of the households that supported themselves from nonagricultural trades. Seventy-five percent of the households of artisans and 69 percent of the poor households were headed by women. In most of these households, women made a living by spinning and weaving cotton cloth. They, with their children, worked as part of a local cottage textile industry.[68] Many were "single mothers," and, judging from the census, they raised their children with little or no support from the children's fathers. Thus, in the town center of Parnaíba, and to a lesser extent in the budding town centers in the parishes of Araçariguama and São Roque, poor women could be found in house after house spin-

ning thread, weaving cloth, and making clothing. This gave the
town center a different character than the surrounding rural areas
where households tended to be nuclear families (see table 14).

Families who continued to farm in 1820 found conditions re-
markably different from those in 1775. Families that had survived
for generations as squatters, tenant farmers, and small landowners
saw their traditional rights erode. Their tenuous position became
clear when they tried to defend their rights to land. In 1820, three
tenants on a religious estate attempted to use the legal process to
regain control over their lands. They claimed that they had worked
their lands for over forty years and that in 1816, they had let João
Rodrigues Fam open a small farm (*rancho*) on these lands. Then
João, in turn, had let Captain Joze Manoel Tavares plant large
fields and graze his cattle on the same land. In 1819, the plaintiffs
stated that the captain had farmed all of the woodlands, leaving
"not a foot of room" for them to plant their corn. Since the captain
was a rich man while they were poor, the plaintiffs asked the
crown magistrate of São Paulo to "ensure that the Captain renounce his power over their lands and remove his animals . . .
and obligate João Rodrigues Fam to leave as well."[69] When asked
to investigate the situation, a local official in Parnaíba replied that
the lands in question actually belonged to the Monserate religious
estate and that the plaintiffs had no claim to the land other than
that they had been born there and had been tenants of the estate.[70]
While we do not know the eventual outcome of this suit, it would
seem, based on the local official's opinion, that the tenants would
have a difficult time regaining their lands since they had never formally owned them.

As families lost their lands, significant changes in family life
took place. Households became smaller. The average size decreased
from 4.8 persons in 1775 to 4.3 persons in 1820. Fewer households
had retainers who supplied extra farm labor. Households headed
by women increased from 24 percent of all households in 1775 to
28 percent in 1820. The number of single women with children also
grew from 3 percent in 1775 to 7 percent in 1820. Not surprisingly,
the number of babies born to women and "unknown fathers" increased dramatically. The priest baptized five babies in the parish
of Santana in 1775 for whom he listed the father as "unknown";

Table 14. Households Headed by Men and Women,
Peasant Population, 1820

Households	Male Heads of Household		Female Heads of Household	
	N	%	N	%
Rural	512	81	75	31
Urban	118	19	170	69
Total	630	100	245	100

Source: 1820 census, Parnaíba.
Chi-square = 205.00; DF = 1; probability = 0.000.

these babies accounted for 10 percent of all baptisms in that year. In 1820, one-third of all babies baptized by the parish priest had unknown fathers.[71]

Most of these changes in family structure occurred in the households found in the town center. There households headed by women were more common, households were smaller, and women outnumbered men. In the rural districts of the town, however, the nuclear family remained the cornerstone of agricultural life (see table 15).

These changes in the families of peasants between 1775 and 1820 illustrate the degree to which the expanding sugar economy had affected their lives. The rise in the number of households headed by single women is a compelling example. As competition for land reduced the size of farms, families began to slough off dependent members. Concomitantly, demand for labor on the frontier, as well as the availability of land there, caused many men to migrate west. This left numerous women behind. These women moved into the towns, where they were poor more often than not. Many never married but still gave birth to several children. Their daughters often remained in Parnaíba, too, and repeated the pattern set by their mothers. The sons of these women tended to leave home, either for the city of São Paulo or for the frontier. Thus, the households headed by women had a high ratio of women to men, which further limited their ability to survive. Deprived of the protection and labor normally provided by men, these female-headed households were among the most marginal in the town.[72]

Women moved into the town centers not because they could

Table 15. Urban and Rural Family Structure,
Peasant Population, 1820

	Rural		Urban	
Average household size	4.8		3.6	
Sex ratio[a]	88		56	
Households of nuclear families	363	(62%)	56	(21%)
Households with agregados	81	(14%)	30	(11%)
Households headed by women	75	(13%)	168	(62%)

Source: 1820 census, Parnaíba.
[a] Men per 100 women

not manage farms but because they owned little or no property. Women had managed ninety-seven farms in 1775, while thirty-four women headed households that supported themselves by spinning, weaving, or begging for alms in the town center. By 1820, women ran seventy-three farms, but the vast majority of households headed by women appeared in the town center, where the women and children worked as spinners, servants, or were simply "poor" (see table 16). The growing number of women who headed households in the town center suggests that either families could no longer support single and widowed women and, as a consequence, women flocked to the town centers and made do as best they could or that as families lost their lands, men moved on to the frontiers while women remained behind.

The life story of Paula Soares illustrates how these changes occurred. In 1775, Paula's father, Felis Soares, appeared in the census with his wife, Thomazia, and children, Joze and Izabel, living by favor and cultivating corn. By 1798, twenty-three years later, Paula had been born, and the family continued to live as subsistence farmers, harvesting and selling corn and beans. Joze had married and lived nearby with his wife and two children as subsistence farmers. In 1820, twenty-two years later, Felis, now an old man of 70 years, was a widower. He lived with Paula and her two children. Paula, it seems, had never married, for she appears in the census as a *solteira*, a single woman. The household supported itself by spinning cotton, a task probably done by Paula and her daughter, Roza. Her brother, Joze, now 50, lived next door with his wife and children. They still farmed, planting and harvesting a small amount of corn. While we do not know exactly what hap-

Table 16. Female-headed Households, Peasant Population,
1775 and 1820

Households	1775		1820	
	N	%	N	%
Farmers	97	74	73	30
Laborers/artisans/poor	34	26	169	70
Total	131	100	242	100

Source: 1775 and 1820 censuses, Parnaíba.

pened in this family, it seems likely that Felis had lost his farmland
or had given at least part of it to his son, Joze, who continued to
farm. In his old age, he lived with his daughter who with her
brother supported him as best they could—Paula by spinning
thread and Joze with food from the farm. After Felis died, Paula
would undoubtedly continue to work as a spinner, most probably
in the town center. Joze and his family would continue to farm.[73]

As the population of Parnaíba grew and as land became scarce,
the traditional ways in which families had survived became increasingly difficult. Moreover, the strategies that many families
had used in 1775 to cope with the changes taking place in Parnaíba
had only temporarily solved their problems. Those families who
had moved from Parnaíba in 1775, for example, seeking to preserve a traditional way of life farther west, had simply delayed, not
eliminated, the moment of reckoning. To move west from Parnaíba
to the town of Itú, or from the parish of Santana into the western
parish of São Roque, resolved only fleetingly the problem of access
to land and freedom from social control. Since the sugar economy
moved in waves, gaining momentum as it pushed west, it affected newer frontier communities even more profoundly than the
older sugar centers. Itú became a more important sugar center than
Parnaíba had been a generation before, just as the parishes of
Araçariguama and São Roque eventually outproduced the older
parish of Santana. Those who elected to move to these areas in
search of land bought themselves time—but not for long. Families
would have to move again and again to maintain access to free
frontier lands.[74]

Similarly, the strategy of fostering ties to planters also had its
limitations. Such ties depended on the benevolence of planters.

While traditionally planters may have seen it in their interests to defend the rights of peasants, as the sugar economy spread, it was increasingly not in their interests to do so. Peasants occupied lands, sometimes valuable lands, that sugar planters could use for planting cane. Increasingly, planters saw themselves as different from peasants, and the bonds between them weakened. In 1820, 48 percent of the heads of peasant households were recorded in the census as "browns" (pardos) or as "blacks" (*pretos*); whereas, in the census of 1775, 73 percent of the heads of peasant households were presumed to be "white." Some peasants who were presumed white in the 1798 census had become brown in the 1820 census.[75] These categorizations suggest that the individuals who collected the census information had changed the way they viewed color. More clearly defined class barriers had emerged by 1820. Planters no longer saw peasants as their poor white kin. Increasingly, they saw them as belonging to a different class, set apart from themselves by color.

Thus, peasants articulated very different strategies for survival in the Parnaíba of 1820 than in that of 1775. By 1820, it was next to impossible to live by favor in Parnaíba. Land boundaries were clearly drawn, and valuable lands were coveted by sugar planters. Neither could peasants live "behind the forest" as they had once done during the days of the Morgado de Mateus. By 1820, their place in agrarian society was a tenuous one, constantly encroached on by the expanding sugar planters. The more intimate and patriarchal world in which peasants had once sought the benevolence of planters had given way. Peasants began to live within their own world, a world defined by their class. They saw other peasant families as their closest allies and selected them as the godparents for their children. But they also saw other peasant families as their immediate competitors.[76]

Whereas the peasantry once depended on ties to planters as an important means of maintaining their position in the town, by 1820, peasants had practically abandoned such strategies. Many fewer families selected godparents for their children from the ranks of the rich and powerful. Rather, godparents tended to be chosen from within the same economic stratum. Most of the peasant children baptized between 1819 and 1821 had one or both godparents from the same social class as their parents. Thirty-eight percent had godparents drawn from the poor planters, and only 20 percent had godparents who owned more than ten slaves (see table 13, above).

As the numbers of peasant families grew and as the lands around them filled in, families lived in greater proximity to one another. Whereas in 1775, peasants still lived relatively dispersed in the town, by 1820, well-defined neighborhoods had taken shape. In these neighborhoods (*bairros*), inhabited mostly by peasants, families lived close to one another. They found little privacy. It was "public knowledge" in 1806 that João Duarte de Moura beat his wife.[77] Tongues wagged in 1805 when Izabel Leme "vented her anger" on Floriana Maria and clobbered her with a piece of wood.[78] Anna Maria de Oliveira complained to anyone who would listen of the poor treatment she received from her husband, Joze Rodrigues, who had abandoned her for two years.[79]

Peasants fought among themselves for land and space, often resolving their differences through the intervention of local officials. Few families had used local institutions to pursue their interests in 1775, but by 1820, families had become quite skilled at manipulating the local judicial courts. Many of these cases focused on disputes over land or harvests, beatings, robberies, or family problems. Peasants sought out the justices of the town council or sometimes militia officers and priests to mediate such disputes. Usually, the local justices were able to come to a settlement. Izabel Leme, guilty of hitting Floriana Maria over the head with a piece of wood, was sent to the town jail. João Duarte de Moura, who beat his wife and then poisoned her, was sent there as well. When local officials could not resolve local disputes, families pursued higher authorities. João Francisco Pais and Antonio Teles, neighbors in São Roque, first asked the military district captain of São Roque to mediate a disagreement between them. When he was unable to settle the dispute, the case was forwarded to the general magistrate in São Paulo.[80]

The independent, roving farmers who "lived in laziness and liberty" behind the curtain of the forest had virtually disappeared in Parnaíba by 1820. Many were pushed out to the frontier as the sugar economy rolled through the town. Others moved into the town center or even to the larger towns and cities. Those who

remained behind farmed smaller plots of land that supported reduced households. When the sugar economy began to decline as
the virgin forests were cut and the lands were rapidly stripped of
their organic compounds, sugar planters moved on. A few planters
remained in Parnaíba and planted coffee, but by and large, by
1850, the agricultural focus of the town was subsistence farming.
Those who continued to survive as farmers turned their attention to producing for a new market, that of the growing city of
São Paulo.[81]

By the middle of the nineteenth century, then, peasants had devised new strategies to survive in Santana de Parnaíba. They tried
to limit the division of their lands among their children in order to
maintain their farms intact. Since land had become a valuable resource, they no longer claimed and abandoned lands. Instead,
they farmed the same lands and, like the small slaveholders,
waged a constant battle against the dispersal of productive family
property among too many heirs. More of the peasants began to
write wills, grant dowries to their daughters, and have their property inventoried by the local orphan's judge. They encouraged
heirs to share land and forced others to migrate to the city or to
the frontier, all to reduce pressure on finite resources.[82]

The transformation of Parnaíba's peasantry from roving swidden farmers to sedentary market-garden producers occurred slowly
from the end of the eighteenth century to the middle of the
nineteenth century. This process was not unique to Parnaíba. It
represented the common experience of communities throughout
São Paulo as the spread of sugar and coffee cultivation subjected
them to a boom and bust economic cycle. For families who had little public influence, each stage of that cycle placed them at risk,
for they could not defend their land.[83] When the free resources of
the frontier on which the traditional life-style of peasants depended ran out in Santana de Parnaíba, those who remained in
the town became more like the peasant class of Europe than the
American frontiersmen. Peasants had to change many aspects of
their lives to survive. These adjustments can be seen in family,
community, and farm life. But even as the wilderness disappeared
in Parnaíba, it still beckoned poor men and women from the town,
who, like the sons of planters, followed the frontier west in search
of cheap or free lands. There, on new land claimed from the wil-

derness, they reproduced a lifeway their parents and grandparents had once practiced in the town of Parnaíba.

By the early nineteenth century, the traditional life-style of peasants had become a memory in Parnaíba. Families such as Bento Cardozo Correa's found themselves pulled in different directions: to the town, the city, or the frontier. Some of Bento's children probably did continue to live much as he and his wife, Maria, had, either in Parnaíba or farther west. A Bento Joze Cardozo appeared in the census of 1798 in the parish of São Roque as a subsistence farmer; he was married and had one daughter. This Bento could have been Bento Cardozo Correa's son, two years old in 1775. Similarly, a Joze Alves Cardozo, forty-seven years old in 1820 and a subsistence farmer, may have been Bento Cardozo Correa's son, six years old in 1775. At least three of Bento Cardozo Correa's children, however, lived very different lives from their parents. In the last two years of the century, Bento's two daughters, Joanna and Roza, still had not married. Given their ages (40 and 37), they probably never would. After their father died, they would continue to live in Parnaíba's town center, eking out a living as spinners and weavers. Their brother Francisco (35) also had not married in 1798. Unless he moved out to the frontier, he would probably remain in Parnaíba's town center "living by his wits." If he married, he might move with his wife to the frontier and reestablish the life he had known as a boy on his father's small farm in Parnaíba. The rest of Bento's children are buried in the census lists as wives or servants or had left Parnaíba altogether. By 1822, the year that Brazil's independence was declared in São Paulo, Bento's children were, most probably, spread throughout the province. Some still lived in Parnaíba, in the town center, or on the outskirts of the town as subsistence farmers. Others moved on, to the receding frontier, now well beyond Parnaíba. A few may have moved to the city of São Paulo. Thus, the dispersal of Bento's family is itself perhaps the best indication of how the families of the peasantry adapted to the changes afoot in São Paulo at the end of the eighteenth century.

6

Families of Slaves

When Mariana Dias (great-great-great-great-granddaughter of Suzana Dias) died in 1776, her husband, Antonio Correa de Lemos Leite, captain major of Parnaíba, began the probate proceedings after one month's time, as required by law. Antonio reported that the couple's community property included seventeen slaves: Joaquim married to Euzebia, Pedro married to Leonarda, Venturo married to Joanna, three Africans not married to anyone, and eight children, five of whom presumably were the children of the three married slave couples. The three other slave children were listed in the inventory as "mulattoes," which suggests that they had a white father; their mother was not named. Thus, three nuclear slave families and possibly a matrifocal family existed on Mariana and Antonio's farm.

Mariana's death began the process of inheritance. The appraisers first evaluated each of these slaves, then the orphan's judge oversaw the division of the slaves among the heirs or their sale to cover the couple's debts. Pedro and Leonarda were both to be sold to repay outstanding loans. Joaquim and Euzebia were to be co-owned by the three heirs, Barbara, Benta, and Anna Esmeria. Joanna and Venturo and four other slaves were to remain with Antonio, as part of his half of the community property. The other slaves went to the other heirs or to cover the couple's debts.[1]

In 1782, when Antonio died, the family property again underwent evaluation and division by the orphan's judge. All of the slaves had to be distributed to heirs or sold to meet any outstanding debts at this time. Pedro and Leonarda, who were supposed to have been sold to cover the family's debts in 1776, had not been sold and had remained with Antonio until his death. Pedro, now fifty, was sick in bed, and according to the assessor, "waiting to die." Leonarda, his wife, was to go to Antonio's daughter, but their son, Francisco, was slated to be sold. Venturo and Joanna, who had remained with Antonio after his wife's death, were to be split up, Venturo going to one daughter and Joanna to another. The couple's daughter, Rita, was to be divided between Antonio's son and the outstanding debts; that meant that she would probably be sold. The other slaves were to go to heirs or to cover debts, except for the three young mulatto boys whom Antonio had decided to free, possibly because he recognized them as kin. This action angered his sons-in-law, who attempted to revoke the manumission.[2]

Thus, of the three slave families that had lived on Mariana's and Antonio's estate during their lives, none remained together after their deaths. The process of breaking up slave families actually began when Mariana died because the Portuguese laws of inheritance went into effect then, but the real breakup occurred after Antonio's death, when all of the couple's community property had to be transferred to the next generation or liquidated to repay any creditors. Tracing Antonio's heirs in later censuses further reveals the dissolution of these slave families. Antonio's daughter and son-in-law, Joze de Medeiros de Souza, were the only heirs who remained in Parnaíba. The other heirs had moved west, to Itú in the developing sugar frontier, and had taken their slaves with them. Joze inherited the largest share of the family farm, and in 1798, he and his wife owned ten slaves. Yet none of the slaves they owned in 1798 were the same slaves that Antonio had owned at his death.[3]

The division of estates according to Portuguese laws of inheritance placed virtually insurmountable stresses on slave family life. After the division of family property, slaves found it extremely hard to maintain family ties, especially if heirs took family members out of Parnaíba to the developing western frontiers. This created the fundamental difference between the family lives of slaves and nonslaves: a slave's status as property far overshadowed his or her right to a family life. Moreover, external factors over which slaves had no control, such as the death of their masters, had a massive impact on family life.

Family life for slaves did not revolve around the essentially free wilderness resources needed for family businesses, as it did for the planters, or around the traditional frontier agriculture of peasants but around the work demanded by the master and the few rights and privileges conceded in return. Because slaves only rarely owned property and had virtually no independence, the family life of slaves diverged in very basic ways from that of planters and peasants.

Since slave family life contrasted so fundamentally from that of planters and peasants, the strategies that slaves developed to create and maintain a family and a community are distinctive. Whereas both the planters and peasants perceived the frontier as a source of wealth and opportunity, slaves did not see the frontier in the same way. With no possibility of acquiring the resources of the frontier, slaves did not view it as integral to their survival. Rather, slave strategies focused on survival at a much more rudimentary level: how to physically endure the work, the violence, and the psychological dehumanization brought into their lives by slavery.

Family life was central to the strategies that slaves developed to survive. It provided slaves with one of the few means to establish a separate, private existence, independent from the master. Even if the master interfered in slave family life, he or she could not own the emotions that tied slave families together. Family life also granted slaves a means to create their own community, likewise separate from their masters. Ties between blood kin, or the ties between godparents and children, joined slaves together. Through the creation of families, slaves bridged the enormous differences among themselves—between the nations of Africa from which they came and between those of African and Brazilian birth. And finally, family life served as the vehicle through which slaves passed their culture from one generation to the next. Thus, family life is key to understanding how slaves survived the physical and emotional violence of slavery.

Because slaves were property, property that belonged to families, their lives were intimately bound up with the lives of the families to which they belonged. Slaves and their children accompanied their masters and their masters' descendants through time. Many aspects of the family lives of masters, therefore, affected the family lives of slaves. To reconstruct the lives of slaves, the historian must also reconstruct the lives of the slave owners. Thus, not only in the past but in the present, as historians search for the story of their lives, are slaves bound to their masters.

Events in the lives of the masters undermined the family lives of slaves, and as Caribbean historian Barry Higman has shown, slave family life tended to be highly correlated with levels of economic development and the slave trade. In developing plantation areas in the Caribbean, where the slave trade from Africa supplied the majority of the slaves for the plantations, male slaves predominated, and few slaves lived in families. In mature plantation areas where the native-born slave population had had a chance to grow, the number of male and female slaves equalized, and more slaves lived in families.[4]

In Santana de Parnaíba, as in many other towns in colonial Brazil, the presence of the frontier also affected slave family life. In the seventeenth century, the Indian slaves of the colonists built the town, cleared the forests, planted the fields, and harvested the wheat that brought a modest prosperity to the town. In the eighteenth century, African slaves likewise made it possible for planters to exploit the wilderness. Africans accompanied the men of planter families to Minas Gerais, Mato Grosso, and Goiás where they mined for gold, traded cattle, or were sold for handsome profits. In the second half of the century, African slaves opened up new sugar estates in São Paulo which finally brought this southern region into the orbit of the Portuguese Atlantic economy. The historic links of Parnaíba's economy to the frontier affected slaves profoundly. Just as planter and peasant families constantly followed the frontier, so, too, did Africans.

For most slaves, migrating with the frontier meant forced relocation and leaving behind family and an established slave community. Still, the wilderness might bring freedom, even if temporary. Runaway slaves headed for the wilderness, where they hid from Portuguese society in maroon communities known as quilombos. In the mining regions, slaves accumulated gold that they could use to purchase their freedom. When André de Goes Leme wrote his will in 1738, he noted that he owed gold to four slaves— 24 *oitavas* (86.4 grams) to Agostinho, 8 oitavas (28.8 grams) to Joze, 10 oitavas (36 grams) to João, and 6 oitavas (21.6 grams) to Faustino. One of these slaves entrusted André with the money for safekeeping, but the others apparently loaned him the sums. These slaves had accumulated this property from the mines of Cuiabá. Thus, some slaves did benefit from the frontier, even though most did not pursue the frontier as a strategy for survival.[5]

Slaves left few visible records of their family lives. Yet, for slaves, as for peasants and planters, family life wielded an enormous influence over upbringing, socialization, and everyday life. When studied as a group, slaves, like peasants and planters, pursued common goals. They sought to establish order and stability in their lives through their families and to construct a slave community. They sought their freedom from slavery through a variety of means. These strategies shaped the lives of their descendants, future slaves and free blacks alike. Slave strategies, like those of peasants and planters, affected the community life of Santana de Parnaíba.

What constituted a slave family? While historians have used the households of planters and peasants enumerated in the manuscript censuses to reconstruct the basic contours of the households of these social groups, no comparable households of slaves appear in the census lists. Since census takers recorded slaves as property, it is never clear if the order in which they listed slaves corresponded to actual slave families. In the 1775 census, for example, the census recorders noted only the number of slaves owned by each master. In the 1798 and 1820 censuses, slaves are individually named and marriages between slaves usually appear, but rarely are slave children coupled with their parents. For example, the slaves who belonged to the Reverend Francisco Lopes Sa, his widowed mother, and his six brothers and sisters, as recorded in the 1798 census, are difficult to arrange into discrete families (see fig.6).

On closer examination of this list, two slave families appear: those formed by the marriages of Pedro and Thereza and of Domingos and Maria. João, the slave from Guiné, had no visible family ties. Francisca, Antonia, Simão, Joze, and Thomé, however, may well have been the children of Pedro and Thereza or Domingos and Maria. Given the racial classifications given to each slave (mulatto and pardo usually referred to slaves lighter in color; Creole, to those who were black), one might reconstruct two families for the slaves on this estate (see fig. 7). Were these the

Pedro, mulatto, married, 60 years old
Thereza, mulatta, his wife, 58 years old
Domingos, Guiné, married, 30 years old
Maria, Creole, his wife, 19 years old
João, Guiné, single, 40 years old
João, mulatto, single, 20 years old
Francisca, mulatta, single, 30 years old
Antonia, mulatta, single, 16 years old
Simão, Creole, single, 15 years old
Joze, Creole, single, 7 years old
Thomé, Creole, single, 2 years old

Source: 1798 census, Parnaíba.

Figure 6. Slaves of Rev. Francisco Lopes Sa, 1798

slave families that formed in and around the family of the Reverend Francisco Lopes Sa? The difficulty of knowing for certain points to the problems faced by historians when attempting to reconstruct the families of slaves with the sources that work well for reconstructing the families of the free population.

The property inventories so meticulously kept by the orphan's judges are another important source of information on slave family life. Since slaves accounted for the largest single investment made by their masters, assessors always carefully described and evaluated each slave. Often, but not always, it is possible to discern the existence of slave families from these lists of slaves. For example, eleven slaves appeared in the inventory of Antonio Francisco Lima, who died in 1758.[6] They are listed in the following order:

João	Angola	30 years
Roza	Benguela	30 years, his wife
Thereza	Creole	11 years
Guiteria	Creole	10 years
Francisco	Benguela	45 years
Ignacia	mulatta	22 years, his wife
Rita	Creole	8 years
Joaquim	mulatto	2 years
Angelo	Creole	12 years
Francisco	Creole	4 years
João	Angola	35 years

Slave Family #1

Pedro, mulatto, 60 years old	(husband)
Thereza, mulatta, 58 years old	(wife)
João, mulatto, 20 years old	(son)
Francisca, mulatta, 30 years old	(daughter)
Antonia, mulatta, 16 years old	(daughter)

Slave Family #2

Domingos, Guiné, 30 years old	(husband)
Maria, Creole, 19 years old	(wife)
Thomé, Creole, 2 years old	(son)

Slaves without Families

João, Guiné, 30 years old	(single)
Simão, Creole, 15 years old	(single)
Joze, Creole, 7 years old	(single, possibly Maria's son)

Figure 7. Slave Families of Rev. Francisco Lopes Sa

From the order of the slaves listed in the inventory, two clear slave families lived with Antonio: one formed by the marriage of the Angolan João and Roza and one created by that of the Benguelan Francisco and his wife, Ignacia. But since the relationship of the children is not given in the inventory, their parentage must be inferred. It seems likely that most of the slave children were Roza's: Angelo, 12, Thereza, 11, Guiteria, 10, Rita, 8 and Francisco, 4. The mulatta Ignacia's only child would have been the young mulatto, Joaquim, 2 years old. But since precise information is not given in the inventory, it is impossible to know for sure.

Precise information on family ties does appear in some of the inventories. In the largest estate inventoried in Parnaíba in the eighteenth century, that of Manoel Correa Penteado, who died in 1745 and owned 110 slaves at his death, the listing of slaves shows that all but 15 slaves on his estate lived in families. The majority of the slaves on his estate, 54 percent, lived in nuclear families, that is, composed of a married couple and their children.[7]

The inventories of some planters thus can be used quite successfully to gain an idea of how their slaves lived. While many of the inventories do not provide an exact picture of slave family life,

combined with the censuses, they do allow the historian to reconstruct in broad outlines the families of the slaves who lived on the
farms and plantations of Santana de Parnaíba.

To understand the family lives of slaves, it is first necessary to
reconstruct the history of the slave population itself. The ability of
slaves to form families depended on many factors beyond their
control, such as the number of slaves in a given area and the ratio
of men to women. It would be hard for slaves to form families if
men outnumbered women by a wide margin. Similarly, the historian would expect to find few families if the average age of the
slave population was old. Since slavery was essentially a forced
migration of Africans, the slave population in a town like Parnaíba
overrepresented men and adults relative to children. Thus, the
basic demographic structure of the slave population had a major
impact on slave families.

Where slaves lived also affected their family life. Those who
lived on large plantations would have a better chance of forming
enduring family ties than those who lived on small farms or in
towns and cities. Historians have found that nuclear and extended
families predominated on large plantations. Richard Graham's
analysis of the Jesuit estate of Santa Cruz, which had 1,300 slaves,
reveals that 55 percent lived in nuclear families.[8] Stuart Schwartz
finds that on the Santana estate in Bahia in 1731, an estate with
178 slaves, 47 percent of the family units constituted some form
of nuclear or extended families. On the same estate in 1752, the
number of nuclear and extended families reached 72 percent.[9] In
the United States, Herbert Gutman documents that on the Good
Hope plantation of South Carolina, nearly all 175 slaves of the estate were related by blood or marriage in 1857.[10] Slaves in towns
and cities, however, often worked as servants, artisans, or laborers
and usually belonged to masters with only a few slaves. They
therefore did not live in an environment as conducive to forming
families as slaves in rural areas. Mary Karasch's discussion of slave
family life in Rio de Janeiro bears this out. She finds little evidence
of stable slave families in this teeming port city in the nineteenth
century. In Rio, the effects of the slave trade created an unbalanced
sex ratio, masters resisted slave marriages, and slave families
found it difficult to find a place to live, all of which militated
against the formation of slave families.[11]

In Parnaíba, the slave population changed its composition over time depending on external economic factors. In the early eighteenth century, when slaves of African origin were first introduced into the town, slaves were primarily African and male. Planter families, enriched by their investments in the mining regions, purchased male slaves from slave traders. At first, these slaves had a difficult time forming families. Not only had they been uprooted from their tribal homelands in Africa but they were mixed with slaves from many different nations. Africans could not easily communicate with each other. In addition, slave traders preferred to traffic in males. Thus, not all male slaves who wished to find a woman to marry (legally or not) could do so. For example, when André de Goes Leme's estate was inventoried in 1738, twelve slaves appeared. Only three of these slaves were women, and two of these women were girls under the age of ten. All but one of André's male slaves were African, but of four different nations.[12]

As the century progressed and as slaves married and had children, proportionally more of the slaves in Parnaíba were born in Brazil. The growing "Creole" population meant that more and more slaves had family ties—slaves born in the New World had New World kin, which African-born slaves acquired only when they married. Gradually, the ratio of male to female slaves equalized, making it easier for male slaves to find mates. Slaves newly arrived from Africa still found it difficult to communicate with other slaves, but they found in Brazil an extant slave community that facilitated their integration into communities such as Santana de Parnaíba. This process can be seen on Antonio Francisco Lima's estate, discussed above. Inventoried in 1758, twenty years after André's, only four of his eleven slaves had been born in Africa. Six of his eleven slaves were men; five were women. All but one of the adult men were married. Thus, one of the most important influences on slave family life was the growth of a Creole slave community that created the conditions that allowed slave families to form.[13]

The importance of these demographic factors for the ability of slaves to form families can be seen in the manuscript censuses that provide a snapshot of the slave population at a given moment in time. The censuses show that the population of slaves born in Africa looked very different from the population of Creole slaves.

In the 1820 census, for example, slaves born in Africa accounted for 27 percent of all slaves living in Parnaíba. These slaves came from a variety of African homelands, the most common being Angola, the Congo region, and west Africa. Compared to Creole slaves, African slaves tended to be older, and more were men. The Creole slaves, however, tended to be born in Parnaíba, had a more equal ratio of men to women, and were younger (see table 17).

The age pyramids constructed by demographers to illustrate the structure of a population at a given time clearly depict these differences in the Creole and African populations in 1820. Among the African slaves, men outnumbered women in virtually all age cohorts. The largest age cohorts of the African population were those between the years of 15 and 35, the prime laboring years in men's and women's lives. These characteristics resulted from the slave trade, for slave dealers bought more men than women and more slaves of certain ages because they commanded higher prices in Brazil.

The African population contrasts sharply with the age pyramid of the Brazilian-born slaves. In the Creole slave population, the largest age cohorts appear at the bottom of the age pyramid, between birth and 15 years. Children outnumber adults, making the average age of all Creole slaves young. The ratio of men to women is relatively constant throughout each of the age cohorts. The age pyramids of the Creole slave population resemble what demographers would consider a more "normal" population for a preindustrial agricultural society (see fig. 8).

In slave societies, the economic development of new regions had a major impact on the formation of slave families. As a sugar economy spread into new areas, planters purchased African slaves, and as the region matured, Creole slaves increased in numbers. This relationship between economic growth and slave family life can be seen in the town's parishes. The parish of Santana, as the center of the town, developed first, followed by Araçariguama and São Roque. In 1820 when the sugar economy was in decline in the parish of Santana, Creole slaves outnumbered African slaves by six to one, but in Araçariguama and São Roque, where the sugar economy was stronger, Creole slaves outnumbered Africans by only two to one. Santana parish, which included the town center, had the most extensive slave community: three black brotherhoods

Table 17. African and Creole Slaves, 1820

	Creole Slaves	African Slaves	All Slaves
Sex ratio[a]	102.5	163.7	115.1
Average age	20.1	29.7	22.6

Source: 1820 census, Parnaíba.
[a] Men per 100 women.

had formed to serve the interests of slave and free black religious confraternities.[14] But fewer slaves in Santana had married because they tended to live in the town center and to be owned by poor planters. In the more rural parishes of Araçariguama and São Roque, where large agricultural estates predominated, slaves were more likely to marry.

Historians have argued long and hard over the most common "type" of slave family household. Some claim that nuclear families predominated, others that matrifocal families were the norm.[15] In Parnaíba, it is clear that slaves lived in nuclear families, in matrifocal families, and as solitary individuals. Polygamous families, common in Africa, especially among wealthier men, are almost impossible to discern in Parnaíba. Because of the dearth of women for slaves to marry, the Christian beliefs of the masters, and the absence of wealth among Parnaíba's slaves, polygamous families probably rarely formed in this town. However, the possibility that polygyny may have existed among slaves cannot be rejected, for in the Caribbean, Higman finds evidence of it.[16]

Nuclear families constituted the most common slave family type in eighteenth-century Parnaíba. Like peasant and planter families, slave couples married in recognized Catholic ceremonies performed by the parish priest. With the birth of children, also baptized by the priest, slave nuclear families formed. Such families fragmented when older kin died. The major difference between the "slave" and the "free" family cycle, therefore, was not so much its outer form but the fact that slaves had much less control over their family cycles than did other social classes.

In Santana de Parnaíba, unlike many other towns, cities, and villages where slaves lived in the New World,[17] slaves married without restrictions in the parish churches. While many historians claim that few slaves married in colonial Brazil, an examination of

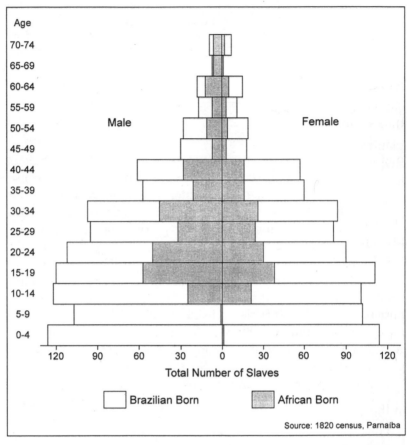

Figure 8. Population Pyramid of the Slave Population, 1820.

the property inventories, censuses, and parish marriage registers clearly reveals this not to be the case for this town. As we have seen, the censuses noted the civil status of slaves as well as free persons, and inventories usually declared which slaves were married and to whom. Entries in the marriage registers of Santana parish further document that between 1726 and 1820, priests celebrated 400 marriages between slaves living in the parish. In addition, the priest also married Indian administrados, primarily during the first half of the eighteenth century. Marriages between slaves and administrados, slaves and Indians, and slaves and free persons also appear in the marriage register. A typical entry reads, "On the eleventh day of the month of August of 1737 in this mother church [igreja matriz] of Parnaíba, after the mass of the day, proceeding with the denunciations, and in the form of the Holy Council of Trent, were married before me by spoken word (*palavras de presente*) João and Jozepha, slaves of the Lieutenant Manoel Rodrigues Fam de Jesus. The witnesses were Bento Pereira, administrado of the deceased Paula Moreira, Antonio, slave of the said Lieutenant, both of whom signed with me, and Maria de Almeida, Indian of the aldeia of Baruerí, and Maria, slave of the said Lieutenant, who being women, did not sign."[18]

The number of slaves who married each year in the parish of Santana varied considerably, from only one marriage in 1781 to fourteen in 1737 and 1759. On average, priests celebrated four marriages between slaves in the parish church each year. For the decades of the 1770s, 1790s, and 1810s, it is possible to calculate the crude marriage rates for slaves and free persons in the parish of Santana by linking the marriage registers with the censuses. In the 1770s, slaves actually had a marriage rate comparable to that of free persons. In the 1790s and 1810s, however, the marriage rate for free persons outpaced slave marriages in the parish church (see table 18).

Almost all slave marriages, 94 percent, conducted by the parish priest in Santana parish, occurred between slaves of the same master. Some masters appear over and over in the marriage ledgers: Antonio Francisco de Andrade (17 times), Baltazar Rodrigues Fam (10 times), Bartolomeo Bueno Pedrozo Leme (10 times), João Gonsalves Seixas (10 times), Manoel Fernandes Soutto (11 times), and Manoel Rodrigues Fam (8 times). These were the large planters

Table 18. Crude Marriage Rates, Slave and Free Populations[a]

	1775	1798	1820
Slaves	6.6	7.0	7.4
Free	6.7	9.4	9.2

Source: Average number of marriages, Santana parish, 1770–1779, 1790–1799, 1811–1820, and censuses of Santana parish, 1775, 1798, 1820.
[a] Marriages per 1,000 individuals.

who saw many of their slaves marry each other. The majority of slave owners, however, appeared only a few times in the marriage registers, as one, two, or three slave couples on their estates sought to marry. These slaves were able to form families on their masters' estates, but they did not live in the slave communities such as existed on the larger farms. Instead, their lives were more entwined with the families of their masters.

A surprisingly large number of slaves in eighteenth-century Parnaíba married free persons. These marriages usually occurred between slaves and free blacks, or occasionally between slaves and Indians. Twenty-one percent of all marriages involving slaves occurred between slaves and free blacks; 9 percent, between slaves and Indians (see table 19). Most of the free blacks whom slaves married lived with the same master as a servant or a retainer. While free black servants and retainers were dependent on the master in many of the same ways that slaves were, they still had a very different social status both on the farm and in the community. Free blacks often had their own plots of land and could move about freely. For example, Rafael, slave of Vicente Correa de Barros, married Anna de Assumpção, a free black woman. The two lived on the same estate—Rafael as a slave, Anna as a retainer. But, in addition, their master had obtained for them a small plot of land that they rented from the town council of Parnaíba. In the rental contract, Vicente, the master, obligated himself to pay the rent if the couple were unable to do so.[19] Thus, a marriage between a slave and a free black gave slaves access to the world of peasants. It provided a means of social mobility for slaves and their children.[20]

Marriages between free blacks (or Indians) and slaves posed some complex questions for family life. Beginning in the early

Table 19. Slave Marriages, Santana Parish, 1726–1820

	N	%
Slave to slave	400	70
Slave to free black·	117	21
Slave to Indian	52	9
Total	569	100

Source: Slave Marriage Registers.

nineteenth century, the parish priest made the free spouse promise to accompany the captive spouse wherever he or she was taken. When Bento Francisco Vieira, a free black man of eighteen, married Maria, a seventeen-year-old slave of Anna Ribeira de Castro, the parish priest wrote in his ledger that "he promised and obligated himself to follow his wife in whatever way her captivity permits."[21] Nineteen years later, it may be possible to catch a glimpse of this marriage. The household of Anna Ribeira, a single white woman of sixty-six, appeared in the 1820 census. She owned four slaves: Mariana, a married slave (Maria of the slave marriage?), two young slave children, probably Mariana's, and a young black slave, João. Living with her was a free retainer named Bento, also listed as married. Quite possibly, this is the same Bento and Maria whom the priest had married many years earlier. If so, Bento had indeed fulfilled his agreement and had "accompanied" his wife's captivity by becoming a retainer of her mistress.

Marriages between slaves and free persons made a tremendous difference when children were born. Of the free black spouses, women outnumbered men by a small margin (78 to 69). Children of these free women, even though their husbands were slaves, would be born free according to law. While the law gave the children of free men who married slaves to the woman's master as property, it was possible for fathers to free their children. A father could gain control over his children's lives, particularly if he purchased the freedom of his children while they were young and of no immediate value to the master.[22] Thus, for slaves, mixed marriages offered a means of social mobility, especially for their children.

The picture of slave marriage that emerges in the parish registers corresponds to what the census tells us about the number of married slaves compared to the number of married free individuals. The censuses reveal that while many slaves were married, not as many slaves married as did free persons. In the parish of Santana in 1820, for example, 138 slaves over the age of fifteen were married, or 33 percent of all slaves, compared to 470 free persons over the age of fifteen, or 43 percent of all free persons. While slaves married, then, they married less frequently than free persons.

While one might have expected fewer African slaves to be married than Creole slaves, this was not the case in Parnaíba in 1820. Thirty-five percent of all Creole slaves over the age of fifteen were married in 1820, compared to 41 percent of Africans. Roughly the same percentage of Creole males and African males were married (35%), but African women were far more likely to have married than Creole women—51 percent compared to 35 percent. Why did African women marry more easily than Creole slave women? Perhaps men preferred them as marriage partners. Or perhaps the majority of African women lived on larger estates where they had greater opportunities to marry, while the majority of Creole slave women lived with poor planters and therefore had less of a chance to marry. Because virtually all African women were married, African slaves were more likely to be married than Creole slaves in all of the parishes except Araçariguama in 1820. Thus, the higher ratio of Africans to Creoles in Araçariguama and São Roque does not seem to have had an effect on the ability of slaves to form families.

Slaves married in their twenties: women on the average at twenty-two years; men, at twenty-nine. Once married, slaves began the process of forming nuclear families, which might become extended families over time. The most important factor affecting the character of these new families was the wealth of the master. Those who belonged to masters who owned many slaves found it easier to marry. They stood a better chance of marrying a slave from the same estate and could continue to live together after the marriage. For example, the largest slave owner in Parnaíba at the end of the eighteenth century, planter Antonio Francisco de Andrade, owned ninety-one slaves. Between 1761 and 1795, seventeen slave marriages took place between the slaves on his estate. By the time he died, a large number of his slaves would have lived in families and would have had kinship ties to other slaves. Slaves who belonged to masters such as Antonio formed small slave communities on their masters' estates. These families had many ties with each other; they served as witnesses at marriages of slaves and as the godparents of slave children. Many slaves had personal ties to the master, to members of his family, or to free retainers living on the estate. Stable nuclear families and an enduring slave community were common on such estates.

The existence of nuclear families can be documented for other large estates in Parnaíba, such as those of planters Manoel Correa Penteado, Rodrigo Bicudo Chassim, and Domingos Rodrigues de Fonseca Leme, all inventoried in the 1740s.[23] Two hundred thirty-four slaves lived on these three estates. Sixty-five percent of all the adult slaves over the age of fifteen were married, or 38 percent of all slaves on the plantations. Nuclear families far outnumbered any other household arrangement, accounting for 44 of 52 families. Sixty-one percent of all slaves on these three estates lived in nuclear families (see table 20).

A variation on the common pattern of slave nuclear families occurred when slaves married slaves living on other estates or when they married free blacks. These persons could form nuclear families, but their families differed from the more usual slave nuclear family settled on the estate of one master. Only 6 percent of the slave marriages celebrated by the parish priest occurred between slaves who belonged to different masters.[24] Masters with few slaves may well have discouraged their slaves from marrying, which may account for the fewer number of marriages between slaves of different masters.[25] Of the forty-six married couples living on the three large estates inventoried in the 1740s, none were married to slaves belonging to other masters. Slaves who were married to slaves belonging to different masters generally had once lived on the same estate but had been separated after inheritance. This can be seen in the inventory of Angela Ribeira Leite, daughter-in-law of Manoel Correa Penteado. Angela had two slaves married to slaves who belonged to other masters. The spouses of both belonged to Angela's brothers-in-law, who had inherited them from their father, Manoel Correa Penteado. The slaves had been married and living together on the same estate until the process of inheritance separated them.[26] For married slaves who lived apart, ties

Table 20. Slave Families on Three Large Estates, 1740s

Households	No. of Households		No. of Slaves	
	N	%	N	%
Nuclear families	31	60	143	61
Married couples	15	29	29	12
Single-parent families	5	10	21	9
Complex families	1	2	3	1
Solitary slaves	–	–	38	16
Total	52	100	234	100

Source: Inv. Domingos Rodrigues de Fonseca Leme, 1738, Rodrigo Bicudo Chassim, 1743, and Manoel Correa Penteado, 1745.

between the families of the masters facilitated the maintenance of slave family ties. For example, Antonio and Elena belonged to two cousins, while Manoel, a slave of Joze Rodrigues Fam, married Maria, a slave of Joze's uncle. While all of these slaves had different masters and lived apart, their bonds to each other were strengthened by the kinship ties between their masters.[27]

Nuclear families were the most common form of slave family structure for slaves who lived on the largest plantations in the eighteenth century. Because masters did not place significant obstacles in front of slaves wishing to marry other slaves on the same estate, significant numbers of slaves on the largest plantations married and formed nuclear families. A small portion of these nuclear families were those in which slaves belonged to different masters or where one spouse was free. In each case, the attitude of the master toward the slave family made a tremendous difference for the ability of the slaves to maintain a stable family life.

Given the ownership patterns of eighteenth-century Parnaíba, most slaves did not live on large plantations. A poor area in comparison to the northeastern sugar areas of the century before or the coffee estates (*fazendas*) of the nineteenth century, the average number of slaves owned by planters in 1775 was 6.4. Planters with more than 10 slaves, thirty-six in all in 1775, owned 700 slaves, or 59 percent of all slaves in the town. Still, the average size of the slave labor force of this privileged group reached only 19.4. Thus, only 135 slaves, or 11 percent of the slave population in 1775, lived on the largest slave plantations, those with more than 50 slaves. On these estates, the average number of slaves owned reached 68, thereby creating a community from which slaves could form families. But many slaves could not take for granted that they would be able to form their families on their masters' estates.

Matrifocal families were a second common family structure for slaves in Parnaíba. Such families appear in the censuses and in the inventories, particularly on smaller estates. Among Agostinha Rodrigues's twenty-two slaves, only two slave families appeared in her inventory of 1757, both matrifocal families: Luzia, a Creole woman of forty, and her two children, and Elena, a Creole woman of twenty, with her daughter, Ursula.[28] In Barbara Pais de Queiroz's inventory, only three slave families are visible among her eighteen slaves, all matrifocal families: Roza with her ten-year-old daughter, Maria with her two children, and Angela with her four children.[29]

The sexual exploitation that slave women experienced and were expected to accept was one of the primary reasons that matrifocal slave families formed. As women who were considered property by their owners and racially inferior by whites, slaves were extremely vulnerable to sexual advances by their masters, their masters' kin, and white men in general. Some slave women were able to become recognized mistresses of free men and obtained recognition and favors from them. Such women sought their own freedom as well as freedom for their children.

Slightly more than half of all slave children baptized by the parish priest in the parish of Santana had "unknown fathers" (*pais incógnitos*). Some fathers, on learning of their paternity, did free their children, but others did not.[30] These children grew up as mulatto slaves in the matrifocal families visible in the inventories and censuses. In these families, the father or fathers of the children remained nebulous figures on the fringes of the family.

The slave woman Guiteria headed a matrifocal slave family in Parnaíba which illustrates many of the characteristics of matrifocal slave families. Guiteria had several children, most by unknown fathers. Despite the informal nature of her relationships to these men, she convinced her children's fathers to free them while young. Over several years, Guiteria freed not only her five children, all born of different fathers, but herself as well. First, she gave her master, Manoel Fernandes Ramos, 89,600 reis for her own freedom and later 128,000 reis for her daughter Anna. At her son Francisco's baptism, his father paid for the baby's freedom. The fathers of Guiteria's children Maria and Manoel also purchased their freedom while they were still young children. Still later, Manoel Fernandes Ramos received 64,000 reis for Guiteria's daughter Rita. Once Manoel registered all freedoms with the town notary, Guiteria and her children became free persons in Parnaíba.[31] Thus, although Guiteria never married, and her children all seem to have had different fathers, she still managed to maintain her family ties and to secure freedom for all.

Matrifocal families probably also appeared when slave women were young and having their first children. Not all of the babies of "unknown fathers" could have been the children of free men. Undoubtedly, many were the children of slave men. In other slave populations, historians have found that slave women often had their first children before they married.[32] Later, they married and formed nuclear families with their mates and their children. This may have been the case in Parnaíba. These matrifocal families would therefore have been of short duration and later would have evolved into nuclear families. By the same token, nuclear families undoubtedly became matrifocal families when slaves were sold or when slave fathers died. Thus, matrifocal families appear to have been a common stage in the family cycle of slave women and their children.

Matrifocal slave families were often favored when planters wrote their wills. Since a mother and her mulatto children composed many of the matrifocal slave families, these were the slaves most likely to be freed by masters. The Reverend Felippe de Santiago Xavier, one of the parish priests of Santana parish, wrote in his will, "I declare that the five young mulattoes Floriano, Caetano, Luciano, João, and Maria, I leave free from all and any slavery with the condition that they serve Antonio Bernardinho or one of his heirs. I declare that Anna, their mother, I leave to the said mulattoes, her children, so that she may finish raising them as she has done until now."[33] By leaving Anna to her freed children, the reverend inadvertently expressed many of his own perceptions and attitudes toward matrifocal slave families composed of slave women and their mulatto children. He clearly viewed the status of the mulatto children as superior to that of their black mother. By granting the mother to the children, the reverend prevented her from being sold and therefore kept the family together. But one wonders why he did not free the mother as well as her children. This omission suggests that the reverend could not free himself from the attitude that blackness and slavery went hand in hand.

The third kind of family life for slaves in Parnaíba was solitary. These slaves lived with other slaves with whom they had no blood or kinship ties. Solitary slaves could be found on all estates, large and small, but a greater proportion of slaves on the smaller estates did live outside of visible families. Being isolated from a family probably was a common part of the life course of slaves—for Africans when they arrived in the town and for Creoles when they had been sold and relocated to a new estate or town. On the larger plantations, these solitary slaves inhabited barracks segregated by sex.[34] On smaller farms, they may have been housed together communally, perhaps sharing a shed. Slaves belonging to masters with only one or two slaves probably resided with the masters' family, much as servants. The characteristics of these solitary slave families are the most difficult to describe. For many slaves, it was a temporary state that endured until they married or had children. Yet during this time, they undoubtedly formed strong friendships and attachments to other slaves. Just as members of "families" depended on their kin for love, support, and compassion, so, too, did these solitary slaves seek such things from each other. Perhaps the existence of so many solitary slaves facilitated the development of a slave community.

Each of these family types influenced the lives of slaves and each had an impact on the formation of slave community. While it is impossible to arrive at any realistic estimate of how many slaves lived in nuclear families versus matrifocal families or solitary families, nuclear families appear to have been the most common. We know that by their thirties, more than 50 percent of the slaves living in the town in 1820 had married (see fig. 9). Therefore, they and their children lived in nuclear families. Yet, according to the baptismal register for the parish of Santana in 1820, 51 percent of the slave babies baptized had unknown fathers. Thus, half of slave children began their lives as the children of single mothers, living in matrifocal families. Some, but we do not know how many,

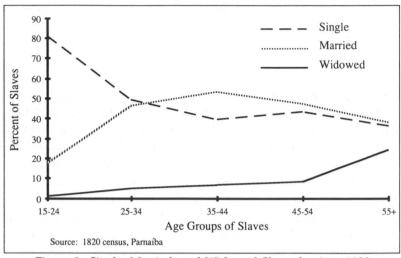

Figure 9. Single, Married, and Widowed Slaves by Age, 1820

later became part of nuclear families when their mothers married. Others lived through their childhood in matrifocal families. We also know that a very high number of slaves never married, some 40 percent. These slaves did not necessarily live outside of families. Rather, many probably were part of extended family and kin networks. But they themselves never married and thus never formally established their own families. A portion of these slaves who never married lived in solitary families, without any visible family relationships to other slaves.

Slave families developed in response to events in their own lives, such as marriages, the births of children, and the deaths of the aged. Yet since similar events in the lives of masters also affected the families of slaves, they lived within two family cycles, one of their own making and another of their masters'. The family cycle intrinsic to slaves began when they married and created nuclear families. These families endured until they became extended with the addition of kin or fragmented due to the death of a spouse. Because the nuclear family was not as dominant in the slave population as in the free population, alternate slave family cycles, such as a matrifocal family cycle, also developed. Such a family cycle began when a young slave woman became a mother. Her simple matrifocal family persisted until she married, at which time it became a nuclear family, or until the family became extended, such as might occur if her daughter became a single mother herself.

Very few slave families passed through an uninterrupted cycle, since they were so tightly bound up in the events taking place in their masters' families. Nuclear and matrifocal families both came under a great deal of stress at times that coincided with critical moments in the life cycles of the masters. These stresses fragmented slave families and contributed to the high number of solitary individuals in the slave population. The event with the greatest impact on slaves was clearly inheritance. Since the laws of inheritance called for an equal division of family property among all the heirs of the deceased, slaves, by law, had to be divided evenly. Just as propertied families feared the effect of probate law, which divided working estates, so did slaves, for inheritance dissolved slave families. While the propertied families often gave slaves the most space to form their own families and community, they could not offer slave families stability over time. Instead, slave families and communities were broken up at inheritance.

The division of Manoel Correa Penteado's estate in 1745 provides many clues to what happened to slaves when their masters died.[35] As one of the largest estates in eighteenth-century Parnaíba, it offered the space for many slave families to form. At Manoel's death, he owned 110 slaves. Twenty-five slave families existed on the estate. The majority of these (13) were nuclear families, followed by married couples (8) and households headed by a single parent (4). When the estate was inventoried and divided, one heir, Fernão Pais de Barros, managed to consolidate almost half of the slaves into his hands. In addition to the slaves he inherited in his own right, Fernão bid on and purchased slaves from the estate when they were auctioned.

What happened to the slave families after the death of their master? The first observation that can be made is that the orphan's judge and the heirs refrained from separating married slaves. All but one of the slave couples remained together after Manoel died. Ignacio and Catharina, marked for the free third, were purchased by Fernão, as were Antonio and Luiza, Silvestre and Felicia, Gracis and Irya, Manoel and Izabel, Antonio and Anna, and Vitoria who was married to a freedman already living in Fernão's house. In addition, Fernão inherited the slave couples Antonio and Mariana, Ignacio the weaver and his wife, Escolastica, Faustina who was also married to a freedman of his household, Antonio and Ignacia, Claudio and Roza, and João the Congo king and his wife, Eugenia.

But the orphan's judge and the heirs did not take the same pains to maintain the family tie between parents and children. Antonio and Luiza's two children ended up with Fernão's brother, Manoel. Two of Silvestre and Felicia's three children went to a purchaser at the auction, as did their one-year-old baby. Fernão inherited three children of the widow Eugenia, while Manoel inherited the widow Eugenia herself. Fernão inherited the two-year-old son of Maria do Rozario, whose matrifocal family was completely divided among six heirs and purchasers at the auction. Other slave families fared better. Vitoria and Faustina, both married to freedmen already living in Fernão's household, went to Fernão with all of their children. Estevão, son of João, the Congo king, remained with his parents. All of Antonio's and Ignacia's children went to Fernão, as did the children of Antonio and Anna, Manoel and Izabel, and Gracis and Irya. Three of Claudio's and Roza's children also went with them to Fernão's estate, but their fifteen-year-old daughter Izabel was sold.

In 1749, only four years after Fernão Pais de Barros consolidated his estate by purchasing or inheriting forty-eight slaves from his father, his wife, Angela Ribeira Leite, died. As required by law, their community property underwent the process of inheritance. From Angela's inventory, it is possible to trace the slave families that Fernão inherited or purchased in 1745. This inventory thus allows the historian to accompany slave families during the most vulnerable time in the family cycle, that which followed the death of their master.[36]

When the slave lists in Angela's and Manoel's inventories are compared, many of the same slave families are visible. Silvestre and Felicia, whom Fernão Pais de Barros had purchased from the auction, appear in Angela's inventory with three children. Claudio and Roza also appear in Angela's inventory with four children. Eugenia, a widow with five children in 1745, is in Angela's inventory as well. Antonio and Luiza likewise show up in Angela's inventory with a daughter. The evaluators described Vitoria, married to a freedman in Fernão's household, and her two children.

Gracis and Irya, whom Fernão purchased in 1745, surface in Angela's inventory of 1749. The couples Ignacio and Catharina, childless in 1745, and Antonio and Mariana, also childless in 1745, similarly emerge in the inventory of 1749.

Some slave families slated to be sold or separated in Manoel's inventory emerge partially intact on Fernão's farm in 1749. Angelo and Polonia, a couple who appeared to have been separated in the division of Manoel Correa Penteado's estate, actually went to Fernão and remained together. By 1749, twenty-two-year-old Polonia had given birth to a son, Leonardo. Antonio and Anna, the only married couple separated by the orphan's judge in 1745, are visible in Angela's inventory in 1749. But the couple was not living together. Anna belonged to Angela and Fernão and her husband, Antonio, to Fernão's brother, Manoel. In 1749, they had three children living with Anna.

Thus, many of the same families perceptible in both inventories lead one to suggest that slave families weathered the storm of death and inheritance. But on closer inspection, major changes did take place in the family lives of these slaves. The widow Eugenia, who had five children in 1745, had only two young children with her in 1749. Only one of her children appears in both inventories. Thus, in the four-year period between the inventories, she had lost four of her children. Similarly, the three children who appear with Silvestre and Felicia are not the same children listed with their parents in 1745. According to Manoel's inventory, all of their children had been sold away from the couple in 1745. One of those children, Benedito, however, had been somehow acquired by Fernão, for he appears with his parents in 1749. In the interval, Felicia had given birth to Ilario and Gertrudes. But Polonia, seven years old in 1745, and Lourenço, one year old in 1745, do not appear. Although this family remained "nuclear," two children had been sold from their parents after Manoel's death. The story is the same for virtually all of the slave families who appear in both inventories. Nearly all had lost some children. These slave children had been inherited by heirs, sold at auction, or possibly had died.

After Angela's death, the slaves were not divided again; rather, they remained with Fernão, who as Angela's widower and guardian of their children, continued to manage the estate. The slave families would not be divided again until Fernão provided dowries for his daughters or until he himself died. But the division of slaves after the death of Manoel and the ability to see many of the slave families in the inventory of Angela suggest some very important observations about slave family life.

Despite the prevailing interpretations of the low birthrates of female slaves in Brazil, the slave women on these estates certainly bore children. Slave families did not appear any larger because children were separated from their parents at inheritance. Most of the children described in Angela's inventories had been born since Manoel's death. Rarely did all of a slave woman's children appear with her in a property inventory. Thus, while nuclear families predominate in both Manoel's and Angela's inventory, this does not mean that slave families were stable. Rather, the structure of family life remained the same, but the older children of the family disappeared. Because their families were tied to events in the families of their masters, particularly the mortality of the masters, slave families did not often become large, complex, or extended.

Yet, in spite of the impact of inheritance on the slaves of Manoel Correa Penteado, many slave families did remain at least partially intact. Half of the slave families living on Angela's and Fernão's estate were families that appeared in Manoel's inventory. These eleven families were almost half of the slave families extant on Manoel's estate in 1745.

Because of the nature of Portuguese inheritance law, slave families were especially vulnerable when the second spouse died. The law decreed that property would be evaluated and divided after the death of each partner, but, in fact, the true division came when the surviving spouse died. Angela's inventory sheds a great deal of light on the slaves living on her and Fernão's estate, but those slaves would not be divided until Fernão himself died. Slave families could thus expect a relatively stable environment in which to form their families which would endure until both their master and their mistress died. When that time came, they would be divided among the heirs of the next generation, and their families would be separated.

The impact of the family events of the propertied on the slaves is but one example of the tremendous influence the families of planters had on the community of Santana de Parnaíba. Their influence, both overt and implicit, cast a long shadow on the lives of many in the community. In his research on slave families on the Cohoon estate in Virginia, historian Herbert Gutman illustrates similar relationships between slave families and the life cycles of their masters. When Virginia planter John Cohoon was a young man, he put together his slave labor force, destroying many extant slave families in the process. In his adulthood, however, as his estate prospered, his slaves formed new families. Yet when he died, slave families broke apart again as the estate was inherited or sold. Thus, according to Gutman's model (simplified in fig. 10), slave families could only look forward to a period of stability roughly commensurate with the life span of one master.[37]

Cohoon owned some forty-seven slaves at his death, a plantation comparable to the larger estates in Parnaíba, estates where slaves were able to marry other slaves on the same farm, form nuclear and even extended families, and establish a slave community. The fact that Cohoon's slaves were only able to maintain stable family lives during the lifetime of their master suggests how limited slave family stability could be, even for the stablest of slave family types.

Inheritance also affected matrifocal slave families tremendously. Like nuclear slave families, matrifocal families could remain together for long periods of time and knit themselves into the broader slave community. But at inheritance, the bonds between mothers and children were overpowered by the judge's mandate to divide property equally among all the heirs. Moreover, since the women who headed matrifocal families were not married, the one relationship that was customarily respected, marriage, did not exist. As a result, matrifocal families rarely survived inheritance intact. Like nuclear families, the form of a matrifocal family might endure, but the members of that family rarely did.

The slave woman Mariana's family illustrates how matrifocal families came under stress when masters died and inheritance began. We know about her family because in 1816 she petitioned the governor of São Paulo, complaining that she and her children had been wrongfully denied their freedom by her late master's widow.[38] While Mariana's own words have been lost, it is clear from what others said about her case that she believed that her master had freed her and her children in recognition of her good services to him. At his death, she was to receive her freedom as

	Planter's Age		
	Young Adult	*Middle Age*	*Old Age/Death*
Slave family	destroyed	reconstructed	dispersed
Family stability	low	high	low

Source: Gutman, *The Black Family*, 138.

Figure 10. Gutman's Model of the Slave Family Cycle

well as a piece of land to live on with her children. Mariana's freedom and the grant of land were stated in a written document that her master stored among his papers in a strongbox in the house. After her master died, however, the charter of freedom never appeared, and Mariana not only remained a slave but was sold away from her children. Believing herself wronged, she initiated her appeal to the governor.

In the investigation that ensued, a question put to various witnesses was if Mariana's master had been the father of her children; if he "had a family" with her. His widow claimed that her late husband was not the father of Mariana's children, for if he were, he would have freed them. Instead, he freed only one of Mariana's children, Joze, not, she said because Joze was his son but because he was the son of his brother. Other witnesses, however, declared it to be common knowledge that Mariana's master was in fact the father of her children. If Mariana's children were those of her master, then they were legally "natural" children and entitled to inherit his property, as his "necessary heirs" (*herdeiros forçados*).

The executor of Mariana's master's estate defended his decision to sell Mariana. He stated that in the will, no mention had been made of freedom for Mariana or for any of her children except Joze, who was freed because he was the master's nephew, and Gertrudes, a daughter freed at baptism. Since no mention had been made of other slave freedoms, the executor felt that he had done right to sell Mariana and to place her children, both slave and free, to serve in the household of her master's widow.

By searching for Mariana's master in previous census returns, some interesting facts come into focus which suggest that he was the father of her children and she his mistress. In the census of 1798, eighteen years before Mariana brought her petition to the governor general, her master's household appeared. The census taker recorded it thus:

Amaro Pereira, single, 45 years old
  slaves: Mariana, black, single, 33 years old
          Benta, mulatta, 6 years old
          Ursula, mulatta, 3 years old
          Maria, mulatta, 2 years old

Was Amaro or his brother the father of these children, plus the children whom we know were later freed—Joze and Gertrudes? The father of Mariana's children may well have been a white man in order for the census taker to list the color of the children as "mulatto" and that of Mariana as "black." Perhaps Mariana did live as Amaro's mistress and benefited from his patronage while he was alive. She believed herself to be in possession of a letter of freedom and a piece of land—a privileged position for a slave woman. Late in life, however, Amaro decided to marry. According to his brother, he was sick when he married and died soon after. Then his legal wife, as co-owner of the community property, was entitled to half of the property, the bulk of which consisted of his slaves: Mariana and her children. Mariana's freedom papers mysteriously disappeared and she was sold. Why? One witness testified that Amaro had told him that he intended to revoke Mariana's freedom because she had disobeyed him. Mariana thought her mistress had maliciously destroyed the papers. If Mariana's children were Amaro's natural children, they would inherit all of Amaro's property, while his wife would receive nothing. Whatever happened, Mariana's family disintegrated after her master died. She took what steps she could to hold it together. Unfortunately, we do not know the outcome of her petition. Nonetheless, her story suggests the hardships faced by matrifocal families when changes took place in the status of their masters' families, as well as the difficulty slave mothers had in trying to keep their families together during times of death and inheritance in their masters' families.

The less formalized bonds that solitary slaves created with each other were also deeply affected by events such as inheritance. Since the solitary slaves tended to be younger and male, they commanded the highest prices and thus stood the most at risk to be sold at inheritance to cover estate debts. As they moved on to a new estate, they would have to begin again to form ties to new slaves and free blacks. Their emotional lives, therefore, were probably the least stable and the least predictable. Not surprisingly, these slaves were the most likely to run away or to commit crimes. The image of the slave Manoel, whom the slave catcher apprehended in 1790 and sent to the town jail, conveys the desperate life of some of these slaves. The jailer described Manoel:

> [He is] twenty years old. I found him in the jail with a metal collar around his neck, manacles on his hands, and a shackle known as "round the world" on his feet. This prisoner is of ordinary height, with a thick neck, a round face, dark eyes, a flat nose, disheveled hair, and a low forehead. He was wrapped in an old hammock without any other clothes at all.[39]

Given the pernicious effect of inheritance on slave families, one might expect that on estates not affected by inheritance, slaves could have established stable and enduring families. In Brazil, only two kinds of estates could provide slaves with such an environment: morgados (entailed estates) and religious estates. Morgados rarely appeared in Brazil. Religious estates thus would be virtually the only place where slave families could expect to live without fear of the division of their families. On one such estate, one of the largest farms in Parnaíba in the eighteenth century, the Araçariguama fazenda, slaves should have been able to establish long-lasting families and enduring kinship ties, but they were unable to do so. The estate had belonged to the Jesuits, who inherited it from a very rich Indian holder and merchant, Guilherme Pompeo de Almeida, in 1713. Because a religious order owned it, the estate never underwent the process of division caused by inheritance and thus slaves would have been rarely sold. But because of external political factors, even this estate proved to be a place where slave families and networks could not last over time.

Organized to produce corn, beans, wheat, peanuts, cotton, manioc, honey, wine, cane brandy, and rice to support the Jesuit school in the city of São Paulo, the fazenda remained in Jesuit hands only until 1759. Then, after Portugal's prime minister, the Marquis de Pombal, expelled the Jesuits from all of Brazil, the estate became part of the extensive Jesuit holdings confiscated by the crown. At that time, 102 African slaves and 101 Indian administrados lived and worked on it. It is likely that these slaves and Indians lived in nuclear families and had formed extensive kinship networks. After the expulsion of the Jesuits, the estate began to deteriorate, and this dramatically affected the lives of the slaves. The crown rented the fazenda to wealthy individuals in Parnaíba, who milked it for their own profit. The number of slaves on the estate dropped alarmingly as slaves died or ran away. Twenty slaves fled in 1779 alone. In 1801, the town council of Parnaíba wrote that during the time that Policarpo Joaquim de Oliveira rented the estate, he abused it to such an extent that it was worth only one-third of what it had been assessed at in 1760 when the Jesuits left. In 1815, an inventory of the fazenda revealed its sorry state. It consisted of a chapel, a large house in ruins, twenty slave quarters in poor condition, and only thirty-five slaves, three of whom had run away. Clearly, the conditions on the Araçariguama estate had disintegrated to such an extent that slaves preferred to run away and break family ties rather than to remain. Thus, on this large estate where one would have expected stable slave families to form, slave families could not endure over time. Once again circumstances beyond the reach of slaves determined the character of their family lives.[40]

Given that slaves had so little control over their family lives, how is it possible to speak of slave strategies for survival? Many historians have concluded that slave family life was so unstable and so unpredictable that family life was virtually nonexistent.[41] Yet in eighteenth-century Parnaíba, it is clear that while slaves had less control over their family lives than other social groups, they did experience long periods of relative stability. These were the times when nuclear families formed and grew or when single mothers reared their children. The times of stress that fractured family life occurred at very specific times: when masters ran into financial difficulties and sold slaves and when the community property owned by husband and wife came to an end with the death of the last living spouse. During other times, slaves could and did shape their families and develop their own strategies to survive in their very constrained world.

To understand how slaves developed strategies to survive, it is first necessary to distinguish between the two very different worlds in which slaves lived: the world of their masters, which demanded that they behave in one way, and the world of other slaves, which allowed them to behave quite differently. Both worlds were a fundamental part of slave life, and no slave, except the·runaway, lived isolated from either one. Slave family life thus had two faces: one, the relationships that developed between the slaves themselves, and the other, the relationships between slaves and their masters' families.[42]

Since so many aspects of the lives of their masters affected slaves, slave families could not be and never were independent from their masters. But masters never completely dominated their slaves. This duality of slave life affected how slaves pursued strategies to ameliorate their lot and how they socialized their children. Despite the violence inherent in slavery—violence expressed through whippings, beatings, and manaclings—slaves saw their masters as a source of favors that might lead to freedom, to permission to marry, or to the right to socialize with other slaves on other farms. Yet, aware of the chasm that separated them from their masters, they bonded to other slaves in the community for mutual support and assistance. Slaves saw themselves in two worlds, and they developed strategies to survive in each.

A shared dream among slaves was the possibility of achieving freedom. How slaves accomplished this reflects how well they manipulated their relationships to their masters. Freedom was obtained through a variety of means, all aimed at achieving social mobility for themselves and their children. Slaves in Brazil found it easier to receive their freedom or to purchase it than those in other slave societies such as the United States. Unlike the United States, where relatively few slaves bought their freedom and where in some regions laws restricted masters from freeing their slaves even if they wished to do so, Brazilian slavery was more flexible.[43] Masters could free their slaves if they so desired, and slaves could buy their freedom. This gave slaves an important stake in the community, because they could dream that one day they would become free black members of it. It also gave them an incentive to maintain good relationships with their masters.

Most of the slaves who obtained their freedom received it from their masters, as a favor, usually in recognition of "good service" and "obedience." Luzia Leme de Barros freed her slave Lourença in 1781 because "she had served her so well and because of the

love she has for her slave."[44] João Ribeiro de Magalhaes freed all
of his slaves before he died—Ignacio, Felisberto, Manoela, Ignacio,
and all the children of João—"because of the good services that he
had received." He stipulated that they were to be "free as if they
had been born free."[45] On her deathbed, Thomazia de Almeida
told Rita Antonia da Silva Serra that it was her last wish to free
her young mulatta slave, Catharina. She asked Rita to take care of
Catharina, to raise her and educate her until she married. When
she married, she was to receive her freedom.[46] Such examples indicate that masters did have emotional ties to their slaves and desired
to help them in their wills. The fact that masters did free slaves
signaled to slaves that "obedience" and "good service" might have
their rewards.

The majority of masters who freed their slaves made that freedom contingent on continued good service. They saw the freeing
of slaves not purely as a humanitarian gesture but as a pragmatic
one as well. Antonia, freed by her mistress for "good service" and
"rectitude," still had to continue to serve her mistress until her mistress died.[47] Mariazinha received her freedom in a clause of Maria
de Abreu's will, with the stipulation that she serve Francisca Xavier
until the latter married.[48] The Reverend Felippe de Santiago Xavier
freed his slave, Manoel, in 1796 but gave him the responsibility of
serving him while he still lived, and after he died, of taking care
of the altar of Our Lady of Sorrows in the church. To help him
fulfill this mission, the reverend gave him half of the yard behind
his house to construct his own house.[49]

Slaves who received their freedom as gifts from their masters
benefited from their humanity, goodheartedness, and paternalism.
Not surprisingly, these slaves tended to be older slaves, women,
and young children; the slaves to whom masters had become attached either through having received a lifetime of faithful service,
or because of the innocence and ingenuousness of young slaves,
or because they knew mulatto slaves to be their kin.[50] It was harder
for men and women of prime working age to receive their freedom
as outright gifts from masters. Too valuable to free, such slaves
usually remained in the possession of their masters. Yet some
could gain their freedom by purchasing it themselves. The slave
woman Benta gave her mistress 100,000 reis for her freedom, a sum
that indicated she was still in her prime working years.[51] João and

Liberata, part of an estate inventoried in 1793, paid their assessed value in the inventory to their new master in return for their freedom.[52] Other slaves, such as Francisco, who came up with 153,600 reis for his freedom in 1801, or Bento, who raised 89,600 reis for his freedom in 1798, also succeeded in liberating themselves from slavery.[53]

To achieve freedom, slaves pursued different strategies. Some appealed to the benevolence of their masters; others attempted to raise the sums of money required. Still, most slaves remained slaves until they died. While for many slaves, to be free did not radically alter the conditions under which they worked, it did make a tremendous difference to them. Freed slaves could "live where they pleased," were "free from all suggestion of captivity," and were "free as if they had been born so."[54] This meant that freed slaves could live with their families and were no longer subject to the dehumanizing treatment slaves normally received. Perhaps the best indication of how much slaves wanted their freedom is conveyed in the words of a slave, Francisco, who petitioned the governor of São Paulo in 1822 asking for his intervention so that he could buy his freedom. Francisco had been evaluated in the property inventory of his master at 25,600 reis. He wished to pay his mistress this sum, but she refused. His petition stated that,

> because of habitual and incurable illness . . . slavery weighs heavily on him, and so that he can pass the remainder of his days more commodiously, he has sought all means possible to get his mistress to agree to receive his assessed value of 25,600 reis for his freedom.[55]

From other documents, we know that Francisco was sixty-five years old, that he had served his masters for over thirty years, that he was married to a free black woman, and that he wanted his freedom to "take care of his salvation" and live out the remainder of his days in peace.[56] Not only had he hired a scribe to write his petition for him but he may even have retained a lawyer as well, for his petition to the officials of São Paulo concluded with a striking appeal:

> He asks your excellencies, as fathers of mercy, to see fit to make the said mistress understand that the law of ownership that she has over the supplicant cannot contradict the natural law of equity and much less Christian charity [which speak] in favor of his liberty and, as a result, concede to the supplicant that which he asks her for, his just evaluation in the property inventory.[57]

That a sixty-five-year-old slave should go to such lengths to obtain his freedom before he died is a reflection of how much slaves desired their freedom, even if only for their few final years.

Slaves who had been promised freedom by their masters often had to defend their right to freedom in the face of potential heirs who desired to keep them as slaves. When Antonio Correa de Lemos Leite died in 1782, his heirs discovered that he had freed three slaves before his death. Two of Antonio's sons-in-law, upset that he had thereby reduced the inheritances their wives would receive, petitioned the probate judge to disallow this stipulation. They argued that since Antonio had died intestate, Antonio had no free third to distribute as he wished. Therefore, the slaves should be part of the property that went automatically to Antonio's heirs.[58]

Not too many years later, another slave of African descent named Maximiano Antonio spent the money to initiate a petition to the governor of São Paulo. In his petition, he stated that he had been born free because his mother, a slave, had been granted her freedom by her master, Manoel Rodrigues Fam. However, after his death, Manoel's heirs burned the freedom papers and subjected him to slavery. Since he knew himself to be a poor man, Maximiano asked that a judge in Parnaíba be instructed to pursue for him his claim for freedom. When directed to investigate the matter, the local judge interviewed the captain major of Parnaíba, the orphan's judge, and two militia officers, all of whom stated that they had always known Maximiano as a slave. Moreover, on reading the will, the judge reported to the governor that no mention had been made of a slave freedom for Maximiano's mother; rather, she and her children all appeared in the will as slaves.[59]

These two cases reflect the situation of slaves who had been promised their freedom by their masters but who had their freedom challenged by the masters' heirs. Such cases demonstrate how tied slaves were not only to their masters but to their masters' families. Because slaves were valuable property, heirs fought against the slave freedoms conceded by their parents. In such situations, slaves could only keep their freedom if they had documented proof. In the two cases cited above, the slaves of Antonio Correa de Lemos Leite did retain their freedom, but it is likely that Maximiano did not.

The duality of slave family life can also be seen at key times in the life cycle. At times of marriage, slaves asked other slaves as well as their masters to serve as witnesses.[60] Similarly, when slaves baptized their children, they selected godparents for their children from among other slaves, free blacks and whites among the peasantry, and even planters. The strategy followed by slaves appeared to be either to connect their children horizontally to other slaves or to link them vertically to members of the planter class. Each strategy made sense: by giving their child a free godfather, possibly a slave owner, they hoped to provide their children with access to more powerful individuals in the community. By choosing slave godfathers for their children, they tied them to the slave community.

As Stephen Gudeman and Stuart Schwartz have shown, in eighteenth-century Bahia, "in no instances did masters serve as godparents for their own slaves."[61] In Parnaíba as well, no master appeared as the godparent of his or her slave except once. In that instance, a slave baby about to die was baptized by his own master, who performed the role of godfather as well as that of priest.[62] Gudeman and Schwartz attribute the absence of masters among the godparents of slaves to the conflict between the church and slavery: how could a master perform as the spiritual adviser to his slaves when at the same time he owned them as property? Hence, they argue, the conflict between baptism and slavery was resolved by skirting the issue, by not having masters serve as the godparents of their slave children.[63] While masters did not serve as godparents in Parnaíba, occasionally their children did sponsor the slave children who belonged to their parents. Six times in the 115 baptisms of slave children did the unmarried children of masters become the godparents for slaves that they might someday inherit.[64]

Who were the godparents, then? Analysis of the baptism records from the parish of Santana reveals that 32 percent of the godfathers and 34 percent of the godmothers of babies born to slaves were themselves slaves.[65] These slave godparents came from the same parish as the baby, most of them were unmarried, and most, therefore, were young. Slaves tended to sponsor the children of married slaves, rather than the children of single mothers. They sponsored more boys than girls. The majority of the godparents of slave babies, however, were free persons living predominantly in the parish of Santana. Most of the free godparents, like the slaves, were single persons. Of these, thirty-six godfathers and nineteen godmothers were planters, usually poor planters who owned less than ten slaves. In each case, they tended to be the young unmarried children of planter families in the parish. Interestingly enough, these godparents were more likely than slaves to sponsor the children of single mothers (see table 21).

Since single mothers sought godfathers from the free population—planters and peasants alike—this may mean that the "godfathers" of the children were actually the children's natural fathers. Or it may reflect the fact that matrifocal families tended to pursue vertical strategies that tied them to the more powerful, rather than the horizontal strategies that linked them to other slaves. Nuclear slave families, however, selected godparents from among slaves. Perhaps nuclear families formed the basis of the slave community and wanted their children to have spiritual and emotional guidance from other slaves. Whichever option parents chose, they were consistent, for children rarely had godparents of very different social status; rather, if a child had a slave godfather, his godmother was also a slave; if her godfather was a free person, so, too, was her godmother.

Because slaves pursued both horizontal and vertical strategies, they managed to secure freedom in increasing numbers in each successive generation. As a result, the free black community in Parnaíba grew. By 1820, 37 percent of the free households in the town were headed by men and women considered by the census taker as pardo (brown) or preto (black). While most of those classified as pardo would have been of Indian or mameluco descent, many were undoubtedly mulattoes. For example, 28 percent of the Creole slaves in the same census had their color described as pardo; these were mulatto slaves. Therefore, it is logical to assume that a portion of the pardo free households were in fact those of free mulattoes. The growth of this free black community created an important buffer between masters and slaves. It allowed slaves to strive for their freedom, and it allowed masters to see blacks in roles other than that of slave. It meant that the strategies of slaves in Parnaíba had an impact on the formation of the social structure of the community.

While slaves pursued strategies to ameliorate their lives, their

Table 21. Godfathers of Slave Children

| Children | Godfathers | | | |
| | Free | | Slave | |
	N	%	N	%
Legitimate	32	42	23	66
Unknown fathers	44	58	12	34
Total	76	100	35	100

Source: Baptisms of Slaves, 1770, 1798, 1820, Parish of Santana.
Chi-square = 5.34; DF = 1; probability = 0.021.

powerlessness in the community meant that such strategies did not and could not solve the myriad problems they faced. Slaves could not prevent their masters from working them to death, from punishing them for minor offenses, or from selling family members. Their strategies, therefore, could play only a limited role in bettering their lives.

Those frustrations that slaves experienced but could not change were expressed in the violence that existed in the slave community. While the slave community did provide its members with an important source of support and resources, violence was also a part of that community. The suppressed anger that slaves felt toward their masters rarely came out in actions against masters but rather in violent acts committed against other slaves, free blacks, or members of the peasantry.

According to the records kept by the jailers of Parnaíba, 20 percent of those who went to jail from 1720 to 1820 were slaves. The crimes that these slaves committed ranged from murder to witchcraft (see table 22). While 53 percent of the slaves sentenced to jail had attacked or murdered someone, their victims were rarely their actual masters. Only three slaves rose up face-to-face against their masters: Joze, who beat up his master; Ignacio, who severely wounded his master, killed his mistress, and killed their daughter; and Francisco, who, like Joze, attacked his master.[66] The majority of the victims attacked by slaves were peasants (see table 23).

Why would slaves attack peasants more than other slaves or planters? The answer to this question lies partially in the fact that peasants constituted the majority of the population of Parnaíba.

Table 22. Crimes for Which Slaves Went to Jail

	N	%
Assault	26	28
Homicide	23	25
Escaping jail	15	16
Rioting	13	14
Unknown/other	16	18
Total	93	101

Source: Jailer's Ledger, 1720–1820, Parnaíba.

Table 23. Victims of Slave Violent Crimes

Victims	Attacks and Homicides	
	N	%
Peasants	21	43
Slaves	11	22
Planters	10	20
Status unknown	7	14
Total	49	99

Source: Jailer's Ledger, 1720–1820, Parnaíba.

But, in addition to this, hostility flared between these two groups. Peasants looked down on slaves, whom they saw as their social inferiors. Yet the work of peasants paralleled that of slaves in many respects. To separate themselves from slaves, some peasants insulted, taunted, and needled slaves to reinforce their own nagging perception of social inferiority. For example, on a workday on the farm of Anastacio Pereira de Camargo in 1818, a fight broke out between a slave and a peasant. The slave, Francisco, apparently loaned or hired out for the day by his master, worked alongside other peasants from the neighborhood, as well as Anastacio's own slaves. During the day, Rodrigo, a young white peasant farmer, harassed Francisco, twenty years his senior. When Rodrigo called him "trash" (*cisco*), Francisco retorted, "Don't call me that," to which Rodrigo replied that it did no harm to call him what he was. Angered, Francisco insulted Rodrigo by calling him a "son of a whore," to which Rodrigo responded by attacking the middle-aged slave and knocking him to the ground. In a loud voice, Rodrigo declared that if Francisco complained to his master, he (Rodrigo) would go after him with a gun.

After the workday, Francisco's master filed a complaint with Parnaíba's justice of the peace. Three witnesses, all peasants, recounted what happened. The judge ruled against Rodrigo and as punishment, sent him to jail.[67] This episode suggests that much suppressed anger existed between slaves and peasants. Indeed, according to the jailer's ledger, much of the violence against slaves was caused by peasants.

Occasionally, slaves erupted in rebellion, rioting on nearby estates and farms. These riots (*assuadas*) involved groups of slaves and free persons. Thirteen slaves and many more peasants went to jail for participating in three riots that occurred in 1765. Riots occurred on the farms of Miguel Garcia de Carvalho, Joze da Costa Ribeiro, and Sebastião Teixeira in 1765. None was the estate of a large planter; Joze da Costa Ribeiro had only two slaves; Sebastião Teixeira had no slaves. Apparently the riots turned violent, for the sources refer to slaves who beat or knifed others in the rioting. Two other riots occurred earlier in the century, one on the property of Francisco Gonçalves de Oliveira in 1731 and another on that of Paulo Dias da Silva in 1733.[68]

Slaves also went to jail as punishment for minor offenses that occurred on their farms or because they had been apprehended by the bush captain, the town's paid slave-catcher, for being runaways. Once in jail, slaves worked hard to escape. The jailers recorded numerous examples of slaves who burned down parts of the jail, broke through the thick adobe walls, or removed tiles from the roof to escape. The descriptions of how Anna "broke through the roof," or how Benedito escaped from the "dungeon of the jail where he had been locked in stocks and chains," or how Custodia broke out of the jail by "burning the wooden bars in the windows"[69] suggest the variety of ways that slaves attempted to escape from bondage. In a symbolic sense, the jail can be seen as representing slavery. Slaves who escaped from the dungeon sought freedom not just from the jail but from slavery itself.

Slaves expressed their unhappiness by running away and attempting to hide themselves or to pass themselves off as free blacks. Most runaways, however, did not remain at large for very

long. Slaves sometimes ran away to other towns where they had
kin. Leonor and Maria, for example, both twenty years old, ran
away from the Santa Anna estate outside of the city of São Paulo
to Araçariguama in 1775. There Policarpo Joaquim de Oliveira took
possession of and reported them.[70] Other slaves ran into the wilderness, where they attempted to survive by living off the land.
Manoel, a slave who ran away from his mistress in the neighboring
town of Itú, came to Parnaíba, where he built himself a shack and
a garden somewhere on the lands of Maria Franca da Cunha. But
Manoel was unable to survive, for he was found dead of hunger
or illness in 1820.[71]

Small runaway slave communities (quilombos) existed outside
of virtually every major settlement in colonial Brazil. In 1775, the
governor of São Paulo gave permission for "anyone to attack the
maroon community forming near Parnaíba."[72] Eleven years later,
Anna Maria Xavier Pinto da Silva ordered twelve of her own slaves
to clear the land around a maroon community, perhaps even the
same one, located between Parnaíba and the next town, Jundiaí.
After three months of work, her slaves reached the deserted community, but the slaves had already fled. Having displaced the
slaves, Anna Maria petitioned for possession of the lands as her
reward.[73] Although usually for only a short time, runaway slaves
survived as long as they remained out of sight and could grow
enough food to support themselves.

While family life in the slave community provided slaves with
an important source of stability and support, it did not alleviate the
hard life they faced. The harshness of that life emerges in document after document from Parnaíba. The assessors of Agostinha
Rodrigues's slaves described her Mina slave André as "broken"
(*quebrado*) in 1757.[74] Baltazar Rodrigues Fam's slave Jacinto "had
an arm eaten by the sugar mill."[75] João Paulo Correa, overseer of
Colonel Policarpo Joaquim de Oliveira, killed one of Policarpo's
slaves in 1802. Joze Fernandes Mota killed two of his own slaves
in 1727. Manoel Antonio, a soldier from the city of São Paulo, killed
a slave named Domingos when he was the overseer of the bishop's
estate in 1815. Francisco Ignacio, a transient, killed Manoel, a
slave, in 1763. Three other men went to jail in Parnaíba for murder-
ing slaves and five went to jail for attacking slaves in the eighteenth
century. Slaves, as valuable property, might be stolen. Five men

went to jail for stealing slaves. Thus, slaves were the victims of considerable violence in eighteenth-century Parnaíba.[76]

Nonetheless, in the dangerous, violent, and harsh world in which slaves lived, by the early nineteenth century, the slaves of Parnaíba had successfully established a stable community in the town. Slaves married, baptized their babies, and buried their dead in the parish churches. They had formed their own religious confraternities dedicated to Our Lady of the Rosary, Our Lady of Assumption and Good Death, and St. Benedict in which they participated along with free blacks. They knew how to petition higher officials and how to seek their own freedom. Thus, despite the odds against them and the myriad uncertainties of their lives, the slaves of Santana de Parnaíba did succeed in using their families as a means to counter the painful effects of slavery and to ameliorate their daily lives.

Conclusion

Family and Frontier at Independence

When Napoleon's armies crossed the border between Spain and Portugal in 1807, the Portuguese king, Dom João VI, the royal family, and his court feverishly packed their belongings and prepared to abandon Lisbon. As Napoleon's armies camped on the outskirts of the city, the entire court sailed out of Lisbon under the escort of the powerful British navy. After the difficult Atlantic crossing, described by a modern historian as "a nightmare . . . the royal party suffered from overcrowding, lack of food and water, lice (the ladies had to cut off their hair) and disease,"[1] they disembarked in Rio de Janeiro. Over the next few months, João transformed Rio into the capital of the Portuguese empire. This unusual and symbolic reversal marked the beginning of Brazil's transformation from colony to nation.

Dom João's arrival in Rio de Janeiro heralded the end of Brazil's "colonial period." Dom João opened Brazil's ports to trade with all friendly nations. Ships loaded with Brazilian sugar no longer had to stop at Portugal to pay duties before sending their cargoes on to other ports in Europe. British merchants could dispatch their goods directly to Brazil and bypass Portugal entirely. João established the Council of State, the Supreme High Court, the Court of Appeal, the Royal Treasury, the Council of the Royal Exchequer, and other important institutions in Rio de Janeiro. He created Brazil's first bank. When, in 1815, Brazil became a kingdom, equal with Portugal, Brazil not only ceased to be a colony but appeared to have replaced Portugal.[2]

Apparently content in Brazil, Dom João only returned to Portugal in 1821, when the Constituent Assembly (*Cortes*), resurgent in Lisbon after Napoleon's defeat at Waterloo, threatened to take drastic measures if he did not return. The members of the Cortes had become indignant that João seemed oblivious to Portugal's degeneration since 1808 to a colony of Brazil and a protectorate of England. Dom João left behind his son, Pedro, as regent of Brazil. Back in Portugal, Dom João found the Cortes, which did include representatives from Brazil, determined to return Brazil to its old colonial status. When the Cortes ordered Pedro back to Portugal in 1822, he refused to go. Instead, a few months later, on the plains outside of the city of São Paulo, Pedro declared Brazil's independence from Portugal and became Brazil's first emperor, Pedro I.[3]

These momentous events scarcely reverberate in the sources from which this history of Santana de Parnaíba has been compiled. For the social historian, the great events of history, such as the arrival of Dom João in Rio or Dom Pedro's declaration of independence, do not always immediately change the lives of ordinary people. In Parnaíba, the outward behavior of peasants and slaves changed little. Peasant families continued to burn their fields, to plant corn, beans, and cotton; while in the town center, artisans still made cloth, hats, and shoes and worked at odd jobs. Slaves labored in the fields, in the mills, and in the houses of their masters irrespective of the portending political changes in Brazil's status. Even families of planters, the class most likely to be informed of the events transpiring in Rio de Janeiro and São Paulo, continued their lives virtually unaffected by these larger forces.

The sources that reveal so clearly the family lives of ordinary people in Parnaíba do not disclose what these people thought as independence approached and ensued. The form of documents such as wills, land sales, slave freedoms, property inventories, censuses, and the town council minutes suggest that business remained virtually unchanged. Notaries still began their contracts with the same preambles; judges continued to inventory and divide estates according to the same laws. The captain majors carried on compiling the annual censuses of their towns; the priests proceeded without interruption to register the births, deaths, and marriages in the parishes. Even the officials remained the same. The officers of the local and provincial militia did not change, nor did the governor of the state of São Paulo. The latter, João C. A. de Oeynhausen, simply became the provincial president of São Paulo after 1822.[4]

Although independence would bring changes to Brazil and to the people of Santana de Parnaíba, in 1822, the forces of continuity far outweighed those of change. At the time of independence, the manuscript censuses of the town portray the traits of a class structure that had evolved over the course of two hundred fifty years. The resources from the wilderness—land, Indians, and precious minerals—had made a small planter class powerful and wealthy. The planters learned in the seventeenth century to live off of large estates, farmed by slaves, and to maintain their wealth by continuing to exploit the wilderness. In the eighteenth century, their descendants formed the powerful class of planters that dominated the resources of the town and its local government. This planter class accounted for 15 percent of the total population of the town in 1820.

Slavery constituted a ubiquitous and unquestioned way of life from the first days of settlement in Santana de Parnaíba. In the seventeenth century, Indians from the interior served Portuguese and mameluco masters as servants and de facto slaves. When the Indian population declined because of disease, planters, gold miners, and merchants turned to the slave trade from Africa. By the early decades of the eighteenth century, African slaves supplied the labor on the agricultural estates of planters in Parnaíba and on their mining claims in the interior. Living in bondage with few rights, slaves performed the backbreaking labor that sustained the wealth of the planter class. Thus, slavery had formed a second class of persons in colonial Santana de Parnaíba. In 1820, slaves constituted 27 percent of the population of the town.

In the seventeenth century in Santana de Parnaíba, the first evidence surfaces of a third social class, the peasantry. Then occupying an intermediate world between planters and slaves, the peasants often lived as dependents of planter families. In the eighteenth century, the peasantry became a separate class, which lived from subsistence farming. Descended from the planters, free Indians, and freed slaves, peasants lacked political influence, power, and secure legal title to land. As the commercialization of agriculture increased in the late eighteenth century, peasant farmers became increasingly vulnerable. Planters forced peasants to sell their lands, or evicted them by force, to expand their own estates. Lacking a firm stake in the town, many peasants left the community altogether, moving to the towns and city of São Paulo or to the far western frontier. Two years before independence, the peasantry accounted for the majority of the inhabitants of Santana de Parnaíba, 59 percent.

The class structure that emerged in Santana de Parnaíba during the seventeenth and eighteenth centuries and that is visible in 1822 at independence can be linked to the larger forces characteristic of Portuguese colonialism, forces that encouraged the development of cash-crop economies based on crops such as sugar. But the class structure that evolved in Parnaíba also owed much to the strategies pursued by families. The family strategies that each social class used to further its interests can be seen in the implicit and unacknowledged patterns of family life.

The strategies of planter families contributed most directly to the creation of an inegalitarian class structure. Families of planters were large and hierarchical. They maintained their property and social position over generations by colonizing new frontiers and by dividing their property in Parnaíba unequally among their children. Planter families carefully planned for marriage, inheritance, and migration. They favored one heir, usually a daughter, who received a large dowry at marriage, and as a result, her husband became the representative of the family in Parnaíba in the next generation. Many sons typically moved on to the frontier where they too married into established families. Some daughters moved west too, but others remained in Parnaíba in "reduced circumstances." Thus, planter families preserved their social position over time but only by "streaming" many of their descendants into a subgroup of the planter class, the poor planters. Owners of only a few slaves, the poor planters rarely commanded much economic clout, but they identified with the wealthy planters.

The peasantry adapted their strategies for survival in a frontier environment where land could be freely obtained and where the agents of local and royal authority remained weak. For the free peasantry, nuclear families predominated as the best-adapted family structure for subsistence agriculture. Peasant women gave birth to many children, all of whom served their families as agricultural laborers. Dramatic changes occurred in the lives of the peasantry during the eighteenth century. Their traditional frontier existence came under fire in Santana de Parnaíba as the sugar economy spread. They adapted by moving west to the frontier or by flocking to nearby towns and cities. Relatively few managed to retain their lands in Parnaíba. The group that kept their lands in Parnaíba became sedentary subsistence farmers and produced crops for local markets. Those who moved west continued to live as frontiersmen on the edges of the wilderness. Still a third group took up residence in the towns and cities and worked as artisans, as laborers, or as servants, or begged for alms. As these changes occurred, traditional family strategies could no longer support all members of the family. Women became particularly vulnerable. Many were forced into the towns and the nearby city of São Paulo where they made do as best they could "living by their wits."

Of the three classes, slaves had the least stable family lives and the least influence over their own survival. External economic factors, such as the level of economic development in the region, the wealth of individual masters, and the demographic characteristics of the slave population, determined many facets of slave family life. Yet slaves did create strategies to survive their lives as slaves, strategies that directly affected the character of life in the town. The growing free black population in Parnaíba attested to the degree to which slaves successfully negotiated a way out of slavery for some family members each generation. Slaves formed families in much the same way as did planters and peasants. They married in the parish churches and lived in families on the estates of their masters. They baptized their children and selected godparents for them from the ranks of the slave and free population. Slaves established two types of families in Santana de Parnaíba: nuclear and matrifocal. Vulnerable to events in the lives of masters, such as when masters died and Portuguese laws of inheritance that mandated the selling of slaves or their transmission to heirs, nuclear and matrifocal slave families broke apart at these times.

The frontier dominated the lives of virtually every family—slaves, peasants, or planters—in colonial Santana de Parnaíba. In the seventeenth and eighteenth centuries, the inhabitants of the town colonized the wilderness to the north, west, and south. The bulk of these resources came into the hands of an enterprising few who used them to create their own wealth, social position, and political power. The ability to transform the wilderness into sources of wealth according to values of the kingdom was a talent perfected by generations of planter families. Many more families, however, learned to subsist off the resources of the wilderness.

Peasants depended on the free lands of the frontier regions and on the culture of the Indians to live. They claimed lands, planted them with native American plants, and adapted Indian farming techniques to create a life-style that was partially Indian and partially European. The presence of the frontier sustained them and gave them independence. Unlike the planters, peasants did not translate the wilderness into wealth or power.

For slaves, the wilderness sometimes represented independence and freedom. When slaves ran away, they hid in the wilderness where they established their own independent communities, or quilombos. These communities survived as long as slaves successfully resisted the armed soldiers sent to recapture them. For most slaves, the frontier did not signify freedom but the backbreaking work of cutting a new farm or a plantation from the forest under the watchful eye and biting whip of the overseer. Slaves who accompanied their masters into the wilderness were instrumental in its transformation into agricultural towns. Indeed, the metamorphosis of wilderness to town was impossible without them.

Thus, unlike Frederick Jackson Turner's thesis of the equalizing effect of the frontier, in Santana de Parnaíba, the frontier had a dissimilar effect on the three social classes of the town. The frontier brought independence and self-sufficiency to peasants but not equality with the planter class. For the slave-owning planters, the frontier offered a way to constantly expand their base of family property, which in turn allowed them to accommodate more and more of their descendants by sending them into the frontier. The bounty of the frontier only rarely benefited slaves.

For both planters and peasants, the fact that the wilderness existed virtually on the edge of Parnaíba for more than two hundred years meant that traditional patterns of survival endured for generations. The eighteenth-century planters, descended from the bandeirantes of the seventeenth century, inherited a way of life analogous in many ways to that of their forebears of the previous century. The peasants of the eighteenth century similarly continued to live a frontier existence characteristic of their antecedents one hundred years before. The roles of African slaves in eighteenth-century Parnaíba had been prefigured by the lives of Indian slaves in the seventeenth century. Both planters and peasants, and their ancestors, sent generation after generation of descendants, many with slaves, into the frontier. This movement carried lifeways into the wilderness and effectively colonized large areas of what are today western São Paulo, Paraná, Mato Grosso, Goiás, and Minas Gerais.

The history of Santana de Parnaíba in the colonial period clearly illustrates that colonization was not a phenomenon limited to the early sixteenth century. Instead, colonization occurred over and over again in new regions. Enacted with few variations, the drama of colonization consisted of a common cycle of events.

In the first stage, Indians of the wilderness met Portuguese and mameluco colonists. As Indians died from unknown diseases and became the slaves and servants of the colonists, a new hybrid frontier culture took root. In this frontier society, colonists absorbed many of the lifeways of the Indians. Although it showed clear signs of social stratification, society retained a fluidity that allowed for the social mobility of some. This stage of colonization characterizes the seventeenth century in Parnaíba.

In the second stage of colonization, Indians all but disappeared in the town. Of those who survived disease, slavery, and war, only a small minority retained their traditional tribal culture. Most Indians assimilated into the colonists' society and became members of the peasantry, living in the Indian aldeia of Baruerí. African slaves replaced Indians as laborers, primarily on the large estates of the wealthy which produced agricultural crops for sale. A powerful but small group of planters dominated the town, which became a society clearly stratified into the social classes of planters, peasants, and slaves. Some social mobility existed for slaves who purchased their freedom, for peasants who acquired land and slaves, and for immigrants from Portugal who married into established families. This period characterizes the eighteenth century in Parnaíba.

In the last stage of this cycle, as soils depleted and as prime virgin forests disappeared, planters lamented their poverty, but farther west, their sons and grandsons reproduced similar estates in regions still in the earlier stages of the colonization process. At the time of independence, Santana de Parnaíba began its decline relative to the towns farther west.

This drama with its emphasis on a cycle of contact, expansion, and decline underscores the fluidity of Brazilian development. Like the North American west, the Brazilian west was "won" over and over again as colonists launched by their families proceeded into the wilderness and sought to re-create a world they had known. Few of the descendants of Manoel Fernandes Ramos and Suzana Dias today live in Santana de Parnaíba. The vast majority have settled in the west.

How significant were these simple actions of families compared with the larger economic and political forces of the Portuguese colonial empire in determining the character of colonial Brazil? Historians have often emphasized the importance of external factors in shaping the character of colonial Brazil. Such external factors include the character of authoritarian imperial government or the transmission of authoritarian institutions such as the military or municipal government from Portugal to Brazil.[5] The type of economic system implanted by Portugal in Brazil—a mercantilist system designed to maximize the exploitation of the resources of the colony of Brazil for the benefit of the metropolis, Portugal—is another external factor emphasized by historians as responsible for the character of Brazilian development.[6]

Without denying the importance of such external factors, which clearly did shape the environment of colonial Brazil, the history of life in a small town like Parnaíba does suggest that the policies and authority of Portugal remained distant and vague to ordinary persons. In the region of São Paulo, colonists customarily ignored royal orders. In the seventeenth century, colonists deliberately disobeyed royal laws and enslaved Indians.[7] In the eighteenth century, the royal governor, the Morgado de Mateus, became exasperated at the ease and facility with which the residents of São Paulo avoided military service and other royal decrees.[8] The seeming disinterest in the town in the face of the coming of independence in the early nineteenth century similarly suggests widespread ignorance of the political choices that would determine the future political character of Brazil. In the economic realm as well, the colonists of this part of the Portuguese empire are not noted for their adherence to mercantilism. Unlike the other Brazilian settlements, the towns of São Vicente in the sixteenth and seventeenth centuries developed inland, away from the coast. They lacked the infrastructure that would allow them to export commercial crops to Portugal.

Smuggling through Paraguay, the Rio de la Plata, and the silver-mining town of Potosí could not be eradicated. Until the last years of the eighteenth century, very few ships regularly docked in Santos to load crops hauled down the steep coastal escarpment for export abroad. The big boom of commercial agricultural production in São Paulo did not come until after independence, when sugar, followed by coffee, took western São Paulo by storm.

Although historians of the family in Brazil reject Gilberto Freyre's depiction of family life in colonial Brazil as highly impressionistic, Freyre's insistence that it was the family, not the crown and not economic institutions, that colonized Brazil must not be rejected as readily.[9] The families of Parnaíba do not resemble the great sugar-planting families described by Freyre, and the town of Parnaíba did not follow the kind of development characteristic of the sugar-producing northeast. Yet, the planter families of Parnaíba dominated the town in the seventeenth and eighteenth centuries and cast a long shadow over the lives of their slaves and their neighbors, the peasants. As I have shown throughout this book, the way that planter families colonized the wilderness began the process that created inequality in the town. From Parnaíba, descendants of these planter families carried the family patterns they had known in Parnaíba into the western frontiers. Families from this community not only influenced the social structure of Parnaíba itself but affected the development of social structures in the interior as well. Since the actions of families in Parnaíba did have such an impact on the creation of an inegalitarian society in the town, social inequality in Brazil may well lie as much in family strategies as in the larger political and economic forces of Portuguese colonialism.

The advent of independence in 1822 did bring about major changes in Brazil, even if they were dimly perceived by such ordinary people as the residents of Santana de Parnaíba. After independence, the role of the "kingdom" in the tripartite mental construct of "town," "kingdom," and "wilderness" changed. The kingdom became Brazil, not an overseas Portugal, although like Portugal in the eighteenth century, the new Brazilian kingdom also quickly found itself overrun by British merchants. The concept of the town undoubtedly changed as well as the political relationships between towns and provinces became worked out in the new country. But the concept of sertão remained intact after independence, as did the traditional strategies for using the wilderness by the planters and peasants. The process of colonization continued in much the same way as planters claimed the wilderness of western São Paulo for their coffee estates and the peasants moved ever farther west in search of free forest land.

The three social classes of Parnaíba benefited differently from independence. After independence, planter elites consolidated their power throughout Brazil, and São Paulo proved to be no exception. In the new representative institutions of the constitutional monarchy, members of the planter class took their seats and voiced their interests along with their close allies, the merchants and professionals.[10]

In Parnaíba, as elsewhere in Brazil, independence brought few changes in the lives of slaves. Slavery endured in the now-independent constitutional monarchy of Brazil. The rapid expansion of the coffee economy in western São Paulo only transpired because of the massive importation of slaves from Africa and other regions of Brazil. Without such a forced relocation, planters could not clear fields, plant coffee bushes, or harvest the ripe coffee berries.[11] Slavery continued as an unquestioned foundation of society in independent Brazil. Not until 1850 would the Brazilian government limit the slave trade. In 1871, the Law of the Free Womb, which declared all infants born to slave mothers free, finally established that only in the twentieth century would slavery disappear in Brazil. But twelve years before the turn of the century, in 1888, the Golden Law abolished slavery in all of its forms, thus bringing to a close an institution of over three hundred years' duration in Brazil.[12]

At independence, the peasantry of the rural areas throughout Brazil remained isolated from and ignorant of the changes taking place. In the larger towns and cities, artisans, laborers, and muleteers did keep abreast of the political developments and often established clear political positions.[13] But the rural peasantry became even more vulnerable vis-à-vis the planter class after independence. Since the planter class "inherited" independence, they could use their newfound authority to pursue their own interests. Yet because many of their interests collided with those of peasants, peasants found themselves increasingly defenseless. The best example of their exposed and weak position is symbolized in the Land Law of 1850. This law outlawed squatters' rights as a legal means to obtain land. In the wake of this law, planters cleared the way to oust peasants who had traditionally relied on squatters' rights to obtain land.[14]

This book tells the story of people who lived in a simple town poised between kingdom and wilderness. Their story provides a focus for detailed examination of frontier and family life in colonial Brazil. By adopting such a focus, the study reconstructs how individuals and their families survived—both physically and socially— in a New World community. Perhaps the most important characteristic of colonial Brazil that this reconstruction of family life in Santana de Parnaíba reveals is the connection between the frontier and the origin of inequality in Brazil. The inhabitants of colonial Brazil did not share equally in the vast resources of the Brazilian wilderness. The planters of Santana de Parnaíba derived their power from the ability to control the resources of the wilderness, not just by their physical possession of them but through their legal expropriation within the framework of Portuguese law and political institutions. Peasants and Indians who possessed similar wilderness resources could not as easily legitimate their claim to them and thus frequently lost them. African slaves had few opportunities to own such resources, whether physically or legally.

After independence, the resources of the wilderness continued to benefit Brazilians unequally. The cycle of colonization visible in Parnaíba in the seventeenth and eighteenth centuries occurred in western São Paulo in the nineteenth century and even farther west in the twentieth century. Today, a similar cycle can be seen in the rapid colonization of the Amazonian provinces of Rondônia and Acre. Thus, the relationships between family and frontier and between town, kingdom, and wilderness are as compelling today as they were in Santana de Parnaíba when Suzana Dias, the mameluca founder of Parnaíba, died in 1634.

Appendix
A Note on Sources and Methodology

Quantitative analysis using the Statistical Analysis System (SAS) of three major sources—censuses, property inventories, and parish registers—provides the backbone of this book by establishing the basic demographic character of the town, the structure of the ownership of property, and economic change over time. The qualitative reading of many other sources then develops this skeletal outline into a social history of family and community life. Below, I discuss briefly how I approached the sources and integrated quantitative with qualitative analysis.

Manuscript censuses from the late eighteenth and early nineteenth centuries housed in the Arquivo do Estado de São Paulo (AESP) provide the most important statistical source for this study. The manuscript censuses for São Paulo, begun in 1765, have been widely used by historians because of the exceptionally detailed information they offer on households, agricultural production, slaves, and family life. In each of the censuses, all members of a household appear, listed by name, age, race, and marital status. The censuses prior to 1798 do not record the names of slaves, which makes it impossible to study the slave population from the returns; however, the 1775 census does indicate the number of slaves owned. Beginning in 1798, very good data appear for every slave, including age, race, sex, marital status, and often place of birth. The census taker, usually the captain major of the militia, recorded the agricultural production of the household, that is, how much sugar, cotton, corn, beans, and so on, was harvested. From all indications, the censuses served as taxation documents and as lists for military recruitment.

I selected the censuses of 1775, 1798, and 1820 for this study based on the special characteristics of each. The 1775 census is the best census from 1765 to 1798 because it records the number of slaves owned and, of special interest, landownership by household. The 1798 census is of exceptionally fine quality, as is that of 1820. Each of the three censuses canvasses three of the four parishes of the town of Santana de Parnaíba (Santana, Araçariguama, and São Roque). The fourth parish, the Indian community (aldeia) of Baruerí appears separately until the 1820 census; before 1820, the 1804 census was selected as the best available source for analyzing the aldeia.

The censuses, coded by household, provide data for 695 households in 1775, 985 in 1798, and 1,161 in 1820. The 1804 census of Baruerí yields information on 133 households. Variables coded include family structure according to Laslett's typology; the age, sex, marital status, and birthplace of the head of household and his/her spouse; the number of children, slaves, and retainers living in the household; and the agricultural production of the household. Since Laslett's typology of family types does not include matrifocal families (single mothers with children), I added several categories to his scheme to take into account the significant numbers of households headed by single (never married) women.

The 1820 census was coded by individual as well as by household to obtain more detailed demographic information on the population, especially the slave population. Information recorded for every individual in this census includes age, race, sex, relationship to head of household, and civil status.

The analysis of the censuses clearly documents the social structure of the town, the major family characteristics of each social class, and changes in these characteristics over time. With such a clear picture of the town in the late eighteenth century in mind, it was then possible to work backwards to trace how the town had evolved since its settlement.

The property inventories from the seventeenth and eighteenth centuries opened an important avenue for exploring how the town developed. Inventories record all of the property owned by an individual, or more usually by a married couple, and they list individually every item of property with a monetary appraisal. Inventories also record how the family property was divided among the heirs, a process that often took several years. Many, but certainly not all, inventories contain a will written before the individual died. The inventories are housed in two separate collections, Inventários e Testamentos (IT) and Inventários do Primeiro Ofício (IPO) in the AESP. In both collections, inventories from Parnaíba are mixed in with those from other localities, thus making it particularly difficult to immediately separate out those of interest. I focused primarily on the eighteenth-century inventories. First, I sorted hundreds of inventories to locate those from Parnaíba. All of the inventories found from 1733 to 1800 then became part of a data base of 241 inventories that were coded for computer analysis. For the quantitative analysis, I recorded information on slaves, land, agricultural tools, machinery, the value of estates, the size of outstanding debts, and the inheritances paid to heirs.

The inventories were also analyzed qualitatively. A sample of the 241 inventories (55) was analyzed in depth to see what patterns of distribution of family property could be found in the eighteenth century. This sample consists of all inventories from the IT collection. The inventories of planters with ten or more slaves (16 of 55) were then used to determine the inheritance patterns of the planter class. Of these sixteen inventories, only nine had information on how property was divided (two inventories were of single men, two were of individuals who had no children, one was incomplete, and two inventories did not divide the property). The remaining nine, however, provided excellent information on how planter families distributed their property to their heirs. The heirs were then searched for in subsequent censuses or inventories. These nine case studies were supplemented by an analysis of eleven inventories from the larger IPO collection. These eleven inventories were drawn from the fifty-one inventories of planters who owned more than ten slaves. In addition, fourteen inventories of poor planters (those planters with fewer than ten slaves) were studied for inheritance patterns. Thus, of the total of 241 inventories analyzed quantitatively for the data presented in chapter 4 on planter family strategies, thirty-four were analyzed qualitatively using record linkage between the inventories and the censuses.

For the seventeenth century, I did not try to duplicate my quantitative analysis of the eighteenth-century inventories. Instead, I worked closely with an additional fifty-eight inventories from the published collection *Inventários e testamentos* (*IT*) to ascertain how inheritance patterns, property ownership, and family relationships differed from those observed in the eighteenth century.

The wills found in the inventories are an exceptionally important source of information on family and community life. I worked with eighty-four wills from the eighteenth century (all of the wills found) as well as thirty-eight wills from the seventeenth century. Given the variation in the wills, I did not quantify them. Rather, I focused on the information they provide on dowries, landownership, indebtedness, relationships between family members, economic strategies, and personal reflections of the testator.

I found the parish records for Santana parish in the Arquivo da Cúria Diocesana de Jundiaí (ACDJ). I did not find the seventeenth-century registers for Santana or the eighteenth-century registers for Araçariguama, Barueri, or São Roque (although one burial register was found for Araçariguama in the AESP). Thus, my demographic analysis of marriages and births focuses on Santana parish, which was in any case the central parish of the town. I use the marriage records to ascertain the marriage patterns of free men and women and of slaves in the eighteenth century. Given the volume of the records, I coded the free population in alternating decades: 1730–1739, 1750–1759, 1770–1779, 1790–1799, 1810–1819. This provided a data base of 274 marriages. For slaves, I coded all marriages from 1726, when the register began, to 1820. This yielded a data base of 610 marriages involving at least one slave partner.

The baptismal registers are used to understand the relationship of godparentage among peasants and slaves. Because the baptismal registers do not give the social status of parents and godparents (except in the case of slaves), I linked the baptismal records to the censuses. For slaves, I used all baptisms for 1770, 1798, and 1820. (The baptisms for 1775 were not found; thus, I linked 1770 to the 1775 census.) For peasants, I created a larger data base because of the greater difficulty of finding peasants in the censuses. For this data base, I used all baptisms from the year of the census, plus the years immediately preceding and immediately following. Thus, all baptisms of free children from 1774 to 1776, 1797 to 1799, and 1819 to 1821 are included.

Record linkage plays an important part in this study because of the way I analyze families by class. While all sources identify slaves as slaves, few sources distinguish consistently between planters and peasants. Since the ownership of slaves is the key difference between planters and peasants in this study, I needed to find a way to distinguish which individuals owned slaves and which did not. I solved this problem by creating a master index of names drawn from the censuses and inventories, the two sources that do record information on slave ownership. Using the merge feature of SAS, I compiled an index of names with information on age, slave ownership, and parish of residence. I then used the index as a means of ascertaining the social class of individuals discussed in other sources. This index proved invaluable in the qualitative analysis, for it made it possible to ascertain the social class of virtually everyone who appeared in other documents. For example, an individual who appeared in a case heard before the local justice of the peace, if found in the index, could be assigned a social status. The index made it possible to ascertain the social status of the godparents of the babies born to free and slave parents. In addition, it allowed for tracing the changes in households over time.

Many other sources appear in this study, such as notarial records, judicial cases, divorce cases, town council deliberations, land grants, official correspondence, and the Portuguese legal code. The majority of these sources are found in the AESP in an extensive collection of 194 books (LP) kept by the town council of Parnaíba from the late seventeenth century to the early twentieth century. These sources allowed me to answer many of the questions brought out by the quantitative analysis. By always having in view the synchronic and diachronic framework supplied by the quantitative analysis, I was able to place many different qualitative sources into a larger context and to use them to their fullest advantage.

Notes

INTRODUCTION: FAMILY, FRONTIER, AND
THE COLONIZATION OF THE AMERICAS

1. Frederick Jackson Turner, *The Frontier in American History* (Tucson: University of Arizona Press, 1986).

2. Ibid., 4.

3. Ray Allen Billington and Martin Ridge, *Westward Expansion: A History of the American Frontier*, 5th ed. (New York: Macmillan Co., 1982).

4. See Ray Allen Billington, ed., *The Frontier Thesis: Valid Interpretation of American History?* (New York: Krieger Pub. Co., 1977), for representative positions on the debate for and against the Turner thesis.

5. Sérgio Buarque de Holanda, *Caminhos e fronteiras* (Rio de Janeiro: Livraria José Olympio Editôra, 1957) and *Monções*, 2d ed. (São Paulo: Editôra Alfa-Omega, 1976).

6. See Billington, *The Frontier Thesis*, as well as Harry N. Schieber, "Turner's Legacy and the Search for a Reorientation of Western History: A Review Essay," *New Mexico Historical Review* 44(1969): 231–248; Jackson K. Putnam, "The Turner Thesis and Westward Movement: A Reappraisal," *Western Historical Quarterly* 7(1976): 379–404, and Martin Ridge, "Frederick Jackson Turner, Ray Allen Billington, and American Frontier History," *Western Historical Quarterly* 19(1988): 5–20, for three reviews in different decades of this literature and controversy. In "Turner, the Boltonians, and the Borderlands," *American Historical Review* 91(1986): 66–81, David Weber argues that the Turner thesis has never been very influential in the study of Mexico's northern frontier or the U.S.–Mexico borderlands because of Turner's (and his students') failure to address ethnicity on the frontier.

7. David A. Brading, *Miners and Merchants in Bourbon Mexico, 1763–1810* (Cambridge: Cambridge University Press, 1971); Doris M. Ladd, *The Mexican Nobility at Independence, 1780–1820* (Austin: University of Texas Press, 1976); Richard B. Lindley, *Haciendas and Economic Development: Guadalajara, Mexico, at Independence* (Austin: University of Texas Press, 1983); Susan E. Ramírez, *Provincial Patriarchs: The Economics of Power in Colonial Peru* (Albuquerque: University of New Mexico Press, 1985); Fred Bronner, "Peruvian Encomenderos in 1630: Elite Circulation and Consolidation," *Hispanic American Historical Review* 57(1977): 633–659; Robert B. Keith, *Conquest and Agrarian Change* (Cambridge: Harvard University Press, 1976). Similar

landowning elites evolved in frontier regions as well. See Charles H. Harris III, *A Mexican Family Empire: The Latifundio of the Sánchez Navarros, 1765–1867* (Austin: University of Texas Press, 1975), Robert J. Ferry, *The Colonial Elite of Early Caracas: Formation and Crisis, 1567–1767* (Berkeley, Los Angeles, Oxford: University of California Press, 1989), and Diana Balmori, Stuart F. Voss, and Miles Wortman, *Notable Family Networks in Latin America* (Chicago: University of Chicago Press, 1984). For an excellent review of the formation and consolidation of this elite, see Susan E. Ramírez, "Large Landowners," in *Cities and Society in Colonial Latin America*, ed. Louisa Hoberman and Susan Socolow (Albuquerque: University of New Mexico Press, 1986), 19–45.

8. Stuart B. Schwartz, *Sovereignty and Society in Colonial Brazil: The High Court of Bahia and Its Judges, 1609–1751* (Berkeley, Los Angeles, London: University of California Press, 1973); Schwartz, *Sugar Plantations in the Formation of Brazilian Society: Bahia, 1550–1835* (Cambridge: Cambridge University Press, 1985); Rae Jean Dell Flory and David Grant Smith, "Bahian Merchants and Planters in the Seventeenth and Early Eighteenth Centuries," *Hispanic American Historical Review* 58(1978): 571–594.

9. See Sedi Hirano, *Pre-capitalismo e capitalismo* (São Paulo: Editôra Hucitec, 1988), for a review of how the terms "estate," "class," and "caste" are used historically and in recent sociological and historical work on colonial Brazil.

10. Peter Laslett and Richard Wall, eds., *Household and Family in Past Time* (Cambridge: Cambridge University Press, 1972).

11. Kenneth A. Lockridge, *A New England Town, The First Hundred Years: Dedham, Massachusetts, 1636–1736* (New York: W. W. Norton & Co., 1970), and Philip J. Greven, Jr., *Four Generations: Population, Land, and Family in Colonial Andover, Massachusetts* (Ithaca: Cornell University Press, 1970). Two other influential studies of New England towns appeared in the same year: John Demos's *A Little Commonwealth: Family Life in Plymouth Colony* (New York: Oxford University Press, 1970) and Michael Zuckerman's *Peaceable Kingdoms: New England Towns in the Eighteenth Century* (New York: Vintage Books, 1970).

12. Stephen Innes, *Labor in a New Land: Economy and Society in Seventeenth-Century Springfield* (Princeton: Princeton University Press, 1983), xv–xvi.

13. Ibid., xvi.

14. Ibid.

15. Lois Green Carr and Lorena S. Walsh, "The Planter's Wife: The Experience of White Women in Seventeenth-Century Maryland," in *The Chesapeake in the Seventeenth Century: Essays on Anglo-American Society and Politics*, ed. Thad W. Tate and David L. Ammerman (Chapel Hill: University of North Carolina Press, 1979), 25–57.

16. Darrett B. and Anita H. Rutman, "'Now Wives and Sons-in-Law': Parental Death in a Seventeenth-Century Virginia County," in *The Chesapeake in the Seventeenth Century*, 153–182.

17. Lorena Walsh, "'Till Death Do Us Part': Marriage and Family in Seventeenth-Century Maryland," in *The Chesapeake in the Seventeenth Century*, 126–152.

18. Darrett B. Rutman, "Assessing the Little Communities of Early America," *William and Mary Quarterly*, 3d ser., 43(1986): 163.

19. Ibid., 167.

20. Jack P. Greene, *Pursuits of Happiness: The Social Development of Early Modern British Colonies and the Formation of American Culture* (Chapel Hill: University of North Carolina Press, 1988).

21. Gilberto Freyre, *The Masters and the Slaves [Casa-Grande & Senzala]: A Study in the Development of Brazilian Civilization*, trans. Samuel Putnam, 2d ed. rev. (New York: Knopf, 1966), 26.

22. Ibid., 43.

23. Freyre's model of colonization has been developed by Oliveira Vianna, Luís de Aguiar Costa Pinto, Antônio Cândido, and others. For an excellent review of this literature, see Eni de Mesquita Samara, *As mulheres, o poder, e a família: São Paulo, século XIX* (São Paulo: Editôra Marco Zero, 1989), 15–45.

24. Elizabeth Anne Kuznesof, *Household Economy and Urban Development: São Paulo, 1765 to 1836* (Boulder: Westview Press, 1986), 158–159.

25. Iraci del Nero da Costa, *Vila Rica: População (1719–1826)* (São Paulo: IPE-USP, 1979), 164.

26. Donald Ramos, "Marriage and the Family in Colonial Vila Rica," *Hispanic American Historical Review* 55(1975): 200–225.

27. Maria Odila Leite da Silva Dias, *Quotidiano e poder em São Paulo no século XIX—Ana Gertrudes de Jesus* (São Paulo: Brasiliense, 1984), and Elizabeth Anne Kuznesof, "The Role of the Female-Headed Household in Brazilian Modernization: São Paulo 1765 to 1836," *Journal of Social History* 13(1980): 589–613.

28. Kuznesof, *Household Economy and Urban Development*, 158; Donald Ramos, "Consensual Unions and the Family in Nineteenth-Century Minas Gerais, Brazil," paper presented to the Social Science History Association, November 1989.

29. Arlene J. Díaz and Jeff Stewart, "Occupational Class and Female-Headed Households in Santiago Maior do Iguape, Brazil, 1835," *Journal of Family History* 16(1991): 299–313.

30. Samara, *As mulheres, o poder, e a família*, 15–45, and Darrell E. Levi, *The Prados of São Paulo, Brazil: An Elite Family and Social Change, 1840–1930* (Athens: University of Georgia Press, 1987), 1–16.

31. Linda Lewin, *Politics and Parentela in Paraíba: A Case Study of Family-based Oligarchy in Brazil* (Princeton: Princeton University Press, 1987); and Levi, *The Prados of São Paulo*. See also Elizabeth Kuznesof's portrayal of elite families in São Paulo in "A família na sociedade Brasileira: Parentesco, clientelismo, e estrutura social (São Paulo 1700–1980)," in *Família e grupos de convívio*, ed. Eni de Mesquita Samara (São Paulo: ANPUH/Marco Zero, 1989).

32. "Dinamica familiar da elite paulista (1765–1836)," M.A. thesis, University of São Paulo, 1987.

33. Carlos de Almeida Prado Bacellar is working in this direction; see "Os senhores da terra—família e sistema sucessório entre os senhores de engenho do oeste paulista, 1765–1855," M.A. thesis, University of São Paulo, 1987.

34. Eni de Mesquita Samara, "Famílias e domicílios em sociedades escravistas (São Paulo no século XIX)," paper presented to the Conference on the Population History of Latin America, Ouro Preto, June 1989; Donald Ramos, "Single and Married Women in Vila Rica, Brazil, 1754–1838," *Journal of Family History* 16(1991): 261–282; Elizabeth Anne Kuznesof, "Sexual Politics, Race, and Bastard-Bearing in Nineteenth-Century Brazil, A Question of Culture of Power?," *Journal of Family History* 16(1991): 241–260; Dias, *Quotidiano e poder;* and Samara, *As mulheres, o poder, e a família.*

35. Maria Luiza Marcílio, *Caiçara: Terra e população, estudo de demografia histórica e da história social de Ubatuba* (São Paulo: Edições Paulinas—CEDHAL, 1986).

36. Mary Karasch, *Slave Life in Rio de Janeiro, 1808–1850* (Princeton: Princeton University Press, 1987), 287–298.

37. See the special issue of *Estudos Econômicos,* "Demografia da Escravidão," 17, 2(1987).

1: INDIANS, PORTUGUESE, AND MAMELUCOS:
THE SIXTEENTH-CENTURY COLONIZATION
OF SÃO VICENTE

1. Inv. Suzana Dias, 1634, *IT* 33:11–21.

2. Luiz Gonzaga da Silva Leme, *Genealogia Paulistana,* 9 vols. (São Paulo: Duprat, 1903–1905), 7:224.

3. James W. Wilkie and Stephen Haker, *Statistical Abstract of Latin America,* 21 (Los Angeles: UCLA Latin American Center Publications, 1981), 30.

4. Paulo Pereira dos Reis, *O Indígena do Vale do Paraíba,* Coleção Paulística, XVI (São Paulo: Governo do Estado de São Paulo, 1979), 41.

5. Before sailing west in 1492, Columbus secured a very favorable contract that gave him extensive administrative and financial powers in any new lands discovered. See "The Capitulations of Santa Fe: The Title—Conditional grant of titles and privileges to Columbus," in *New Iberian World: A Documentary History of the Discovery and Settlement of Latin America to the Early 17th Century,* 5 vols., ed. John H. Parry and Robert G. Keith (New York: Times Books, 1984), doc. 14:2, 2:19.

6. "Pedro Vaz de Caminha to the King of Portugal, describing the Portuguese landing at Porto Seguro," in *New Iberian World,* doc. 57:1, 5:14.

7. Ibid., 5:6.

8. Ibid., 5:10.

9. Ibid., 5:13.

10. On the Spanish background, see Jaime Vicens Vives, *An Economic History of Spain,* trans. F. M. López-Morillas (Princeton: Princeton University Press, 1969); Derek W. Lomax, *The Reconquest of Spain* (New York: Longman, 1978); J. H. Mariéjol, *The Spain of Ferdinand and Isabella,* trans. and ed. Benjamin Keen (New Brunswick: Rutgers University Press, 1961).

11. For an overview of this period of Portuguese history, see Victorino Magalhães Godinho, *A economia dos descobrimentos henriquinos* (Lisbon: Liv. Sa da Costa, 1962); Bailey W. Diffie and George D. Winius, *Foundations of the Portuguese Empire, 1415–1580* (Minneapolis: University of Minnesota Press, 1977); and A. H. de Oliveira Marques, *A History of Portugal,* 2d ed. (New York: Columbia University Press, 1976).

12. J. F. de Almeida Prado, *Primeiros povoadores do Brasil, 1500–1530,* 2d ed., Brasiliana, 37 (São Paulo: Companhia Editôra Nacional, 1939), 59–130; Alexander Marchant, *From Barter to Slavery: The Economic Relations of Portuguese and Indians in the Settlement of Brazil, 1500–1580* (Baltimore: Johns Hopkins University Press, 1942; repr. ed., Gloucester, Mass.: Peter Smith, 1966), 28–47.

13. John Hemming, *Red Gold: The Conquest of the Brazilian Indians* (Cambridge: Harvard University Press, 1978), 487–501.

14. John Hemming, "The Indians of Brazil in 1500," in *The Cambridge History of Latin America,* ed. Leslie Bethell (Cambridge: Cambridge University Press, 1984), 1:119–143; see also Hemming, *Red Gold,* 24–28.

15. There are many accounts of the ritual cannibalism practiced by the Tupi groups of Brazil, the most famous of which is that of Hans Staden in the 1550s; see Hemming, *Red Gold,* 28–34, for a fuller discussion of the practice as well as its eyewitnesses.

16. Frei Gaspar da Madre de Deus, *Memórias para a história da Capitania de São Vicente* (Lisbon: 1797; repr. ed., Coleção Reconquista do Brasil, vol. 20, Belo Horizonte: Editôra Itatiaia, 1975), 29–110; Marchant, *From Barter to Slavery,* 49–52; Almeida Prado, *Primeiros povoadores,* 81–108.

17. Silva Leme, *Genealogia Paulistana,* 7:224.

18. Madre de Deus, *Memórias,* 91.

19. J. F. de Almeida Prado, *São Vicente e as Capitanias do Sul do Brasil: As origens (1501–1551),* Brasiliana, 314 (São Paulo: Companhia Editôra Nacional, 1961), 467.

20. H. B. Johnson, "The Portuguese Settlements of Brazil, 1500–80," in *The Cambridge History of Latin America,* 1:261–267; and H. B. Johnson, "The Donatary Captaincy in Perspective: Portuguese Backgrounds to the Settlement of Brazil," *Hispanic American Historical Review* 52(1972): 203–214; see also the "Donation and charter for the captaincy of Pernambuco to Duarte Coelho," *New Iberian World,* doc. 58:2, 5:44.

21. Marchant, *From Barter to Slavery,* 94.

22. See, e.g., the letters of Pero de Góis, donatário of Paraíba do Sul, and Duarte Coelho, donatário of Pernambuco, written in the 1540s, which describe the early conditions of the settlements and the difficulties en-

countered, in *New Iberian World*, docs. 58:3, 58:4, 58:5, 5:52–58. Marchant, *From Barter to Slavery*, 48–80, provides an excellent analysis of this period.

23. Francisco Adolfo de Varnhagen, *História geral do Brazil*, 3 vols., 10th ed. (São Paulo: Editôra Itatiaia, 1981), 1:168, n. 8.
24. Marchant, *From Barter to Slavery*, 71–72.
25. Madre de Deus, *Memórias*, 91.
26. Hemming, *Red Gold*, 97–118.
27. See the laws of 1570 and 1574 briefly described in Johnson, "The Portuguese Settlement of Brazil," 274, and in Hemming, *Red Gold*, 151. For a wider discussion of the laws pertaining to Indian slavery, see Hemming, *Red Gold*, 149–160, and Stuart Schwartz, "Indian Labor and New World Plantations: European Demands and Indian Responses in Northeastern Brazil," *American Historical Review* 83(1978): 43–79.
28. Hemming, *Red Gold*, 139–146.
29. Nóbrega to P. Simão Rodrigues, 1552, in Serafim Leite, S.I., *Novas cartas jesuiticas: De Nóbrega a Vieira* (São Paulo: Companhia Editôra Nacional, 1940), 27; Nóbrega to Rodrigues, 1553, in Leite, *Novas cartas*, 35.
30. Nóbrega to P. Luiz Gonçalves da Câmara, 1553, in Leite, *Novas cartas*, 45.
31. Affonso d'Escragnolle Taunay, *São Paulo nos primeiros anos (1554–1601), ensaio de reconstituição social* (Tours: Imprimerie E. Arrault, 1920), 188.
32. Ibid., 185–186.
33. Nóbrega to P. General Diogo Láinez, 1561, in Leite, *Novas cartas*, 112.
34. Anchieta to St. Francis Borgia, 1570, quoted in Helen G. Dominian, *Apostle of Brazil: The Biography of Padre José de Anchieta, S.J.* (New York: Exposition Press, 1958), 236.
35. Ibid.
36. Nóbrega to Câmara, 1553, in Leite, *Novas cartas*, 46.
37. Madre de Deus, *Memórias*, 122; Hemming, *Red Gold*, 42; Dominian, *Apostle of Brazil*, 70.
38. Nóbrega to Láinez, 1561, in Leite, *Novas cartas*, 106–107.
39. Letter of Anchieta, quoted in Dominian, *Apostle of Brazil*, 165.
40. Ibid.
41. Letter of Pero Correia, 1554, in Leite, *Novas cartas*, 175.
42. Hemming, *Red Gold*, 140.
43. Dominian, *Apostle of Brazil*, 212.
44. Alfred W. Crosby reports that mortality from smallpox in a nonimmunized population is 30 percent. Of those who survived the epidemic, more would die because of the famine that generally followed. See *The Columbian Exchange: Biological and Cultural Consequences of 1492* (Westport: Greenwood Press, 1972), 44.
45. Robert Southey, *History of Brazil* (London: 1822; repr. ed., New York: Greenwood Press, 1969), 298–299; Dominian, *Apostle of Brazil*, 168–170; Hemming, *Red Gold*, 126–128; Reis, *O Indígena*, 44–50.

46. Hemming, *Red Gold*, 119–138.

47. Taunay, *São Paulo nos primeiros anos*, 188; 195–196.

48. Description of life in a Bahian Jesuit aldeia from a letter of Ruy Pereira, 1560, quoted in Marchant, *From Barter to Slavery*, 111, n. 46.

49. On the transformation from Indian to African slavery, see Schwartz, *Sugar Plantations and the Formation of Brazilian Society: Bahia, 1550–1835* (Cambridge: Cambridge University Press, 1985), 51–72.

50. Ibid., 65.

51. Ibid., 68.

52. Marchant, *From Barter to Slavery*, 136–137; Schwartz, *Sugar Plantations*, 35–43.

53. Johnson, "The Portuguese Settlements of Brazil," 279.

54. Ibid., 285.

55. Ibid., table 2, 285.

56. Silva Leme, *Genealogia Paulistana*, 7:224.

57. The Tupi and Guaraní word for water is *parana*; hence, "para-naiba" refers to water, possibly waterfall.

58. The original land grants for these lands no longer exist, or cannot be found, however, in Suzana Dias's inventory, two land grants (*sesmarias*) are listed as part of her property. Inventory and will, Suzana Dias, 1634, *IT* 33:17.

59. "Informação das minas de São Paulo e dos çertõens da sua Capitania desde o ano de 1597 até o prezente de 1772 com rellação chronologica dos administradores dellas," Papeis do Brasil, C16 E147 P6, Codice 3, ff. 2–4, ANTT.

60. Pasquale Petrone, "Os aldeamentos paulistas e sua função na valorização da região paulistana: Estudo de geografia histórica," Tese de Livre Docência, Universidade de São Paulo, 1964.

61. Mons. Paulo Florêncio da Silveira Camargo, *História de Santana de Parnaíba*, Coleção História, 15 (São Paulo: Conselho Estadual de Cultura, 1971), 29–43; Silva Leme, *Genealogia Paulistana*, 7:224–258; John Monteiro, "São Paulo in the Seventeenth Century: Economy and Society," Ph.D. diss., University of Chicago, 1985, 87–90.

62. Alcântara Machado, *Vida e morte do bandeirante*, Coleção Reconquista do Brasil, 8 (Belo Horizonte: Editôra Itatiaia, 1980), 69–76.

2: TOWN, KINGDOM, AND WILDERNESS

1. Antonio de Morais Silva's *Diccionario da Lingua Portugueza*, 8th ed. (Lisbon: Editôra Empreza, 1890), defines *villa* as "(do Lat.) Povoação de menor graduação que a cidade, mas superior à aldeia."

2. The definition of *reino* given in Morais is, "O estado de um rei ou soberano."

3. Morais's definition of *sertão* is, "O interior, o coração das terras; é opp. ao *maritimo, praias, e costa*."

4. This description is reconstructed from a late eighteenth- or early

nineteenth-century description of the church written by the then parish priest. The church was partially rebuilt in 1812, and a completely new church, which now dwarfs the seventeenth- and eighteenth-century houses that still stand on the town square in Parnaíba, was finished in the 1870s. Book of Records, Church of Santana de Parnaíba, liv. 524:3–6, ACDJ.

5. See Sérgio Buarque de Holanda's essay, "A lingua-geral em S. Paulo" in *Raízes do Brazil*, 2d ed., Coleção Documentos Brasileiros (Rio de Janeiro: Livraria José Olympio Editôra, 1948), 88–96, for an analysis of the essentially hybrid (Indian/Portuguese) character of life on the Piratininga plateau in the seventeenth century.

6. Holanda underscores this point in his essay, "A lingua geral," 95.

7. There is a voluminous literature on these men known as *bandeirantes*. While the early histories (usually written by Jesuits) emphasized the ruthlessness of their exploits, later generations of historians, particularly in the 1920s, extol their activities. See Affonso d'Escragnolle Taunay's massive *História geral das bandeiras paulistas*, 11 vols. (São Paulo: Typ. Ideal H. L. Canton, 1924–1950). Alcântara Machado's interesting social history of the bandeirantes uses the wills and inventories of the seventeenth century; see *Vida e morte do bandeirante*, Coleção Reconquista do Brasil, vol. 8 (Belo Horizonte: Editôra Itatiaia, 1980). Richard Morse has collected and translated many useful documents about the bandeirantes as well as examples of the literature written about them in *The Bandeirantes: The Historical Role of the Brazilian Pathfinders* (New York: Knopf, 1965). Recent generations of historians are once again critical of the bandeirantes; see Hemming's chapters in *Red Gold: The Conquest of the Brazilian Indians* (Cambridge: Harvard University Press, 1978), 238–282, and John Monteiro, "From Indian to Slave: Forced Native Labor and Colonial Society in São Paulo during the Seventeenth Century," *Slavery and Abolition* 9(1988): 105–127.

8. Mario Gongora points out the similarities between the bandeiras and the early conquests of Spanish conquistadors in his essay "Algunos pontos de vista comparativos," in *Los grupos de conquistadores en Tierra Firme (1509–1530): Fisonomía historio-social de un tipo de conquista* (Santiago, Chile: Editorial Universitaria, 1962).

9. Some of the first bandeiras were not expressly slaving expeditions but exploratory expeditions outfitted by Portuguese crown officials in search of gold and precious minerals. Organized from São Paulo beginning·in the 1590s, the expeditions set out to the north in search of fabled mountains of silver in the headwaters of the São Francisco River. Although they failed to find gold or silver, those on the expeditions returned from the wilderness with Indian captives. These expeditions created a precedent for later expeditions, which had as their primary goal the capturing of Indians while masquerading as searches for precious metals. See Monteiro, "São Paulo in the Seventeenth Century," 176–179.

10. Muriel Nazzari emphasizes the family-oriented character of the

bandeiras and cites examples where men from the same family or kin group participated in the same bandeira. See "Women, the Family and Property: The Decline of the Dowry in São Paulo, Brazil (1600–1870)," Ph.D. diss., Yale University, 1986, 38–44.

11. Hemming, *Red Gold*, 259–260.

12. Ibid., 268–271.

13. Silva Leme, *Genealogia Paulistana*, 7:225, 226, 248.

14. Hemming, *Red Gold*, 256.

15. Ibid., 268; Affonso d'Escragnolle Taunay, *A grande vida de Fernão Dias Pais* (São Paulo: Melhoramentos, 1977).

16. The wills and inventories from seventeenth-century Parnaíba clearly show that Indians captured from the wilderness became the primary labor force for the agricultural estates of the town. The town council stated the same in a letter to Pope Urban VIII in the 1640s; see Serafim Leite, S.I., *História da Companhia de Jesus no Brasil*, 10 vols. (Lisbon: Livraria Portugália, 1938), 6:264–267.

17. John Monteiro argues that the Indian laborers of seventeenth-century São Vicente did form a class of slaves that made possible the rapid agricultural development of seventeenth-century São Paulo. See "From Indian to Slave," and "Celeiro do Brasil: Escravidão indígena em São Paulo e a agricultura paulista no século XVII," *História: São Paulo* 7(1988): 1–12.

18. Although Brazilian historians have argued that this was the case, in wills and property inventories from Parnaíba, Indians are rarely mentioned as having been sold and in fact are rarely given monetary evaluations at all; see below. Monteiro downplays the significance of an Indian slave trade out of São Vicente and argues that the vast majority of the Indians were destined for use on estates in São Vicente; see "São Paulo in the Seventeenth Century," passim. Stuart Schwartz argues the same; see "Plantations and Peripheries, c. 1580–c. 1750," in *The Cambridge History of Latin America*, ed. Leslie Bethell (Cambridge: Cambridge University Press, 1984), 2:469–470.

19. Papal Bull of Urban VIII, 1639, published in São Paulo in 1640, in Leite, *História da Companhia de Jesus*, 6:569–570.

20. Hemming, *Red Gold*, 279. The Jesuits did return to São Vicente in 1653, but they never fully regained their influence.

21. Letter of the town council of São Paulo to Pope Urban VIII, c. 1645, in Leite, *História da Companhia de Jesus*, 6:264–267.

22. See the definition of armação given by Alcântara Machado in *Vida e morte do bandeirante*, 235, in which he suggests that the name came from the armador, or backer of such expeditions, who supplied the expedition in return for half of the captives. Monteiro has a similar interpretation; see "São Paulo in the Seventeenth Century," 228–231.

23. Inv. 1644, *IT* 14:347–367. See also the will of Antonio Castanho da Sylva, 1648, *IT* 36:105–157. "Blacks" in this context refers to Indian slaves.

24. Royal edict, 1570, in Leite, *História da Companhia de Jesus*, 2:211.

25. "Gibão de armas."

26. Inv. Antonio Gomes Borba, 1645, *IT* 14:347–367. When the band returned, Antonio's widow could not sell the remaining items for the amounts that had been assigned to them in the interior; these items had to be reevaluated for sale in Parnaíba, which underscores how valuable they were in the wilderness.

27. For an excellent treatment of the history of the Indian aldeias around São Paulo, see Pasquale Petrone, "Os aldeamentos paulistas e sua função na valorização da região paulistana: Estudo de geografia histórica," Tese de Livre Docência, Universidade de São Paulo, 1964.

28. See Monteiro's list of land grants conferred in Santana de Parnaíba between 1600 and 1645, in "São Paulo in the Seventeenth Century," 398–415.

29. Departamento do Arquivo do Estado de São Paulo, *Sesmarias*, 3 vols. (São Paulo: Departamento do Arquivo do Estado de São Paulo, 1921), vol. 1, passim.

30. Petition of João Missel Gigante, 1638, *Sesmarias*, 1:264–266.

31. Each town had its rossio, or common lands, which the town council rented to residents. Individuals rented such lands for long periods and even bequeathed them to their heirs. These lands were still being rented in the eighteenth century in Parnaíba. See Land Rentals, LP, 89, 6066–18, AESP. Chapels, such as the one founded by Suzana Dias and her son, André, also had lands. André gave the chapel 440 meters by one-half league of sertão, and Suzana gave the chapel 968 square meters. The rents collected from these lands were used to maintain the chapel and say masses for the souls of the benefactors. See "Igreja Matriz, Freguesia de Sant'anna da villa de Parnahyba," Arquivo Aguirra, Museu Paulista, and Book of Records, Church of Santana de Parnaíba, liv. 524, ACDJ.

32. Inv. Manuel Pinto Suniga, 1627, *IT* 7:331–357.

33. Inv. Ambrosio Mendes, 1642, *IT* 13:477–510.

34. Inv. Manuel de Lara, 1637, *IT* 10:461–491.

35. Inv. Antonio Castanho da Sylva, 1648, *IT* 36:105–157.

36. Nazzari reaches a similar conclusion based on her analysis of the seventeenth-century inventories from São Vicente. Because land and Indians were so undervalued in inventories, she points out that it is difficult to compare the wealth of the paulistas with that of settlers in the northeastern sugar regions of Brazil. It may well be that while "poor" on paper, the paulistas were not as poor as historians have assumed, because only a portion of their assets could be legally given monetary values in inventories. See "Women, the Family and Property," 60–62.

37. While land was not assigned much value in inventories, the inventories clearly stated ownership of land. In this way, the elite carefully reinforced their claim to land, even though they might not be farming it. For example, in Anna da Costa's inventory, three pieces of land were described, even though none was given a value. One was for a square league of land, given as a land grant (sesmaria) in the parish of Itú; the second piece, also received as a land grant, was for two leagues of land,

and the third was for a piece of land downstream on the Tietê River, near the Moixy sandbar and up the Moixy stream to the watershed. It is unlikely that at the time of her death in 1650, Anna and her husband, Domingos Fernandes, son of Suzana Dias, had improved much, if any, of this land. But they continued to hold title to it, even if they did not actually farm all of it. Inv. Anna da Costa, 1650, *IT* 40:35–46.

38. Inv. Antonio Furtado de Vasconcellos, 1628, *IT* 7:5–38.

39. Inv. Paschoal Leite Pais, 1664, *IT* 27:123–160; Inv. Maria de Oliveira, 1665, *IT* 17:5–24.

40. In Morais, *servo/serva* is defined as "he/she who lives in a state of servitude; slave."

41. Inv. Antonio Bicudo, 1648, *IT* 15:25–48.

42. Inv. Salvador Moreira, 1697, *IT* 24:79–114.

43. Inv. Paschoa Leite, 1667, *IT* 17:161–175.

44. Inv. Paschoal Leite Pais, 1664, *IT* 27:123–160.

45. Warren Dean, "Indigenous Populations of the Rio de Janeiro Coast: Trade, Aldeamento, Slavery, and Extinction," *Revista de História* 117(1984): 3–26.

46. Inv. Isabel de Barcelos, 1648, *IT* 36:219–259. See also Monteiro's research on the high mortality rates for Indians in the São Paulo region: "São Paulo in the Seventeenth Century," 258–264.

47. The War of Emboabas pitted those from São Vicente, who had discovered the gold washings, against the newcomers from other regions. The paulistas lost out in this clash, and many moved out of Minas Gerais to Mato Grosso and Goiás. See Charles Boxer, *The Golden Age of Brazil, 1695–1750: Growing Pains of a Colonial Society* (Berkeley and Los Angeles: University of California Press, 1962), 61–83.

48. Boxer, *The Golden Age of Brazil*, 30–83, 254–270.

49. Petition of Bartolomeu Bueno da Silva, João da Silva Ortis, and Domingues Rodrigues do Prado, 1720, São Paulo 148, AHU.

50. See Taunay, *A grande vida de Fernão Dias Pais*, passim.

51. Sérgio Buarque de Holanda describes the long epic trips up and down the rivers of the sertão to the mining towns of Mato Grosso in *Monções*, 2d ed. (São Paulo: Editôra Alfa-Omega, 1976). In some ways, these trips resembled the river trips of the French fur traders in North America, who also traversed great distances by canoe.

52. Wills and inventories from the first half of the eighteenth century are once again an excellent source of information for these changes. References to slaving expeditions disappear almost entirely from them, while allusions to gold, commerce, credit transactions, cattle ranching, and sugar production increase. Eighteenth-century inventories from Parnaíba, IT and IPO, AESP.

53. Inv. Francisco Bueno de Camargo, 1736, IPO #14,568, 690–78, AESP; Inv. Domingos Rodrigues de Fonseca Leme, 1738, IPO #15,085, 740–128, AESP; Inv. Luis Pedrozo de Barros, 1731, in Inv. Agostinha Rodrigues, 1757, IT, 534–57, AESP.

54. J. P. Leite Cordeiro, "Documentação sôbre o 'Capitão Mor Guilherme Pompeo de Almeida, morador que foi na vila de Parnaíba,'" *Revista do Instituto Histórico e Geográfico de São Paulo* 58:525–526; see also Camargo, *História de Santana de Parnaíba*, 193–206, and Boxer, *The Golden Age of Brazil*, 58.

55. Inv. Domingos Rodrigues de Fonseca Leme, 1738, IPO #15,085, 740–128, AESP.

56. Although the church and the crown banned Indian slavery, they extended no such restrictions to Africans. They argued that Indians were "pure," that is, never exposed to Christianity, whereas Africans had been and had rejected it. For a fuller treatment of this contradictory logic and its consequences for Africans, see Leslie B. Rout, *The African Experience in Spanish America: 1502 to the Present Day* (Cambridge: Cambridge University Press, 1976), 3–36.

57. Cordeiro, "Documentação sôbre o 'Capitão Mor Guilherme Pompeo de Almeida,'" 547–548.

58. Kathleen Joan Higgins, "The Slave Society in Eighteenth-Century Sabará: A Community Study in Colonial Brazil," Ph.D. diss., Yale University, 1987.

59. Inv. Domingos Rodrigues de Fonseca Leme, 1738, IPO #15,085, 740–128, AESP.

60. Inv. Jozé Madeira Salvadores, 1733, IT, 514–37, AESP.

61. "Bastards" in this context refers to persons of mixed descent, i.e., mamelucos.

62. Letter of Jozeph Moreira da Silva, 1736, Ordens Régias, 45–1–83, AESP.

63. Minas Gerais became a separate captaincy in 1720; Goiás and Mato Grosso followed suit in 1748. See Heloísa Liberalli Bellotto, *Autoridade e conflito no Brasil colonial: O governo do Morgado de Mateus em São Paulo (1765–1775)*, Textos e documentos, no. 36 (São Paulo: Conselho Estadual de Artes e Ciências Humanas, 1979): 28–36.

64. See, among many others, the works of Bellotto, *Autoridade e conflito*, and Alice Canabrava, "Uma economia de decadência: Os niveis de riqueza na Capitania de São Paulo, 1765/67," *Revista Brasileira de Economia* 26:4(1972): 95–123.

65. Maria Luiza Marcílio, "Crescimento demográfico e evolução agrária paulista, 1700–1836," Tese de Livre Docência, Universidade de São Paulo, 1974.

66. The Morgado de Mateus to the Conde de Oeyras, 23/Dec/1766, *DI* 23:1–10.

67. Ibid.

68. Bellotto, *Autoridade e conflito*, 87–264; Nanci Leonzo, "Defesa militar e controle social na Capitania de São Paulo: As milícias," Tese de Doutoramento, Universidade de São Paulo, 1979.

69. Cargo of *Mercúrio*, 1791, São Paulo 3,307, AHU.

70. Men from families in Parnaíba migrated to Itú, Porto Feliz, Cam-

pinas, and Sorocaba, the major sugar-producing towns of eighteenth- and nineteenth-century São Paulo.

71. Inv. Antonio Correa de Lemos Leite, 1782, IT, 556–79, AESP.

72. Inv. Anna Leme do Prado, 1771, IPO #14,751, 709–97, AESP.

73. The parish priest of Parnaíba in the early nineteenth century, João Gonsalves Lima, remarked in the parish ledger that "this town is today in decadence." Book of Records, Church of Santana de Parnaíba, liv. 524:125, ACDJ.

74. Daniel Pedro Müller, *Ensaio d'um quadro estatístico da província de São Paulo* (São Paulo: 1838; repr. ed., Coleção Paulistica Vol. 11, São Paulo: Governo do Estado, 1978), 126.

3: THE ORIGINS OF SOCIAL CLASS

1. Inv. Thomé Fernandes, 1648, *IT* 38:57–94.

2. Inv. Paschoa Leite, 1667, *IT* 17:161–175.

3. Inv. Antonio Nunes, 1643, *IT* 38:15.

4. Inv. Ambrosio Mendes, 1642, *IT* 13:477–510; Inv. Domingos Fernandes, 1652, *IT* 27:69–119.

5. Inv. Antonio Nunes, 1643, *IT* 38:15.

6. Inv. Maria Bicuda, 1660, *IT* 16:63–156; see a similar statement in the will of Maria de Oliveira, 1627, *IT* 13:149–170.

7. Inv. Pedro Fernandes, 1649, *IT* 40:9–22.

8. Inv. Francisco Pedrozo Xavier, 1674, *IT* 20:291–315; Luis Gonzaga da Silva Leme, *Genealogia Paulistana*, 9 vols. (São Paulo: Duprat, 1903–1905), 7:148.

9. Inv. Paschoal Leite Pais, 1664, *IT* 27:123–160.

10. Inv. Diogo Coutinho de Mello, 1654, *IT* 15:365–405.

11. Inv. Pedro Fernandes, 1649, *IT* 40:9–22; Inv. Domingos Alvres, 1650, *IT* 40:125–128.

12. "Distribuição da riqueza e as origens da pobreza rural em São Paulo (século XVIII)," *Estudos Econômicos* 19(1989): 117–118.

13. Inv. Domingos Fernandes, 1652, *IT* 27:69–119; Inv. Clemente Alveres, 1641, *IT* 14:93–195; Inv. João de Gomes Camacho, 1650, *IT* 40:113–121. Generally, the large Indian holders petitioned for and received land grants, but this did not preclude the smaller Indian holders from doing so.

14. Estimates of Juan de Mongelos, "Acuerdo del Cavildo Justica y Regimento de esta Cuidad de la Asumpcion . . .," in Prefeitura do Município de São Paulo, *Bandeirantes no Paraguai Século XVII*, Coleção Departamento da Cultura, Vol. 35 (São Paulo: Publicação de Divisão do Arquivo Histórico, 1949), 112. See John Monteiro's discussion of Mongelos's figures and other estimates of São Vicente's population in the seventeenth century in "São Paulo in the Seventeenth Century: Economy and Society," Ph.D. diss., University of Chicago, 1985, 332–334.

15. Monteiro illustrates that the majority of the Indian slaves in the towns were women, while men served on the bandeiras and armações

into the wilderness. See "Celeiro do Brasil: Escravidão indígena e a agricultura paulista no século XVII," *História: São Paulo* 7(1988): 1–12.

16. Inv. Antonio Furtado de Vasconcellos, 1628, *IT* 7:5–38. See Pasquale Petrone, "Os aldeamentos paulistas e sua função na valorização da região paulistana: Estudo de geografia histórica," Tese de Livre Docência, Universidade de São Paulo, 1964; and Hemming, *Red Gold,* on the use of such Indians as laborers by the paulistas.

17. See Candido Mendes de Almeida, *Codigo Phillipino, ou Ordenações e leis do reino de Portugal,* 24th ed. (Rio de Janeiro: 1870; repr. ed., Lisbon: Fundação Calouste Gulbenkian, 1985), Liv. 4, Tit. XCII and XCIII, esp. n. 1, 944.

18. Inv. Isabel de Barcelos, 1648, *IT* 36:219–259.

19. Inv. Antonio Bicudo, 1648, *IT* 15:25–48.

20. Liv. 4, Tit. XCII and XCIII, *Ordenações,* 939–947.

21. Inv. Domingos Fernandes, 1653, *IT* 27:69–119.

22. Inv. Bernardo Bicudo, 1649, *IT* 15:173–189.

23. Inv. Thomé Fernandes, 1648, *IT* 38:57–94.

24. These bequests would have come from his free third (*terça*). See chap. 4 for a fuller discussion of how inheritance worked in Parnaíba. Inv. Ambrosio Mendes, 1642, *IT* 13:477–510.

25. Because such bequests came from the terça, which could be allocated however an individual wished, legitimate children could not challenge them.

26. That a daughter should "own" her own mother was not an unheard of practice in seventeenth- or eighteenth-century Parnaíba. Perhaps Aleixo gave his Indian slave mistress to Paula so that she would care for her mother, or perhaps to prevent his mistress from being inherited by his legitimate daughter.

27. Inv. Aleixo Leme de Alvarenga, 1675, *IT* 19:5–39.

28. Inv. Ambrosio Mendes, 1642, *IT* 13:477–510.

29. Others who freed Indian slaves were Antonio Nunes, *IT* 38:15–53; Antonio Furtado de Vasconcellos, *IT* 7:5–38; Dom Diogo de Rego, 1668, *IT* 17:179–188; and Domingos Fernandes, 1652, *IT* 27:69–119.

30. Inv. Isabel de Barcelos, 1648, *IT* 36:219–259.

31. Inv. Antonio Castanho da Sylva, 1648, *IT* 36:105–157.

32. Monteiro finds many similar statements in wills. See his discussion of the master/servant relationship in "São Paulo in the Seventeenth Century," 252–325.

33. Inv. Antonio Furtado de Vasconcellos, 1628, *IT* 7:5–38.

34. Inv. Isabel de Barcelos, 1648, *IT* 36:219–259.

35. Inv. Aleixo Leme de Alvarenga, 1675, *IT* 19:5–39.

36. Inv. Simão Minho, 1649, *IT* 40:49–55. One of Aleixo Leme de Alvarenga's slaves had run away at the time of his death in 1675 as well, *IT* 19:5–39.

37. Silva Leme, *Genealogia Paulistana* 4:542.

38. Inv. Anna da Costa, 1650, *IT* 40:35–46.

39. "Bastard" is the term used in the document, and it is impossible to know if these were "natural" or "spurious" children.

40. Inv. Felippe de Campos, 1682, *IT* 21:227–252.

41. Inv. Antonio Castanho da Silva, 1700, *IT* 25:155–165.

42. Inv. Agostinha Dias, 1648, *IT* 36:9–21. Natural daughters seem to have been more readily accepted and favored within families, for the inventories and wills suggest that fathers seemed more likely to favor their natural daughters over their natural sons.

43. "Carta Régia," 19/Feb/1696, *Revista do Arquivo Municipal* 10(1935): 70–74. As Pasquale Petrone points out, such a decree, even though it attempted to ameliorate an extant practice through regulation, reinforced what the colonists saw as their right to use Indians as servants. See Petrone, "Os aldeamentos paulistas."

44. Câmara of São Paulo to the king, 1725, SP 750, AHU.

45. King to Rodrigo Cézar de Menezes, 1726, SP 750, AHU.

46. By this statement, the plaintiffs meant that Indians from São Paulo were supposed to live as free subjects of the crown in the Indian communities under the jurisdiction of the Jesuits or the crown. Indians conquered from the wilderness were subjected to slavery.

47. Petition to the governor of São Paulo, *Boletim*, 7:37–38.

48. Petition to the governor of São Paulo, 1733, *Boletim*, 7:19–20.

49. Inv. Jozé Madeira Salvadores, 1733, IT, 514–37, AESP.

50. Inv. Anna Vieira, 1735, IPO #15,784, 785–173, AESP.

51. Inv. João Marques de Araujo, 1736, IT, 514–37, AESP.

52. See also the wills and inventories of Violanta da Costa Gil, 1734, IT, 516–39, AESP; Francisco Bueno de Camargo, 1736, IT, 514–37, AESP; Maria de Siqueira, 1736, IPO #15,173, 748–136, AESP; Albano de Goes Leme, 1739, IPO #15,034, 735–123, AESP; Manoel Correa Penteado, 1745, IPO #14,406, 676–64, AESP; Anna Maria Furquim, 1748, IPO #15,614, 744–162, AESP; and Lourenco Franco da Rocha, 1750, IPO #15,095, 742–130, AESP.

53. Petrone, "Os aldeamentos paulistas."

54. Inv. João da Cunha, 1737, IPO #14,600, 693–81, AESP; Inv. Luiza Gonçalves, 1735, IT, 513–36, AESP.

55. Inv. Gabriella Ortis de Camargo, 1736, IPO #14,617, 695–83, AESP; Inv. João dos Santos, 1738, IPO #13,802, 619–7, AESP.

56. Inv. Luiza Gonçalves, 1735, IT, 513–36, AESP.

57. Will, Domingas de Godoy Bicudo, 1731, IPO #14,684, 702–90, AESP; see also the will of Maria Jozeph de Godoy, her aunt, which tells us more about this family, 1739, IPO #14,368, 673–61, AESP.

58. Analysis of all surviving property inventories from eighteenth-century Parnaíba reveals that slaves accounted for more than 50 percent of the total assets of slave owners, while land accounted for less than 10 percent. See chap. 4 for more discussion of the property of the slave owners.

59. 1798 census of Parnaíba, MP, 127–127, AESP.

60. Census of Baruerí, 1804, 2–8–14, 228–2, AESP; this census is also published in *Boletim*, 8.

61. This was João, slave of the parish priest. See LP, 111:92, 6069–21, AESP.

62. Jailer's Ledger, LP, 48:14–53, 6060–12, AESP.

63. Investigation of Policarpo Joaquim de Oliveira, 1779, Ordens Régias, 282–45, AESP.

64. Acts of the town council, 1787, LP, 5:33, 6050–2, AESP.

4: FAMILIES OF PLANTERS

1. Military forces in São Paulo were divided into three lines of defense: the first line, which consisted of the paid royal troops quartered in Santos; the second line, called the *auxiliares*, a provincewide militia made up of able-bodied men not in the royal troops; and the third line, the ordenança, or local militia, which consisted of the remaining men in each township. The capitão mor headed the local militia. Selected by the royal governor from the ranks of elite families, these captain majors worked to implement the directives of the governor, to uphold order, and to resolve conflicts that arose within their towns. See Nanci Leonzo, "As Companhias de Ordenanças na Capitania de São Paulo—Das origens ao governo do Morgado de Matheus," *Coleção Museu Paulista* 6(1977): 125–239, and "Defesa militar e controle social na Capitania de São Paulo: As milicias," Tese de Doutoramento: Universidade de São Paulo, 1979. On the influence of the militia on society, see Elizabeth A. Kuznesof, "Clans, the Militia and Territorial Government: The Articulation of Kinship with Polity in Eighteenth-Century São Paulo," in *Social Fabric and Spatial Structure in Colonial Latin America*, eds. David J. Robinson and David G. Browning (Syracuse: Syracuse University Press, 1979), 181–226.

2. Antonio was from an old family in São Paulo; see Luis Gonzaga da Silva Leme, *Genealogia Paulistana*, 9 vols. (São Paulo: Duprat, 1903–1905), 4:521.

3. Household of Captain Major Antonio Correa de Lemos Leite, 1775 census of Parnaíba, MP, 125–125, AESP.

4. Inv. Escolastica Cordeira Borba, 1756, IT, 533–56, AESP.

5. I found only one woman who actually signed her name, the wife of Domingos Rodrigues de Fonseca Leme; see his inventory, 1738, IPO #15,085, 740–128, AESP.

6. Dispute of Maria da Costa Correia and João Francisco de Paiva, 1772, LP, 97:23–32, 6068–20, AESP.

7. Divorce Case, Joze Vieira Falcão Pedrozo and Francisca de Paula Oliveira, 1810, Divórcios 15–5–73, ACMSP. While not common, divorces were occasionally granted by ecclesiastical courts for reasons such as adultery (committed by either spouse) or maltreatment. In all of São Paulo, some 220 divorce petitions were filed, almost all by women, in the eighteenth and early nineteenth centuries. See Maria Beatriz Nizza da

Silva, *Sistema de casamento no Brasil colonial* (São Paulo: T. A. Queiroz, Editôra da Universidade de São Paulo, 1984), 210–252.

8. Will, Joze Vieira Falção Pedrozo, 1810, Livro de Registros de Testamentos, 571–94, AESP.

9. That husbands could not sell or alienate the property belonging to their wives without their express permission (as evidenced by their written consent) is clearly set out in Portuguese law. See liv. 4, Tit. XLVIII, *Ordenações*, 837–840.

10. Portuguese law stipulated that widows could head the household after their husbands died. But to protect the property that they managed in trust for their children, widows had to present a guarantor (*fiador*) who became liable for any losses sustained under their management. Most of the guarantors selected by widows were their kinsmen. See liv. 4, Tit. XCV, *Ordenações*, 949–954.

11. Inv. Luiz Mendes Vieira, 1793, IT, 565–88, AESP; household of Ignes Barboza, 1798, MP, 127–127, AESP; petition of Anna Caetana de Jesus, 1816, Requerimentos 342–93A:3–15, AESP; household of Anna Caetana, 1820, MP, 133–133, AESP.

12. See the laws pertaining to filho famílias in liv. 4, Tit. LXXXI, no. 3, *Ordenações*, 909; liv. 4, Tit. XCVII, no. 19, *Ordenações*, 979–980. Once married, sons were considered emancipated and outside of their father's authority; see liv. 1, Tit. LXXXVIII, no. 6, *Ordenações*, 209. Fathers were entitled to the income produced by their sons in business ventures until their sons came of age. However, the law made some exceptions in which sons did have rights to income they earned while still minors. These rights are outlined in nos. 17, 18, and 19 of liv. 4, Tit. XCVII, *Ordenações*, 979–980.

13. 1775 census, MP, 125–125, AESP.

14. Ties to the cities of São Paulo, Santos, and Rio de Janeiro can be seen in the seventeenth-century wills of Manuel de Alvarenga, 1639, IT 14:15–49; Domingos Fernandes Coxo, 1648, IT 36:179–216; Antonio Castanho da Sylva, 1648, IT 36:105–157; Felippe de Campos, 1681, IT 21:227–252; Antonio Bicudo de Brito, 1687, IT 26:189–225; and in the eighteenth-century wills of Luis Pedrozo de Barros, 1731, in Inv. Agostinha Rodrigues, IT, 734–57, AESP; Manoel da Costa Homen, 1740, IPO #15,152, 747–135, AESP; Baltazar Rodrigues Fam, 1758, IT, 536–59, AESP, and Domingos Teixeira da Cruz, 1767, Testamentos, 1:12–18, 455–1, AESP.

15. See my article, "Fathers and Sons: The Politics of Inheritance in a Colonial Brazilian Township," *Hispanic American Historical Review* 66(1986): 455–484.

16. Historians of the family in preindustrial Europe and America have explored how families have developed customs, organizational forms, attitudes, and values that played a role in their survival as families. Historians increasingly believe that many patterns of family life were not random but stemmed from strategies that families evolved to protect their resources (generally land and labor). Some very good examples of this

literature on the family are Lutz K. Berkner, "The Stem Family and the Developmental Cycle of the Peasant Household: An Eighteenth-Century Austrian Example," *American Historical Review* 77(1972): 398–418; Jack Goody, Joan Thirsk, and E. P. Thompson, eds., *Family and Inheritance: Rural Society in Western Europe, 1200–1800* (Cambridge: Cambridge University Press, 1976); Philip J. Greven, *Four Generations: Population, Land, and Family in Colonial Andover, Massachusetts* (Ithaca: Cornell University Press, 1970); James Henretta, "Families and Farms: *Mentalité* in Pre-Industrial America," *William and Mary Quarterly*, 3d ser., 35(1978): 3–32; Eleanor Searle, "Seigneurial Control of Women's Marriage: The Antecedents and Functions of Merchet in England," *Past and Present* 82(1979): 3–43; Ralph Trumbach, *The Rise of the Egalitarian Family: Aristocratic Kinship and Domestic Relations in Eighteenth-Century England* (New York: Academic Press, 1978); and Robert Wheaton, "Family and Kinship in Western Europe: The Problem of the Joint Family Household," *Journal of Interdisciplinary History* 5(1975): 601–626.

17. Our knowledge of inheritance customs in historical and contemporary Brazil and Portugal is still somewhat sketchy. For analyses of the different customs of inheritance in Portugal, see Caroline Brettell, "Family Legacies: An Analysis of the *Livros dos Testamentos* in a Portuguese Village, 1750–1860," paper presented to the Society for Spanish and Portuguese Historical Studies, Bloomington, Ind., April 1984; Caroline Brettell, *Men Who Migrate, Women Who Wait: Population and History in a Portuguese Parish* (Princeton: Princeton University Press, 1986); David Kertzer and Caroline Brettell, "Advances in Italian and Iberian Family History," in *Family History at the Crossroads: A Journal of Family History Reader*, ed. Tamara Hareven and Andrejs Plakans (Princeton: Princeton University Press, 1987), 87–120; Brian Juan O'Neill, "Dying and Inheriting in Rural Tras-os-Montes," *Journal of the Anthropological Society of Oxford* 14:1(1983): 44–73; and Robert Rowland, "Family and Marriage in Portugal (16th–20th Centuries): A Comparative Sketch," paper presented to the Social Science History Association, Washington, D.C., October 1983. For Brazil, see the work of Muriel Smith Nazzari, "Women, the Family and Property: The Decline of the Dowry in São Paulo, Brazil (1600–1870)," Ph.D. diss., Yale University, 1986; Margarida Maria Moura, *Os herdeiros da terra: Parentesco e herança numa área rural* (São Paulo: Editôra Hucitec, 1978); Eni de Mesquita Samara, *As mulheres, o poder, e a família: São Paulo, século XIX* (São Paulo: Editôra Marco Zero, 1989); and Metcalf, "Fathers and Sons."

18. These laws of succession can be found in liv. 4, Tit. XCVI, *Ordenações*, 954–956; liv. 4, Tit. XCI, *Ordenações*, 936; liv. 4, Tit. XCIV, *Ordenações*, 947–948.

19. See liv. 4, Tit. LXXXVIII, *Ordenações*, 927–934.

20. Liv. 4, Tit. C, *Ordenações*, 990–993.

21. Liv. 4, Tit. C, no. 5, *Ordenações*, 991.

22. The laws of inheritance for unentailed property, which applied to all property owned by commoners as well as property owned by the

nobility not specifically in morgados, are set out in liv. 4, Tit. XCVI, and liv. 4, Tit. XCVII, *Ordenações*, 954–983. Inheritance laws that differentiated between the aristocracy and the peasantry were common throughout Europe; see Goody et al., *Family and Inheritance*.

23. The laws for these two kinds of marriages are found in liv. 4, Tit. XLVI, and liv. 4, Tit. XLVII, *Ordenações*, 832–837. The laws for marriage by a *carta de ametade* (charter of halves) are quite clear, while those for marriage by a contract of *dote e arras* (dowry and bride gift) are less clear. From the law code alone, it is difficult to ascertain how the marriage contract might have been used. But further evidence helps to clarify the use of the contract of dowry and bride gift. The forms used by notaries to draw up such marriages, for example, make it clear that there would be no joint ownership of family property in such marriages and that the wife had no rights to her husband's property, or to that of her children, if he should die before her. The groom obligated himself to pay his wife a monthly sum for her maintenance (the arras, or bride gift), and after his death, his heirs had to continue these payments until his widow died. According to Maria Beatriz Nizza da Silva, who reproduces the model for the contract used by notaries in *Sistema de casamento*, 98–99, the contract of dowry and bride gift characterized marriages among the nobility, for they used it to protect property and to prevent its division. The commoners, however, sought to join property together to create a viable base for a new family.

24. Liv. 4, Tit. LXXXII, *Ordenações*, 911–915, and liv. 4, Tit. XCI, no. 1, *Ordenações*, 936.

25. Liv. 4, Tit. XCVII, *Ordenações*, 968–983, esp. nos. 1, 3, 4, 5, 6, 14, 15.

26. Liv. 4, Tit. C, *Ordenações*, 990–993.

27. The natural children were those born in a state of nature and were different from spurious children, who had no inheritance rights. See above, 70–74. Liv. 4, Tit. XCIII, no. 1, *Ordenações*, 942–943.

28. Liv. 4, Tit. XCIII, *Ordenações*, 939–943.

29. In "Women and Means: Women and Family Property in Colonial Brazil," *Journal of Social History* 24(1990): 277–298, I explore the legal inheritance from Rome and how law and custom affected women and property in Brazil.

30. While entailed estates were common among the nobility of colonial Mexico, they appear to have been rare in Brazil; see Stuart Schwartz, *Sugar Plantations and the Formation of Brazilian Society: Bahia, 1550–1835* (Cambridge: Cambridge University Press, 1985), 292. One morgado established in Brazil was the sugar mill of Sergipe do Conde with its lands and slaves, which was placed in a morgado by Mem de Sá, the first governor of Brazil, according to his will of 1569. See Instituto do Açúcar e do Alcool, *Documentos para a história do açúcar*, Vol. 3, "Engenho Sergipe do Conde, Espólio de Mem de Sá (1569–1579)" (Rio de Janeiro: Serviço Especial de Documentação Histórica, 1963), 6–8.

31. I found no marriage contracts for couples in Parnaíba. Nizza da Silva, in *Sistema de casamento*, 98, calls marriage by contract in São Paulo

extremely rare. It also appears to have been rare elsewhere in Brazil. One example of a marriage governed by a marriage contract was that between the daughter of Mem de Sá (see n. 28), who inherited the morgado of the Sergipe do Conde sugar mill, and her husband. See Contract of Dowry and Bridegift of D. Filipa de Sá and D. Fernando de Noronha, 1573, *Documentos para a história do açúcar*, 311–321.

32. Stuart Schwartz illustrates that the sugar planters of Bahia and Pernambuco had a similar problem, since they too had to divide their property equally among their children. See *Sugar Plantations*, 287–294.

33. See my discussion of natural children and inheritance, chap. 3.

34. Inv. Salvador Garcia Pontes Lumbria, 1747, IPO #14,519, 685–73, AESP.

35. Inv. Jozeph Pereira Rara, 1742, IPO #14,728, 707–95, AESP.

36. Inv. P. Ignacio de Almeida Lara, 1755, IT, 532–55, AESP.

37. Inv. Daniel Rocha Franco, 1784, IT, 557–80, AESP.

38. Liv. 4, Tit. XLVIII, *Ordenações*, 837–840. See Nazzari's extensive analysis of dowries in São Paulo in the seventeenth, eighteenth, and nineteenth centuries, in "Women, the Family and Property."

39. Frei Gaspar da Madre de Deus, *Memórias para a história da Capitania de São Vicente* (Belo Horizonte: Editôra Itatiaia, 1975), 83.

40. Liv. 4, Tit. XCVII, no. 3, *Ordenações*, 972.

41. Nazzari, "Women, the Family and Property," 68–76.

42. Studies that examine the use of dowries as a means of transmitting family property are few and far between. For a theoretical discussion of dowry and a comparative analysis of its use, see Jack Goody, "Bridewealth and Dowry in Africa and Eurasia," in Jack Goody and S. J. Tambiah, *Brideprice and Dowry*, Cambridge Papers in Social Anthropology, no. 7 (Cambridge: Cambridge University Press, 1973), 1–58. Jean Yver's work illustrates the historical role of dowries in France and how they served to favor one heir (either a son or a daughter) over the others; see *Egalité entre héritiers et exclusión des enfants dotés* (Paris: Sirey, 1966). Useful studies of how dowries were used in different contexts are Stanley Chojnacki, "Dowries and Kinsmen in Early Renaissance Venice," *Journal of Interdisciplinary History* 5(1975): 571–600; Asunción Lavrin and Edith Couturier, "Dowries and Wills: A View of Women's Socioeconomic Roles in Colonial Guadalajara and Puebla, 1640–1790," *Hispanic American Historical Review* 59(1979): 280–304; Eugene H. Korth, S.J., and Della M. Flusche, "Dowry and Inheritance in Colonial Spanish America: Peninsular Law and Chilean Practice," *The Americas* 43(1987): 395–410; and Eni de Mesquita Samara, "O dote na sociedade paulista do século XIX: Legislação e evidências," in *Anais do Museu Paulista* 30(1980/81): 41–53.

43. Inv. Izabel da Cunha, 1650, IT 40:159–175. See also Inv. Manuel Pacheco Gato, 1715, IT 26:445–531, where the endowed heir elected to keep his dowry, worth 200,000 reis plus four slaves, and not enter into the inheritance, while the other heirs received a legitima worth 81,168 reis.

44. Inv. Izabel Mendes, 1633, IT 9:23–32.

45. Anastacio da Costa complained that he never received anything

from the estate of his father-in-law or mother-in-law, will, 1640, *IT* 13:219–243; Ursolo Collaço voiced a similar complaint in his will, 1644, *IT* 39:19–36. See also the inventories of Assenco Luis Grou, 1648, *IT* 36:161–176; Isabel de Barcelos, 1648, *IT* 36:219–259; Paschoal Delgado, 1650, *IT* 40:141–156; Felippe de Campos, 1682, *IT* 21:227–252; and Izabel Velha, 1699, *IT* 26:253–262, where the orphan's judge turned the property over to the widowed spouse who obligated himself or herself to pay the debts.

46. These instructions, written by a visiting judge in 1722, clearly state that the third should go toward the first dowry when it exceeded the daughter's inheritance. Other dowries were not protected by the third. This suggests that orphan's judges were ordered by the visiting judges to limit the degree to which parents could favor sons-in-law through the dowry. "Treslado dos Capitulos de Coreição do Desembargador Antonio Luis Pelleja ao Ouvidor Geral desta Comarca, 1722," LP, 89:1–8, 6066–18, AESP. Nazzari argues that the size of dowries began to decline in eighteenth-century São Paulo until they came close to the real value of an equal share (legitima); "Women, the Family and Property," 196–224.

47. Inv. Mariana Pais, 1740, IPO #14,912, 724–112, AESP. Mariana's son actually did the negotiating with her sons-in-law, thus placing the interests of his sisters above his own. Other examples where the orphan's judge used a similar procedure to give the couple with the first dowry the free third and to compensate the other heirs "from the hands of" the richly endowed sons-in-law can be found in the inventory of Escolastica Cordeira Borba, 1756, IT, 533–56, AESP.

48. Stanley Stein finds a similar ratio of land to labor in Vassouras in the nineteenth century. There the coffee planters had over half of their property invested in slaves, approximately 12 percent in land, and 10 percent in coffee bushes. See *Vassouras: A Brazilian Coffee County, 1850–1890* (Cambridge: Harvard University Press, 1957; repr. ed., New York: Atheneum, 1974), 226.

49. Reconstructed from Inv. Manoel Rodrigues Fam, 1757, IPO #14,712a, 706–94, AESP; Inv. Guilherme Antonio de Athayde, 1746, IPO #14,619, 695–83, AESP; Inv. Maria Marques de Carvalho, 1779, IPO #14,712b, 706–94, AESP; Inv. Joze Rodrigues Fam, 1787, IT, 559–82, AESP; and thirty-five households from the 1775, 1798, and 1820 censuses, MP, 125–125, 127–127, 133–133, AESP.

50. Actually Maria's heirs (her children), as Maria had already died. Her heirs were obligated to repay Maria's mother's estate for the excessive dowry received by their mother. Inv. Maria Marques de Carvalho, 1779, IPO #14,712b, 706–94, AESP.

51. The division of property in this family has been reconstructed from Silva Leme, *Genealogia Paulistana* 6:339–346; Inv. Miguel Bicudo de Brito, 1749, IPO #14,317, 669–57, AESP; Inv. Antonio Barboza Fagundes, 1777, IPO #14,486, 682–70, AESP; Inv. João Martins da Cruz, 1788, IPO #14,301, 668–56, AESP; and eighteen households from the 1775, 1798, and 1820 censuses, MP, 125–125, 127–127, and 133–133, AESP.

52. Reconstructed from Silva Leme, *Genealogia Paulistana* 6:187–199;

Inv. Antonio Francisco de Andrade, 1780, IPO #14,341, 671–59, AESP; Inv. João Franco da Cunha, 1786, IPO #14,160, 655–43, AESP; and eight households from the 1775, 1798, and 1820 censuses, MP, 125–125, 127–127, 133–133, AESP.

53. Inv. Cosme Ferreira de Meirelles, 1760, IPO #14,789, 711–99, AESP; Land Sale, 1790, LP, 56:45–46, 6061–13, AESP; Inv. Joze Pedrozo Navarro, 1794, IPO #14,726, 707–95, AESP; and six households from the 1767, 1775, 1798, and 1820 censuses, MP, 125–125, 127–127, and 133–133, AESP.

54. 1775 census, MP, 125–125, AESP.

55. Will, Bento Pais de Oliveira, 1753, IPO #14,745, 708–96, AESP. By far the majority of the bequests from the third went to women, usually kin, to be used as part of their dowries. Nazzari finds the same pattern in her work on the seventeenth and eighteenth centuries in São Paulo; see "Women, the Family and Property." In Portugal, Caroline Brettell also finds that bequests from the third tended to favor women, but there it was to reward those daughters who had taken care of their parents in their old age. See Brettell, *Men Who Migrate, Women Who Wait.*

56. The conflict between fathers and sons in the patriarchal world of colonial New England is developed by Philip Greven in *Four Generations* and by Nancy Folbre, "The Wealth of Patriarchs: Deerfield, Massachusetts, 1760–1840," *Journal of Interdisciplinary History* 2(1985): 199–220.

57. This is a common pattern throughout Latin America. See David A. Brading, *Miners and Merchants in Bourbon Mexico, 1763–1810* (Cambridge: Cambridge University Press, 1971); Susan Migden Socolow, *The Merchants of Buenos Aires, 1778–1810: Family and Commerce* (Cambridge: Cambridge University Press, 1978); and Rae Jean Dell Flory and David Grant Smith, "Bahian Merchants and Planters in the Seventeenth and Early Eighteenth Centuries," *Hispanic American Historical Review* 58(1978): 571–594.

58. Will, Manoel Rodrigues Fam, 1757, IPO #14,712a, 706–94, AESP.

59. As a result of the investigation, Policarpo was placed under house arrest in Santos but was able to secure his release and return to Parnaíba before his death. Investigation of Captain Policarpo Joaquim de Oliveira, Ordens Régias, 1:100, 282–45, AESP.

60. See my "Women and Means" for a more detailed analysis of women and property in colonial Brazil.

61. Liv. 4, Tit. CII, no. 3, *Ordenações,* 999.

62. Maria Tereza Schorer Petrone, *A lavoura canavieira em São Paulo: Expansão e declínio (1765–1851)* (São Paulo: Difusão Européia do Livro, 1968), 65–66.

63. Schwartz, *Sugar Plantations,* 304.

64. The reconstruction of what happened to Antonio Correa de Lemos Leite's property has been drawn from the following documents: Inv. Antonio Correa de Lemos Leite, 1782, IT, 556–79, AESP; land sale, 1802, LP, 85, 6065–17, AESP; and two households from the 1798 census, MP, 127–127, AESP.

5: FAMILIES OF PEASANTS

1. 1767 census of Parnaíba, MP, 125–125, AESP.

2. The peasants whom I describe in this chapter are the predecessors of the rural *caipiras* of São Paulo today. On the modern peasants of São Paulo, see Antônio Cândido's classic work, *Os parceiros do Rio Bonito: Estudo sobre o caipira paulista e a transformação dos seus meios de vida*, 5th ed. (São Paulo: Livraria Duas Cidades, 1979), as well as Lia Freitas Garcia Fukui, *Sertão e bairro rural: Parentesco e família entre sitiantes tradicionais* (São Paulo: Atica, 1979). On the historical development of the peasantry of São Paulo, see Maria Luiza Marcílio, *Caiçara: Terra e população: Estudo de demografia histórica e da história social de Ubatuba* (São Paulo: Edições Paulinas-CEDHAL, 1986), 62–71, and Maria Sylvia de Carvalho Franco, *Homens livres na ordem escravocrata*, 2d ed. (São Paulo: Atica, 1976).

3. The Morgado de Mateus to the Conde de Oeyras, 23/Dec/1766, *DI* 23:1–20.

4. Ibid.

5. See Alice P. Canabrava, "Uma economia de decadência: Os niveis de riqueza na Capitania de São Paulo 1765/67," *Revista Brasileira de Economia* 26, 4(1972): 103–104, for a discussion of sitios volantes. The Jesuits observed this style of agriculture in the sixteenth century; see Serafim Leite, *Novas páginas de história do Brasil* (São Paulo: Companhia Editôra Nacional, 1965), 26.

6. In all of the inventories from seventeenth- and eighteenth-century Parnaíba consulted for this study, only one reference to a plow appears, in an inventory from the early seventeenth century. The Morgado de Mateus constantly urged the paulistas to adopt the plow. See his letters to the captain major of Parnaíba, 30/Dec/1776, *DI* 67:37–38. On the farming techniques used by peasants in Europe, see Fernand Braudel, *Civilization and Capitalism, 15th–18th Century*, vol. 1, *The Structures of Everyday Life: The Limits of the Possible*, trans. Siân Reynolds (New York: Harper & Row, 1986), 104–182 passim.

7. Iron foundries were very old in São Vicente. In 1584, three blacksmiths worked in the town of São Paulo. In 1607, the first ironworks was established in São Vicente. See Sérgio Buarque de Holanda, *Caminhos e fronteiras* (Rio de Janeiro: Liv. José Olympio, 1957).

8. Daniel Pedro Müller, *Ensaio d'um quadro estatístico da província de São Paulo: Ordenado pelas leis provinciais de 11 de abril de 1836 e 10 de março de 1837*, Coleção Paulística, vol. 11 (São Paulo: Governo do Estado de São Paulo, 1978), 31–32.

9. Ibid., 27.

10. These averages have been drawn from several references to the amount planted and the amount harvested in the 1798 census, MP, 125–125, AESP.

11. Braudel, *The Structures of Everyday Life*, 123.

12. Ibid., 104–182, see esp. 120, 151, 161. For another, equally provoca-

236   Notes to Pages 123–127

tive discussion of "New World" and "Old World" foods, see Alfred W. Crosby, *The Columbian Exchange: Biological and Cultural Consequences of 1492* (Westport, Conn.: Greenwood Press, 1972), 165–207.

13. The "laziness" of the American Indian civilizations, particularly those still living in tribal societies, constantly amazed Europeans. Geographer Carl O. Sauer, in his discussion of the Arawak Indians of the Caribbean, accounts for this by showing how well adapted the Indians were to their environment. See Sauer, *The Early Spanish Main* (Berkeley and Los Angeles: University of California Press, 1969), 45–69.

14. According to Holanda, the monjolo existed in Iberia as well as in Asia; see *Caminhos e fronteiras*, 215–244. See also Carlos Borges Schmidt, *O milho e o monjolo: Aspectos da civilização do milho: Técnicas, utensílios, e maquinaria*, Documentário da Vida Rural, 20 (Rio de Janeiro: Ministerio da Agricultura, Serviço de Informação Agrícola, 1967), for information on corn cultivation and its techniques in Brazil.

15. According to Müller, a piece of land in São Paulo 110 meters by 55 meters yielded 100 alqueires of manioc flour (3,627 liters). Manioc produces one of the highest ratios of calories per hectare planted of any American or European crop: 9.9 million calories, compared to 7.3 for corn and rice, and 4.2 for wheat. See Crosby, *The Columbian Exchange*, 175.

16. "Quadrimestre de Maio a Setembro de 1554, de Piratininga," in José de Anchieta, *Cartas: Informações, fragmentos históricos, e sermões* (Belo Horizonte: Editôra Itatiaia, 1988), 53.

17. This attitude was deeply rooted in São Paulo, as can be seen in the seventeenth-century inventories that evaluate fields of corn, cotton, and wheat, not the actual land. See above, chap. 2.

18. Land grant to Paschoal Fernandes de Sampayo, 1783, Patentes e Sesmarias 22:56v–57v. See also "Cópia do parágrafo respeito às sesmarias," 4/Nov/1799, Ofícios Diversos, TC–1799, 355–105, AESP, which reinforces the right of the first settlers to the lands they cultivate, irrespective of subsequent sesmarias that might include their lands.

19. Land Grant Petition, Anna Maria Xavier Pinto da Silva, 1786, Requerimentos para Sesmarias, 82–4–30, 325, AESP. See also Marcílio's discussion of squatters' rights in *Caiçara*, 62–71.

20. Research by modern sociologists on the peasantry of São Paulo in the twentieth century similarly underscores the relative equality between men and women. Fukui writes that in Laranjeiras in 1964, "it is the general opinion of the rural neighborhood that women can work as much as men and understand farming as much as they do." *Sertão e bairro rural*, 151.

21. Again, modern research underscores the importance of children to peasant families today. In Laranjeiras, "childhood lasts only a short time and never extends past the age of six or seven years, the age at which children become responsible for the jobs given to them. Fukui, *Sertão e bairro rural*, 153.

22. See Berkner's fascinating account of the use of servants in eighteenth-century Austrian peasant families in "The Stem Family and the

Developmental Cycle of the Peasant Household: An Eighteenth-Century Austrian Example," *American Historical Review* 77(1972): 398–418.

23. José Arouche de Toledo Rendon, "Reflexões sobre o estado em que se acha a agricultura na capitania de São Paulo," *DI* 44:195–213. Other allusions to these workdays sometimes appear in documents that inadvertently describe the daily lives of peasants. For example, in 1816, an investigation conducted by the justice of the peace into the beating of Francisco da Penha reveals that Antonio de Gois Leme was on his way to Itú to buy some cane brandy and molasses for a workday (ajuntamento) to hoe his field when he witnessed a crime (LP, 98:33–34, 6068–20, AESP). Another investigation into a crime committed in 1790 reveals that kin worked with each other on each other's farms. When the justice of the peace investigated the assault of Joze Leme, he learned that Joze was working with his brother-in-law hoeing his field when three men came up, attacked him, and stole the medallions from around his neck (LP, 152:3–5, 6077–29, AESP).

24. The practice of mutual aid, or *multirão*, among Brazil's modern peasantry has been discussed by sociologists and anthropologists. See Fukui, *Sertão e bairro rural*, 166, and Cândido, *Os parceiros do Rio Bonito*, 67–71.

25. Helen G. Dominian, *Apostle of Brazil: The Biography of Padre José de Anchieta, S.J.* (New York: Exposition Press, 1958), 88.

26. Fukui, *Sertão e bairro rural*, 166. See also descriptions from the nineteenth century in Cândido, *Os parceiros do Rio Bonito*, 67, and Franco, *Homens livres*, 29–40.

27. "rendido dos pistos."

28. The Morgado de Mateus had a good deal of trouble recruiting men for his various military objectives. The paulistas did not like to enlist in the royal troops and constantly thwarted his attempts to build up these companies. Perhaps the ailments of the adult men of Parnaíba are other examples of ruses to avoid military service.

29. I have found few references to "by favor" in the historical literature. Maria Thereza Schorer Petrone, in *A lavoura canavieira em São Paulo: Expansão e declínio (1765–1851)* (São Paulo: Difusão Européia do Livro, 1968), 55–56, notes that it referred to cultivating freely, without legal title. She also notes that it was most common among those who planted foodstuffs.

30. Land Arrangements, João Ribeiro et al., 1784, Ofícios Diversos, TC–1784, 355–105, AESP.

31. 1775 census, MP, 125–125, AESP.

32. 1775 census, MP, 125–125, AESP; land sale 1796, LP, 57:83–84, 6061–13, AESP. A landowning census of São Paulo taken in the early nineteenth century, the Bens Rusticos, also shows the importance of occupation (*posse*) as a means to acquire legal title to land. Unfortunately, the Bens Rusticos have been lost for Parnaíba as well as for the city of São Paulo. The remaining parts of the census are housed in the AESP. For an

analysis of this census, see Alice Canabrava, "A repartição da terra na Capitania de São Paulo, 1818," *Estudos Econômicos* 2, 6(1972): 77–129.

33. 1775 census, MP, 125–125, AESP.

34. See, above, the example of João Leite de Lima.

35. 1775 census, MP, 125–125, AESP.

36. Inv. Anna Leme do Prado, 1771, IPO #14,751, 709–97, AESP; the heirs of Sipriana Gil made a similar decision, see her inventory, 1770, IPO #14,794, 712–100, AESP.

37. The records for the lands rented by the mother church (igreja matriz) of Parnaíba are found in Livro de Lançamento da Fabrica da Igreja, LP, 72, 6063–15, AESP; those rented by the town council are found in Foros de Terrenos, 1724–1828, LP, 89:40–87, 6066–18, AESP. While references appear in inventories to lands rented from the Indian community, Bauerí, I have not been able to find the actual account books.

38. "Relação dos bens aprehendidos e confiscados aos Padres Jesuitas," 13/Dec/1762, *DI* 44:339–378.

39. São Bento Monastery, Chapel of St. Antonio, 1775 census, MP, 125–125, AESP.

40. Historians and sociologists use the term "family cycle" to refer to the changes that take place in family life over time. These cycles are affected by demography and family customs. Scholars believe that families of similar regions, classes, and ethnicities share common family cycles; see Tamara Hareven, "The Family as Process: The Historical Study of the Family Cycle," *Journal of Social History* 7(1974): 322–329.

41. 1767, 1775, and 1798 censuses, MP, 125–125, 127–127, AESP.

42. Lutz Berkner observes that where land is available, nuclear families tend to be the rule, whereas where land tenure is limited, complex households are more common. See "Inheritance, Land Tenure, and Peasant Family Structure: A German Regional Comparison," in *Family and Inheritance: Rural Society in Western Europe, 1200–1800*, eds. Jack Goody, Joan Thirsk, and E. P. Thompson (Cambridge: Cambridge University Press, 1976), 71–95. See also Robert Wheaton's analysis of the joint family in "Family and Kinship in Western Europe: The Problem of the Joint Family Household," *Journal of Interdisciplinary History* 5(1975): 601–628.

43. 1767, 1775, and 1798 censuses, MP, 125–125, 127–127, AESP.

44. Census of 1775, MP, 125–125, AESP.

45. Ibid.

46. Iguatemí was a frontier outpost and fort constructed by the Morgado de Mateus to protect Portugal's claim to the western boundary of Brazil. Located in the old Jesuit mission territory of Guairá, Iguatemí was deliberately close to Spanish settlements in Paraguay, and it became a bone of contention between Spain and Portugal. The Morgado, determined to keep Iguatemí a viable settlement so that Portugal could claim the region, according to the principle of *uti possedetis*, constantly demanded supplies from the captain majors of São Paulo, as well as men to staff the fort and families to colonize the town. See Dauril Alden, *Royal*

Government in Colonial Brazil: With Special Reference to the Administration of the Marquis of Lavradio, Viceroy, 1769–1779 (Berkeley and Los Angeles: University of California Press, 1968), 462–471; and Kathleeen Joan Higgins, "Iguatemí: A Brazilian Frontier Community, 1767–1777," M. A. thesis, University of Texas, Austin, 1980.

47. Census of 1775, MP, 125–125, AESP.

48. The Morgado regularly demanded that the captain majors of towns like Parnaíba supply him with food. See his letters to Parnaíba and Baruerí demanding food, men, and couples to colonize Iguatemí in *DI* 5:25, 55, 104; 6:68, 91, 117, 178; 8:7, 96, 149.

49. Inv. Francisco de Oliveira Gago, 1755, and Inv. Anna Leme do Prado, 1771, both in IPO #14,751, 709–97, AESP.

50. Baptismal records, 1775, LPS, ACDJ.

51. Mauricio da Rocha Campos vs. Francisco Joze de Paula, 1780, LP, 97:36–41, 6068–20, AESP, and households from the 1775 census, MP, 125–125, AESP.

52. The Morgado de Mateus to the Conde de Oeyras, 23/Dec/1766, *DI* 23:1–10.

53. The Morgado expanded the local militia (ordenança) and created a provincial militia, the auxiliares; see above, chap. 4, n. 1.

54. The Morgado de Mateus to the captain majors of Itú, Parnaíba, Sorocaba, Jundiaí, Mogi, Taubaté, Jacarei, Guaratinguetá, Iguape, São Sebastião, Ubatuba, and São Paulo, 3/July/1765, *DI* 72:27–28.

55. Order of the Morgado de Mateus, 6/Nov/1765, *DI* 65:25–26.

56. The king to the Morgado de Mateus, 22/July/1766, Avisos e Cartas Régias, 1765–1767, 145, 426–62, AESP.

57. Ibid.

58. Martim Lopes Lobo de Saldanha to Policarpo Joaquim de Oliveira, 26/Dec/1775, *DI* 84:59.

59. Investigation of Policarpo Joaquim de Oliveira, 1779, Ordens Régias 282–45, 1:100, AESP.

60. Ibid.

61. Land sales, LP, 56:28–29 and 67–68, 6061–13, AESP; LP, 57:40–41 and 83–84, 6061–13, AESP; LP, 81:40, 6064–16, AESP; LP, 85:np, 6065–17, AESP.

62. Inv. Mariana Dias, 1776, IT, 553–76, AESP; and Inv. Anna Moreira, 1789, IPO #14,241, 662–50, AESP.

63. Investigation of Policarpo Joaquim de Oliveira, 1801, SP 3865, AHU.

64. Investigation of Policarpo Joaquim de Oliveira, 1801, SP 3865, AHU; Sesmaria of Policarpo Joaquim de Oliveira, 1802, Patentes e Sesmarias 13:1–2, AESP.

65. Land sale, 1799, LP, 85:np, 6065–17, AESP (the land actually changed hands in 1775); two households from the 1775 and 1798 censuses, MP, 125–125, 127–127, AESP.

66. 1820 census, MP, 133–133, AESP.

67. 1775, 1798, and 1820 censuses, MP, 125–125, 127–127, and 133–133, AESP.

68. The Morgado de Mateus promoted the production of cotton in São Paulo, and as a result, many peasants began to grow the crop in the late eighteenth century. This gave rise to the cottage industry of spinning and weaving found in all paulista towns by the end of the eighteenth century.

69. Petition of Domingos Francisco Pires et al., 1819, Requerimentos, 4:28, 342–93A, AESP.

70. Ibid.

71. Baptismal Records, 1775 and 1820, LPS, ACDJ.

72. The abundance of female-headed households in 1820 was not peculiar to Parnaíba itself but was common throughout São Paulo. By the very end of the eighteenth century, large numbers of women lived in the town centers of many towns like Parnaíba. See the manuscript censuses of Guaratinguetá, Ubatuba, and São Paulo, MP, AESP. In the city of São Paulo, matrifocal households were particularly apparent; see Maria Odila Leite Silva Dias, *Quotidiano e poder em São Paulo no século XIX—Ana Gertrudes de Jesus* (São Paulo: Brasiliense, 1984), and Eni de Mesquita Samara, *As mulheres, o poder, e a família: São Paulo, século XIX* (São Paulo: Marco Zero, 1989). Elizabeth Kuznesof has linked the large numbers of female-headed households in the city of São Paulo to early stages of modernization, arguing that women were part of a valuable and growing cottage industry. See "The Role of the Female-Headed Household in Brazilian Modernization: São Paulo, 1765 to 1836," *Journal of Social History* 13(1980): 589–613.

73. 1775, 1798, and 1820 censuses, MP, 125–125, 127–127, 133–133, AESP.

74. This phenomenon leads Maxine Margolis to describe a "moving frontier" in Brazil. See her study of peasants in Paraná in 1967–1968 in *The Moving Frontier: Social and Economic Change in a Southern Brazilian Community* (Gainesville: University of Florida Press, 1973).

75. Felis Soares, described above, appeared in the 1775 and 1798 censuses without any color classification, an indication that he was not considered "brown," "black," or Indian. In the 1820 census, however, he appears as pardo, "brown."

76. See the work of Maria Sylvia de Carvalho Franco who emphasizes the violence and competition between peasants of nineteenth-century São Paulo in *Homens livres,* 20–59.

77. Not only did he beat her but at least four men testified that he poisoned her with a "purgative" from which she died. João Montes Ferreira vs. João Duarte de Moura, 1806, LP, 98:np, 6068–20, AESP.

78. Floriana Maria vs. Izabel Leme, 1805, LP, 98:np, 6068–20, AESP.

79. Petition of Anna Maria de Oliveira, 1819, Requerimentos 3:60, 342–93A, AESP.

80. The controversy began when Antonio decided to open a field near João's barn, and on a windy day, without informing João, he burned the

field and inadvertently set fire to the barn. Petition of João Francisco Pais, 1816, Requerimentos, 3:8, 342–93A, AESP.

81. For an interesting comparative analysis of the importance of subsistence agriculture in Brazil in the nineteenth century, see Hebe Maria Mattos de Castro, "Beyond Masters and Slaves: Subsistence Agriculture as a Survival Strategy in Brazil during the Second Half of the Nineteenth Century," *Hispanic American Historical Review* 68(1988): 461–489.

82. Muriel Nazzari finds that the amount of money awarded in dowries in the nineteenth century declined from what women had received in the seventeenth and eighteenth centuries. But since the number of dowries granted increased, it seems likely that peasants began to grant dowries to their daughters to influence who they married. See Nazzari, "Women, the Family and Property: The Decline of the Dowry in São Paulo, Brazil (1600–1870)," Ph.D. diss., Yale University, 1986. On the inheritance strategies used by modern peasants in Brazil, see Margarida Maria Moura, *Os herdeiros da terra: Parentesco e herança numa área rural* (São Paulo: Editôra Hucitec, 1978).

83. See Marcílio, *Caiçara*, where the peasant farmers and fishermen of Ubatuba lost their lands as tourism rapidly inflated beachfront property; Stanley J. Stein, *Vassouras: A Brazilian Coffee County, 1850–1890* (Cambridge: Harvard University Press, 1957, repr. ed., New York: Atheneum, 1974); and Warren Dean, *Rio Claro: A Brazilian Plantation System, 1820–1920* (Stanford: Stanford University Press, 1976), describe how peasants lost lands to coffee growers. This process is so widespread in Brazil that it even can be seen in literature; see Jorge Amado's famous novel, *Terras do semfim* (Rio de Janeiro: Livraria Martins Editôra, 1943), published in English as *The Violent Land*.

6: FAMILIES OF SLAVES

1. Inv. Mariana Dias, 1776, IT, 553–76, AESP.

2. Inv. Antonio Correa de Lemos Leite, 1782, IT, 556–79, AESP. Two of Antonio's sons-in-law, upset that he had thereby reduced the inheritances their wives would receive, petitioned the orphan's judge to disallow the slave freedoms. They would have accepted the slave freedoms if their father-in-law had written a will, they argued, but since Antonio had died intestate, he had no third to distribute as he wished. Therefore, they maintained that Antonio's executor could not free the slaves.

3. 1798 census, MP, 127–127, AESP.

4. Barry Higman, "The Slave Family and Household in the British West Indies, 1800–1834," *Journal of Interdisciplinary History* 6(1975): 261–287. Allan Kulikoff makes a similar point in *Tobacco and Slaves: The Development of Southern Cultures in the Chesapeake, 1680–1800* (Chapel Hill: University of North Carolina Press, 1986), 355–360.

5. Inv. André de Goes Leme, 1738, IT, 516–39, AESP. See Kathleen J. Higgins, "The Slave Society in Eighteenth-Century Sabará: A Community

Study in Colonial Brazil," Ph.D. diss., Yale University, 1987, for a discussion of the strategies developed by slaves in the mining frontier.

6. IT, 535–58, AESP.

7. Inv. Manoel Correa Penteado, 1745, IPO #14,406, 676–64, AESP.

8. Richard Graham, "Slave Families of a Rural Estate in Colonial Brazil," *Journal of Social History* 9(1976): 382–402.

9. Stuart Schwartz, *Sugar Plantations in the Formation of Brazilian Society: Bahia, 1550–1835* (Cambridge: Cambridge University Press, 1985), 395–399.

10. Herbert Gutman, *The Black Family in Slavery and Freedom* (New York: Pantheon Books, 1976), 45–61.

11. Mary Karasch, *Slave Life in Rio de Janeiro, 1808–1850* (Princeton: Princeton University Press, 1987), 287–298. See also, Barry W. Higman, *Slave Populations of the British Caribbean, 1807–1834* (Baltimore: Johns Hopkins University Press, 1984), 226–259.

12. Inv. André de Goes Leme, 1738, IT, 516–39, AESP.

13. This is one of the reasons John Blassingame argues that in the United States South, the "plantation was unique in the New World because it permitted the development of a monogamous slave family." *The Slave Community: Plantation Life in the Antebellum South*, 2d ed. (New York: Oxford University Press, 1979), 149.

14. These brotherhoods had formed at the end of the eighteenth century. They cared for altars in the church, loaned out monies to their members, and secured the right for their members to be buried in the church, as was the custom in Brazil. Book of Records, Church of Santana de Parnaíba, liv. 524:117; 123–125, ACDJ; Brotherhood of Our Lady of Good Death of Slaves and Free Blacks, liv. 530, ACDJ.

15. See Gutman's introduction to *The Black Family*. While Gutman criticizes those who have argued that the slave family was predominantly matrifocal, he does admit that matrifocal families were one type of slave family structure; ibid., 115–116. For a critique of the matrifocal hypothesis in studies of Brazilian slavery, see Robert Slenes, "Escravidão e família: Padrões de casamento e estabilidade familiar numa comunidade escrava (Campinas, século XIX)," *Estudos Econômicos* 17, 2(1987): 221–222.

16. Higman discusses the existence of polygamous families in the Caribbean in *Slave Population and Economy in Jamaica, 1807–1834* (Cambridge: Cambridge University Press, 1976), 165–171. He believes that the predominant family types for slaves in Jamaica were, first, solitary households, second, nuclear families, and third, extended families; ibid., 168. He discounts the importance of the matrifocal family. In Brazil, where slaves did sometimes accumulate wealth in the cities, polygamous families may have formed.

17. According to Kulikoff, "No slaves enjoyed the security of legal marriage" in the tobacco-growing region of the Chesapeake in the eighteenth century; *Tobacco and Slaves*, 353. Higman states that Anglican and Catholic priests performed "relatively few marriages" in the British Caribbean but

that Moravian and Wesleyan missionaries did emphasize the importance of marriage; see *Slave Populations of the British Caribbean*, 369–370.

18. Slave marriage, 1737, LPS, ACDJ.

19. 1820 census, MP, 133–133, AESP; Land Rentals, LP, 89:84, 6066–18, AESP.

20. In Bahia, Schwartz finds a similar pattern; in one parish, 21% of the marriages involving slaves occurred to free persons; see *Sugar Plantations*, 392.

21. Marriage of Bento Francisco Vieira, 1801, LPS, ACDJ.

22. For example, Antonio da Silva, a free mulatto married to Domingas, a slave, freed his three-year-old daughter Juliana for 38,400 reis in 1780. Slave Freedom, LP, 81:np, 6064–16, AESP.

23. Inv. Manoel Correa Penteado, 1745, IPO #14,406, 676–64, AESP; Inv. Rodrigo Bicudo Chassim, 1743, IPO #14,648, 698–86, AESP; Inv. Domingos Rodrigues de Fonseca Leme, 1738, IPO #15,085, 740–128, AESP; see also the estate of Angela Ribeira Leite, 1749, IPO #14,584, 692–80, AESP.

24. Elsewhere, I have reported that marriages between slaves of different masters reached 13%. This figure was based on the inclusion of marriages between slaves and administrados, who also might belong to different masters. I have eliminated these marriages in this analysis of slave marriages. See Metcalf, "Families of Planters, Peasants, and Slaves: Strategies for Survival in Santana de Parnaíba, 1720–1820," Ph.D. diss.: University of Texas, Austin, 1983, 181, and "Vida familiar dos escravos em São Paulo no século dezoito: O caso de Santana de Parnaíba," *Estudos Econômicos* 17(1987): 238.

25. This is a major difference between slavery in Brazil and slavery in the United States. In the U.S. South, "broad marriages" were not uncommon. These were marriages of slaves who lived on different estates in the same region and who were allowed to travel to visit their spouses. See Gutman, *The Black Family*, 131–142 passim, and Kulikoff, *Tobacco and Slaves*, 352–380. Slenes finds a low incidence of marriages between slaves of different masters in Campinas, a coffee-growing region of nineteenth-century São Paulo; see "Escravidão e família," 220. Schwartz finds no evidence of it in Bahia; *Sugar Plantations*, 383.

26. Inv. Angela Ribeira Leite, 1749, IPO #14,584, 692–80, AESP.

27. Other slaves who married slaves belonging to different masters similarly appear to have married slaves who belonged to masters who were related to their own masters. When Victorino married Roza, the priest noted that he belonged to Andreza Buena and she to Antonio Bueno de Azevedo. Manoel and Francisco, who belonged to Antonio Correa de Barros, married two Marias who belonged to Maria Xavier de Barros. It would appear, then, that most of the slaves who married off of their masters' estates married slaves belonging to the same extended white family. These slaves may not have lived very far apart, and families may have ex-

changed slaves to allow them to see each other for extended periods. Slave Marriages, LPS, ACDJ.

28. Inv. Agostinha Rodrigues, 1757, IT, 534–57, AESP.

29. Inv. Barbara Pais de Queiroz, 1761, IT, 539–62, AESP.

30. For example, the mulatto slave Bento (6 years old), Maria (3 years old), Antonio (3 years old), Ricardo (5 months), and Manoel (6 months) were all freed by their fathers or probable fathers in the 1780s and 1790s. See Slave Freedoms, LP, 85, 56, 57, 6061–13, 6065–17, AESP.

31. Slave Freedom, LP, 85, 3/Dec/1800, 6065–17, AESP.

32. Gutman, *The Black Family*, 60–67; Slenes, "Escravidão e família," 220.

33. Will, Rev. Felippe de Santiago Xavier, 1793, Testamentos 6:2–8, 456–2, AESP.

34. Travelers to Brazil described these slave barracks. Iraci del Nero da Costa has collected many of their descriptions in "Os viagantes estrangeiros e a família escrava no Brasil," *Leitura*, São Paulo 7(77) October 1988:9–10.

35. Inv. Manoel Correa Penteado, 1745, IPO #14,406, 676–64, AESP.

36. Inv. Angela Ribeira Leite, 1749, IPO #14,584, 692–80, AESP.

37. Gutman, *The Black Family*, 123–139. João Luis R. Fragoso and Manolo G. Florentino argue, based on their analysis of large slave properties in Rio de Janeiro in the nineteenth century (estates with more than 100 slaves), that slave families were able to weather the storm of inheritance and maintain family ties. They also suggest that masters, especially those who owned large estates, purchased slave families. See "Marcelino, filho de Inocência crioula, neto de Joana cabinda: Um estudo sobre famílias escravas em Paraíba do Sul (1835–1872)," *Estudos Econômicos* 17, 2(1987): 151–173. To what extent they mean *whole* families were able to remain together, or merely *some* individuals of a family, is still not clear.

38. Petition of Mariana, 1816, Requerimentos 72–2–58, 313, AESP.

39. Jailer's Ledger, LP, 48:34–34v, 6060–12, AESP.

40. This history of the Araçariguama estate has been reconstructed from the following sources: report of Manoel da Costa Couto, notary of the sequestration of Jesuit properties, *DI* 84:151–153; Town Council of Parnaíba to the Crown, 1815, São Paulo 3865, AHU; inventory of the Araçariguama estate, 1815, cod. 481:203–221, AN.

41. See, for example, Florestan Fernandes, *A integração do negro na sociedade de classes* (São Paulo: Dominus, Editôra da Universidade de São Paulo, 1965). While an earlier generation of American historians also held this view, as, for example, E. Franklin Frazier, *The Negro Family in the United States*, rev. ed. (New York: Dryden Press, 1948), contemporary historians of slavery emphasize that within the confines of slavery, slaves were able to fashion their own family lives. Examples of these American historians include Gutman, Blassingame, and Kulikoff, and for Brazil, Schwartz, Slenes, and Graham.

42. Here I follow the models of slave family and community life de-

veloped by Eugene Genovese, *Roll, Jordan, Roll: The World the Slaves Made* (New York: Pantheon Books, 1974), and Gutman, *The Black Family*. Genovese emphasizes the vertical ties that slaves had with their masters, ties that developed because of the patriarchal and paternalistic character of slavery; Gutman focuses his attention on the horizontal connections slaves had with other slaves, arguing that the essence of slave family and community life took place in a world separate from that of the masters. I do not find these views mutually exclusive, for slaves survived by learning how to interact with their masters and with other slaves.

43. Carl N. Degler discusses the comparison between the freed slaves in Brazil and the United States in *Neither Black nor White: Slavery and Race Relations in Brazil and the United States* (New York: Macmillan, 1971), 39–47, and concludes that while slaves could and did receive their freedom in the United States, in Brazil, they stood a better chance of being freed or purchasing their freedom.

44. Slave Freedom, LP, 81:39, 6064–16, AESP.

45. Ibid., LP, 85:np, 6065–17, AESP.

46. Ibid., LP, 57:42–43, 6061–13, AESP.

47. Ibid., LP, 81:np, 6064–16, AESP.

48. Ibid., LP, 85:np, 6065–17, AESP.

49. Ibid., LP, 75:68–69, 6061–13, AESP.

50. This was a common pattern in Brazil. See Peter L. Eisenberg, "Ficando livre: As alforrias em Campinas no século XIX," *Estudos Econômicos* 17(1987): 175–216, and James P. Kiernan, "The Manumission of Slaves in Colonial Brazil: Paraty, 1789–1822," Ph.D. diss., New York University, 1976.

51. Slave Freedom, LP, 85:np, 6065–17, AESP.

52. Ibid., LP, 57:8, 6061–13, AESP.

53. Ibid., LP, 85:np, 6061–17; LP, 56:11–12, 6061–13, AESP.

54. Ibid., LP, 57:68–69, 6061–13, AESP; LP, 85:np, 6065–16, AESP.

55. Petition of Francisco, Requerimentos, 72–3–37, 313, AESP.

56. Ibid., and 1820 census, MP, 133–133, AESP.

57. Ibid.

58. Inv. Antonio Correa de Lemos Leite, 1782, IT, 556–79, AESP.

59. Petition of Maximiano Antonio, 1820, Requerimentos, 72–3–52, 313, AESP.

60. Most witnesses at slave marriages were other slaves, but free blacks, Indians, and masters also witnessed these events. For example, Sergeant Major Luis Pedroso de Barros served as one of the witnesses at the marriage of his slaves, Francisco and Dezideria. Slave Marriage, 1728, LPS, ACDJ.

61. Gudeman and Schwartz, "Cleansing Original Sin: Godparenthood and the Baptism of Slaves in Eighteenth-Century Bahia," in *Kinship Ideology and Practice in Latin America*, ed. Raymond T. Smith (Chapel Hill: University of North Carolina Press, 1984), 40.

62. Baptism of Caetano, 1820, LPS, ACDJ. It was not uncommon for a

man to stand in for the priest and baptize babies in extremis—those judged near death.

63. Gudeman and Schwartz, "Cleansing Original Sin."

64. Slave baptisms on 4/11, 7/17, and 8/26, 1798, and 4/9, 4/13, and 11/21, 1820, LPS, ACDJ. Gudeman and Schwartz find the same pattern in Bahia; see "Cleansing Original Sin."

65. Gudeman and Schwartz find that 20% of the godparents of baptized slaves were slaves, 10% former slaves, and 70% free persons; "Cleansing Original Sin," 45.

66. Jailer's Ledger, LP, 133, 6074–26, AESP.

67. Francisco Cruz vs. Rodrigo Joze de Barros, LP, 98:38–40, 6068–20, AESP.

68. Each of the riots was investigated by legal authorities in *devassas*, but I have not been able to find them or any other trial records that pertain to those accused of crimes and sent to the jail in Parnaíba. The only records that we have, therefore, are the entries made by the jailers when the prisoners arrived at the jail. Jailer's Ledger, LP, 133, 6074–26, AESP.

69. Jailer's Ledger, LP, 133, 6074–26, AESP.

70. Governor of São Paulo to Rodrigo Bicudo Chassim, 1775, *DI* 70:25.

71. Captain major of Parnaíba to the governor of São Paulo, 1820, Ordenanças 2:41, 295–57, AESP.

72. Governor of São Paulo to the captain major of Parnaíba, 1775, *DI* 84:51.

73. Land Grant Petition, Anna Maria Xavier Pinto da Silva, 1786, Patentes e Sesmarias, 22:111, AESP.

74. Inv. Agostinha Rodrigues, 1757, IT, 534–57, AESP.

75. Inv. Baltazar Rodrigues Fam, 1758, IT, 536–59, AESP.

76. Jailer's Ledger, LP, 133, 6074–26, AESP.

CONCLUSION: FAMILY AND FRONTIER
AT INDEPENDENCE

1. Leslie Bethell, "The Independence of Brazil," in *The Cambridge History of Latin America*, 3:157–196, ed. Leslie Bethell (Cambridge: Cambridge University Press, 1985), 170.

2. Bethell, "The Independence of Brazil"; A. H. de Oliveira Marques, *History of Portugal*, 2d ed. (New York: Columbia University Press, 1976), 455–457.

3. Bethell, "The Independence of Brazil," 180–183; Oliveira Marques, *History of Portugal*, 429–430, 458–459.

4. Richard M. Morse, *From Community to Metropolis: A Biography of São Paulo, Brazil* (Gainesville: University of Florida Press, 1958), 45–58.

5. Raymundo Faoro, *Os donos do poder: Formação do patronato político brasileiro*, 2 vols., 5th ed. (Porto Alegre: Editôra Globo, 1979), 1:139–240.

6. Faoro, *Os donos do poder*, 1:221–234; Fernando A. Novais, *Portugal e*

Brasil na crise do antigo sistema colònial (1777–1808) (São Paulo: Editôra Hucitec, 1979).

7. In *Os donos do poder*, Faoro argues that the bandeirantes were agents of imperial·policy and control; see vol. 1:146–165.

8. Heloisa Liberalli Bellotto, *Autoridade e conflito no Brasil colonial: O governo do Morgado de Mateus em São Paulo (1765–1775)* (São Paulo: Conselho Estadual de Artes e Ciências Humanas, 1979), 251–261.

9. Gilberto Freyre, *The Masters and the Slaves [Casa-Grande & Senzala]: A Study in the Development of Brazilian Civilization*, trans. Samuel Putnam, 2d ed. rev. (New York: Knopf, 1966), 26.

10. Emilia Viotti da Costa, *The Brazilian Empire: Myths and Histories* (Chicago: University of Chicago Press, 1985), 20–23.

11. See Warren Dean, *Rio Claro: A Brazilian Plantation System 1820–1920* (Stanford: Stanford University Press, 1976), and Stanley J. Stein, *Vassouras: A Brazilian Coffee County, 1850–1890* (Cambridge: Harvard University Press, 1957; repr. New York: Atheneum, 1974), for a clear description of the expansion of coffee in São Paulo and Rio de Janeiro in the nineteenth century.

12. See Katia M. de Queirós Mattoso, *To be a Slave in Brazil, 1550–1888*, trans. Arthur Goldhammer (New Brunswick: Rutgers University Press, 1986), for a more thorough discussion of the abolition of Brazilian slavery in the nineteenth century.

13. See João José Reis, "Slave Rebellion in Brazil: The African Muslim Uprising in Bahia, 1835" Ph.D. diss., University of Minnesota, 1982, 57–123.

14. Costa, *The Brazilian Empire*, 78–93.

Bibliography

ARCHIVES AND MANUSCRIPT COLLECTIONS

Arquivo da Cúria Diocesana de Jundiaí (ACDJ)
    Livros Paroquiais de Santana de Parnaíba
Arquivo da Cúria Metropolitana de São Paulo (ACMSP)
    Divórcios
Arquivo do Estado de São Paulo (AESP)
    Inventários do Primeiro Ofício
    Inventários e Testamentos
    Livros de Parnaíba
    Mapas de População
    Requerimentos
    Sesmarias
Arquivo Histórico Ultramarino, Lisbon (AHU)
    São Paulo
Arquivo Nacional, Rio de Janeiro (AN)
Arquivo da Torre do Tombo, Lisbon (ATT)

PUBLISHED PRIMARY SOURCES

Almeida, Candido Mendes de. *Codigo Phillipino, ou Ordenações e leis do reino de Portugal, recopilados por mandado d'el Rey D. Phillipe I.* 24th ed. Rio de Janeiro: 1870; repr. ed., Lisbon: Fundação Calouste Gulbenkian, 1985.
Anchieta, José de. *Cartas: Informações, fragmentos históricos, e sermões.* Belo Horizonte: Editôra Itatiaia, 1988.
Andrada, Martim Francisco Ribeiro de. "Jornaes das viagems pela Capitania de São Paulo." In *Roteiros e noticias de São Paulo colonial: 1751–1804,* 145–163. Coleção Paulística, vol. 1. São Paulo: Governo do Estado, 1977.
Cordeiro, J. P. Leite. "Documentação sôbre o 'Capitão Mor Guilherme Pompeo de Almeida, morador que foi na vila de Parnaíba.'" *Revista do Instituto Histórico e Geográfico de São Paulo* 58: 491–549.
Departamento do Arquivo do Estado de São Paulo. *Documentos interessantes para a história e costumes de São Paulo.* São Paulo: Instituto Histórico e Geográfico de São Paulo, 1895–.
———. *Inventários e testamentos.* São Paulo: Departamento do Arquivo do Estado de São Paulo, 1920–.

————. *Boletim*. São Paulo: Departamento do Arquivo do Estado de São Paulo, 1942–1948.

————. *Sesmarias*. São Paulo: Departamento do Arquivo do Estado de São Paulo, 1921.

Instituto do Açúcar e do Alcool. *Documentos para a história do açúcar*, 3, "Engenho Sergipe do Conde, Espólio de Mem de Sá (1569–1579)." Rio de Janeiro: Serviço Especial de Documentação Histórica, 1963.

Leite, S. I. Serafim. *Novas cartas jesuíticas: De Nóbrega a Vieira*. Brasiliana, vol. 194. São Paulo: Companhia Editôra Nacional, 1940.

Leme, Luis Gonzaga da Silva. *Genealogia Paulistana*. 9 vols. São Paulo: Duprat, 1903–1905.

Müller, Daniel Pedro. *Ensaio d'um quadro estatístico da província de São Paulo: Ordenado pelas leis provinciais de 11 de abril de 1836 e 10 de março de 1837*. São Paulo, 1838; repr. ed., Coleção Paulística, vol. 11. São Paulo: Governo do Estado, 1978.

Parry, John H., and Robert G. Keith, eds. *New Iberian World: A Documentary History of the Discovery and Settlement of Latin America to the Early 17th Century*. 5 vols. New York: Times Books, 1984.

Rendon, José de Toledo. "Memória sobre as aldeias de Indios da Província de São Paulo, segundo as observações feitas no anno de 1798." In *Obras*, 37–53. Coleção Paulistica, vol. 3. São Paulo: Governo do Estado, 1978.

Saint-Hilaire, Auguste de. *Segunda viagem do Rio de Janeiro a Minas Gerais e a São Paulo (1822)*. Trans. V. Moreira. São Paulo: Livraria Itatiaia Editôra Limitada, 1974.

Valente, José Augusto Vaz. *A carta de Pero Vaz de Caminha: Estudo crítico, paleográfico-diplomático*. Colecão Museu Paulista, Série de História, vol. 3. São Paulo: Fundo de Pesquisas do Museu Paulista da Universidade de São Paulo, 1975.

PUBLISHED AND UNPUBLISHED
SECONDARY SOURCES

Adams, John W., and Alice Bee Kasakoff. "Migration and the Family in Colonial New England: The View from Genealogies." *Journal of Family History* 9(1984): 24–43.

Aguirra, João B. C. "Tombamento de 1817." *Revista do Arquivo Municipal de São Paulo* 12(1935): 77–80.

Alden, Dauril. "The Population of Brazil in the Late Eighteenth Century: A Preliminary Survey." *Hispanic American Historical Review* 43(1963): 173–205.

————. "The Growth and Decline of Indigo Production in Colonial Brazil: A Study in Comparative Economic History." *Journal of Economic History* 25(1965): 350–360.

————. *Royal Government in Colonial Brazil: With Special Reference to the*

Administration of the Marquis of Lavradio, Viceroy, 1769–1779. Berkeley and Los Angeles: University of California Press, 1968.

———. "Vicissitudes of Trade in the Portuguese Atlantic Empire During the First Half of the Eighteenth Century." *Americas* 32(1975): 282–291.

Alden, Dauril, ed. *Colonial Roots of Modern Brazil: Papers of the Newberry Library Conference.* Berkeley, Los Angeles, and London: University of California Press, 1973.

Allen, David Grayson. *In English Ways: The Movement of Societies and the Transferral of English Local Law and Custom to Massachusetts Bay in the Seventeenth Century.* Chapel Hill: Univ. of North Carolina Press, 1981.

Amaral, Antonio Barreto do. *O bairro de Pinheiros.* Série Histórica dos Bairros de São Paulo, no. 2. São Paulo: Departamento de Cultura da Secretaria de Educação e Cultura da Prefeitura do Município de São Paulo, 1969.

Antonil, André João. *Cultura e opulencia do Brasil.* 3d ed. Coleção Reconquista do Brasil, vol. 70. Belo Horizonte: Editôra Itatiaia Limitada, 1982.

Ariès, Philippe. *Centuries of Childhood: A Social History of Family Life.* Trans. Robert Baldick. New York: Knopf, 1962.

———. *The Hour of Our Death.* Trans. Helen Weaver. New York: Knopf, 1981.

Arrom, Silvia Marina. "Marriage Patterns in Mexico City, 1811." *Journal of Family History* 3(1978): 376–391.

———. *The Women of Mexico City, 1790–1857.* Stanford: Stanford University Press, 1985.

Aufderheide, Patricia Ann. "Order and Violence: Social Deviance and Social Control in Brazil, 1780–1840." Ph.D. diss., University of Minnesota, 1976.

Azevedo, Thales de. "Família, casamento e divórcio no Brasil." *Journal of Inter-American Studies* 3(1961): 213–257.

Bacellar, Carlos de Almeida Prado. "Herança em família: A partilha dos engenhos de açúcar no oeste paulista, 1765–1855." *Anais do V Encontro Nacional de Estudos Populacionais* 1(1986): 123–137.

———. "Os senhores da terra—família e sistema sucessório entre os senhores de engenho do oeste paulista, 1765–1855." M.A. thesis, University of São Paulo, 1987.

Bakewell, Peter J. *Silver Mining and Society in Colonial Mexico: Zacatecas, 1546–1700.* Cambridge: Cambridge University Press, 1971.

Balmori, Diana, Stuart F. Voss, and Miles Wortman. *Notable Family Networks in Latin America.* Chicago: University of Chicago Press, 1984.

Bazant, Jan. *Cinco haciendas Mexicanas: Tres siglos de vida rural en San Luis Potosí, 1600–1910.* Centro de Estudios Históricos, Nueva Serie 20. México: El Colegio de México, 1975.

Bellotto, Heloísa Liberalli. *Autoridade e conflito no Brasil colonial: O governo do Morgado de Mateus em São Paulo (1765–1775).* Textos e documentos, no. 36. São Paulo: Conselho Estadual de Artes e Ciências Humanas, 1979.

Bergad, Laird W. *Coffee and the Growth of Agrarian Capitalism in Nineteenth-Century Puerto Rico.* Princeton: Princeton University Press, 1983.

Berkner, Lutz K. "Rural Family Organization in Europe: A Problem in Contemporary History." *Peasant Studies Newsletter* 1(1972): 145–156.

————. "The Stem Family and the Developmental Cycle of the Peasant Household: An Eighteenth-Century Austrian Example." *American Historical Review* 77(1972): 398–418.

————. "The Use and Misuse of Census Data for the Historical Analysis of Family Structure." *Journal of Interdisciplinary History* 5(1975): 721–738.

————. "Household Arithmetic: A Note." *Journal of Family History* 2(1977): 159–163.

Berkner, Lutz K., and F. F. Mendels. "Inheritance Systems, Family Structure, and Demographic Patterns in Western Europe, 1700–1900." In *Historical Studies of Changing Fertility*, 209–223. Ed. Charles Tilley. Princeton: Princeton University Press, 1978.

Berlink, Manuel Tosta. *The Structure of the Family in the City of São Paulo.* Latin American Studies Program, Cornell University, no. 12. Ithaca: Cornell University Press, 1969.

Bethell, Leslie, ed. *The Cambridge History of Latin America.* Cambridge: Cambridge University Press, 1984.

Billington, Ray Allen, ed. *The Frontier Thesis: Valid Interpretation of American History?* New York: Krieger Pub. Co., 1977.

Billington, Ray Allen, and Martin Ridge. *Western Expansion: A History of the American Frontier.* 5th ed. New York: Macmillan, 1982.

Blank, Stephanie. "Social Integration and Social Stability in a Colonial Spanish American City, Caracas (1595–1627)." Ph.D. diss., University of Wisconsin, 1971.

————. "Patrons, Clients, and Kin in Seventeenth-Century Caracas: A Methodological Essay in Colonial Spanish American Social History." *Hispanic American Historical Review* 54(1974): 260–283.

Blassingame, John W. *The Slave Community: Plantation Life in the Antebellum South.* 2d ed. New York: Oxford University Press, 1979.

Bourdieu, Pierre. "Marriage Strategies as Strategies of Social Reproduction." In *Family and Society: Selections from the Annales, Economies, Sociétés, Civilisations*, 117–144. Ed. Robert Forster and Orest Ranum. Trans. Elborg Forster and Patricia M. Ranum. Baltimore: Johns Hopkins University Press, 1976.

Boxer, Chárles Ralph. *Salvador de Sá and the Struggle for Brazil and Angola, 1602–1686.* 1952; repr. ed., Westport, Conn.: Greenwood Press, 1975.

————. *Four Centuries of Portuguese Expansion, 1415–1825: A Succinct Survey.* Johannesburg: Witwatersrand University Press, 1961.

————. *The Golden Age of Brazil, 1695–1750: Growing Pains of a Colonial Society.* Berkeley and Los Angeles: University of California Press, 1962.

————. *Portuguese Society in the Tropics: The Municipal Councils of Gôa,*

Macao, Bahia, and Luanda, 1510–1800. Madison: University of Wisconsin Press, 1965.

———. *The Portuguese Seaborne Empire, 1415–1825.* London: Hutchinson, 1969.

Brading, David A. *Miners and Merchants in Bourbon Mexico, 1763–1810.* Cambridge: Cambridge University Press, 1971.

Braudel, Fernand. *Civilization and Capitalism, 15th–18th Century.* 3 vols. Trans. Siân Reynolds. New York: Harper & Row, 1986.

Brennan, E. R., A. V. James, and W. T. Morrill. "Inheritance, Demographic Structure, and Marriage: A Cross-Cultural Perspective." *Journal of Family History* 7(1982): 289–298.

Brettell, Caroline B. "Family Legacies: An Analysis of the *Livros dos Testamentos* in a Portuguese Village, 1750–1860." Paper presented to the Society for Spanish and Portuguese Historical Studies, Bloomington, Indiana, April 1984.

———. *Men Who Migrate, Women Who Wait: Population and History in a Portuguese Parish.* Princeton: Princeton University Press, 1986.

Bronner, Fred. "Peruvian Encomenderos in 1630: Elite Circulation and Consolidation." *Hispanic American Historical Review* 57(1977): 633–659.

Bruno, Ernai Silva. *Viagem ao país dos paulistas: Ensaio sôbre a ocupação da área vicentina e a formação de sua economia e de sua sociedade nos tempos coloniais.* Coleção Documentos Brasileiros, vol. 123. Rio de Janeiro: José Olympio, 1966.

Camargo, Mons. Paulo Florêncio da Silveira. *História de Santana de Parnaíba.* Coleção História, vol. 15. São Paulo: Conselho Estadual de Cultura, 1971.

Canabrava, Alice P. "A evolução das posturas municipais de Sant'Ana de Parnaíba, 1829–1867." *Revista de Administração* 3(1949): 34–62.

———. "A repartição da terra na Capitania de São Paulo, 1818." *Estudos Econômicos* 2, 6(1972): 77–129.

———. "Uma economia de decadência: Os níveis de riqueza na Capitania de São Paulo, 1765/67." *Revista Brasileira de Economia* 26, 4(1972): 95–123.

Cândido, Antônio. "A vida familiar do caipira." *Sociologia* 16(1954): 341–367.

———. *Os parceiros do Rio Bonito: Estudo sobre o caipira paulista e a transformação dos seus meios de vida.* 5th ed. São Paulo: Livraria Duas Cidades, 1979.

Canny, Nicholas, and Anthony Pagden, eds. *Colonial Identity in the Atlantic World, 1500–1800.* Princeton: Princeton University Press, 1987.

Cardoso, Fernando Henrique. *Capitalismo e escravidão no Brasil meridional: O negro na sociedade escravocrata do Rio Grande do Sul.* São Paulo: Difusão Européia do Livro, 1962.

Carneiro, Robert L. "Slash-and-Burn Agriculture: A Closer Look at Its Implications for Settlement Patterns." In *Men and Cultures,* 229–234.

Ed. A. F. C. Wallace. Philadelphia: University of Pennsylvania Press, 1960.

Carr, Lois Green, and Lorena S. Walsh. "The Planter's Wife: The Experience of White Women in Seventeenth-Century Maryland." *William and Mary Quarterly*, 3d ser., 34(1977): 542–571.

Castro, Hebe Maria Mattos de. "Beyond Masters and Slaves: Subsistence Agriculture as a Survival Strategy in Brazil During the Second Half of the Nineteenth Century." *Hispanic American Historical Review* 68(1988): 461–489.

Chance, John K., and William B. Taylor. "Estate and Class in a Colonial City: Oaxaca in 1792." *Comparative Studies in Society and History* 19(1977): 454–487.

———. "Estate and Class: A Reply." *Comparative Studies in Society and History* 21(1979): 433–442.

Chandler, Billy Jaynes. *The Feitosas and the Sertão dos Inhamuns: The History of a Family and a Community in Northeast Brazil, 1700–1930*. Gainesville: University of Florida Press, 1972.

Chevalier, François. *La formatión des grands domaines au Mexique: Terre e société aux XVIè–XVIIIè siècles*. Paris: L'Université de Paris, 1952.

Chojnacki, Stanley. "Dowries and Kinsmen in Early Renaissance Venice." *Journal of Interdisciplinary History* 5(1975): 571–600.

Coale, Ansley J., and Susan Cotts Watkins, eds. *The Decline of Fertility in Europe: The Revised Proceedings of a Conference on the Princeton European Fertility Project*. Princeton: Princeton University Press, 1986.

Cole, John W., and Eric R. Wolf. *The Hidden Frontier: Ecology and Ethnicity in an Alpine Valley*. New York: Academic Press, 1974.

Costa, Emilia Viotti da. *Da senzala à colônia*. São Paulo: Difusão Européia do Livro, 1966.

———. *The Brazilian Empire: Myths and Histories*. Chicago: University of Chicago Press, 1985.

Costa, Iraci del Nero da. "A estrutura familiar e domiciliária em Vila Rica no alvorecer do século XIX." *Revista do Instituto de Estudos Brasileiros* 19(1977): 17–34.

———. *Vila Rica: População (1719–1826)*. Ensaios Econômicos, no. 1. São Paulo: IPE-USP, 1979.

———. *Minas Gerais: Estruturas populacionais típicas*. São Paulo: EDEC, 1982.

———. "Os viagantes estrangeiros e a família escrava no Brasil." *Leitura* (São Paulo) 7, 77 (October 1988): 9–10.

Costa, Iraci del Nero da, and Horácio Gutiérrez. "Nota sobre casamentos de escravos em São Paulo e no Paraná (1830)." *História: Questões e Debates* 5, 9(1984): 313–321.

Costa, Iraci del Nero da, and Nelson Hideiki Nozoe. "Economia colonial brasileira: Classificação das ocupações segundo ramos e setores." *Estudos Econômicos* 17(1987): 69–87.

Costa, Iraci del Nero da, Robert Slenes, and Stuart Schwartz. "A família escrava em Lorena (1801)." *Estudos Econômicos* 17(1987): 245–295.

Cott, Nancy F. "Eighteenth-Century Family and Social Life Revealed in Massachusetts Divorce Records." *Journal of Social History* 10(1976): 20–43.

Craton, Michael. *Searching for the Invisible Man: Slaves and Plantation Life in Jamaica.* Cambridge: Harvard University Press, 1978.

———. *Testing the Chains: Resistance to Slavery in the British West Indies.* Ithaca: Cornell University Press, 1982.

Craton, Michael, ed. *Roots and Branches: Current Directions in Slave Studies.* Historical Reflections Directions, no. 1. New York: Pergamon Press, 1979.

Crosby, Alfred W. *The Columbian Exchange: Biological and Cultural Consequences of 1492.* Contributions in American Studies, no. 2. Westport, Conn.: Greenwood Press, 1972.

———. *Ecological Imperialism: The Biological Expansion of Europe, 900–1900.* Cambridge: Cambridge University Press, 1986.

Curtin, Philip D. *The Atlantic Slave Trade: A Census.* Madison: University of Wisconsin Press, 1969.

Darnton, Robert. *The Great Cat Massacre and Other Episodes in French Cultural History.* New York: Vintage Books, 1985.

Davidson, David M. "Rivers and Empire: The Madeira Route and the Incorporation of the Brazilian Far West, 1737–1808." Ph.D. diss., Yale University, 1970.

———. "How the Brazilian West Was Won: Freelance and State on the Mato Grosso Frontier, 1737–1752." In *Colonial Roots of Modern Brazil: Papers of the Newberry Library Conference,* 61–106. Ed. Dauril Alden. Berkeley, Los Angeles, and London: University of California Press, 1973.

Davis, J. *Land and Family in Pisticci.* New York: Humanities Press, Inc., 1973.

Davis, Natalie Ann Zemon. *Society and Culture in Early Modern France: Eight Essays.* Stanford: Stanford University Press, 1975.

———. "Ghosts, Kin, and Progeny: Some Features of Family Life in Early Modern France." *Daedalus* 106, 2(1977): 87–114.

Dean, Warren. "Latifundia and Land Policy in Nineteenth-Century Brazil." *Hispanic American Historical Review* 51(1971): 606–625.

———. *Rio Claro: A Brazilian Plantation System, 1820–1920.* Stanford: Stanford University Press, 1976.

———. "Indigenous Populations of the Rio de Janeiro Coast: Trade, Aldeamento, Slavery, and Extinction. *Revista de História* 117(1984): 3–26.

Degler, Carl N. *Neither Black nor White: Slavery and Race Relations in Brazil and the United States.* New York: Macmillan, 1971.

Demos, John. *A Little Commonwealth: Family Life in Plymouth Colony.* New York: Oxford University Press, 1970.

Denevan, William M., ed. *The Native Population of the Americas in 1492.* Madison: University of Wisconsin Press, 1976.

Departamento de Geografía da Universidade de São Paulo. *Pinheiros: Aspectos geográficos de um bairro paulistano.* São Paulo: Editôra da Universidade de São Paulo, 1963.

Dias, Maria Odila Leite da Silva. *Quotidiano e poder em São Paulo no século XIX—Ana Gertrudes de Jesus.* São Paulo: Brasiliense, 1984.

Diaz, Arlene J., and Jeff Stewart. "Occupational Class and Female-Headed Households in Santiago Maior do Iguape, Brazil, 1835." *Journal of Family History* 16(1991): 299–313.

Diefendorf, Barbara B. "Widowhood and Remarriage in Sixteenth-Century Paris." *Journal of Family History* 7(1982): 379–395.

Diffie, Bailey W., and George D. Winius. *Foundations of the Portuguese Empire, 1415–1580.* Minneapolis: University of Minnesota Press, 1977.

Divisão administrativa e divisas municipais do estado de São Paulo. São Paulo: Divisão de Estatística e Arquivo do Estado, 1908.

Dominian, Helen G. *Apostle of Brazil: The Biography of Padre José de Anchieta, S.J.* New York: Exposition Press, 1958.

Dupâquier, J., et al., eds. *Marriage and Remarriage in Populations of the Past.* London: Academic Press, 1981.

Eisenberg, Peter L. "O homem esquecido: O trabalhador livre nacional no século XIX sugestões para uma pesquisa." *Anais do Museu Paulista* 28(1977/78): 153–173.

———. "Ficando livre: As alforrias em Campinas no século XIX." *Estudos Econômicos* 17(1987): 175–216.

Ellis, Alfredo, Jr. *O bandeirismo paulista e o recúo do meridiano.* 3d ed. Brasiliana, vol. 36. São Paulo: Companhia Editôra Nacional, 1938.

Engels, Frederick. *The Origin of the Family, Private Property and the State.* Ed. Eleanor Burke Leacock. New York: International Publishers, 1972.

Estudos Econômicos. "Demografia da Escravidão." 17, 2(1987).

Fairchilds, Cissie. "Female Sexual Attitudes and the Rise of Illegitimacy: A Case Study." *Journal of Interdisciplinary History* 8(1978): 627–667.

Faoro, Raymundo. *Os donos do poder: Formação do patronato político brasileiro.* 2 vols. 5th ed. Porto Alegre: Editôra Globo, 1979.

Farriss, Nancy M. *Maya Society under Colonial Rule: The Collective Enterprise of Survival.* Princeton: Princeton Unviversity Press, 1984.

Felstiner, Mary Alexandra Lowenthal. "The Larrain Family in the Independence of Chile, 1780–1830." Ph.D. diss., Stanford University, 1970.

Fernandes, Florestan. *A integração do negro na sociedade de classes.* São Paulo: Dominus, Editôra da Universidade de São Paulo, 1965.

Ferreira, Manuel Rodriques. *As bandeiras do Paraupava.* São Paulo: Prefeitura Municipal, 1977.

Ferry, Robert J. *The Colonial Elite of Early Caracas: Formation and Crisis, 1567–1767.* Berkeley, Los Angeles, and Oxford: University of California Press, 1989.

Flandrin, Jean-Louis. *Families in Former Times: Kinship, Household, and Sex-*

uality. Trans. Richard Southern. Cambridge: Cambridge University Press, 1979.

Florescano, Enrique, ed. *Haciendas, latifundios y plantaciones en America Latina*. México: Siglo Ventiuno Editores, 1975.

Flory, Rae Jean Dell. "Bahian Society in the Mid-Colonial Period: The Sugar Planters, Tobacco Growers, Merchants, and Artisans of Salvador and the Recôncavo, 1680–1725." Ph.D. diss., University of Texas, Austin, 1978.

Flory, Rae Jean Dell, and David Grant Smith. "Bahian Merchants and Planters in the Seventeenth and Early Eighteenth Centuries." *Hispanic American Historical Review* 58(1978): 571–594.

Fogel, Robert William, and Stanley L. Engerman. *Time on the Cross: The Economics of American Negro Slavery*. 2 vols. Boston: Little, Brown & Co., 1974.

Folbre, Nancy. "The Wealth of Patriarchs: Deerfield, Massachusetts, 1760–1840." *Journal of Interdisciplinary History* 2(1985): 199–220.

Forster, Robert, and Orest Ranum, eds. *Family and Society: Selections from the Annales, Economies, Sociétés, Civilisations*. Trans. Elborg Forster and Patricia Ranum. Baltimore: Johns Hopkins University Press, 1976.

Foster, George M. "Cofradía and Compadrazgo in Spain and South America." *Southwest Journal of Anthropology* 9(1953): 1–28.

Fragoso, João Luis R., and Manolo G. Florentino. "Marcelino, filho de Inocência crioula, neto de Joana cabinda: Um estudo sobre famílias escravas em Paraíba do Sul (1835–1872)." *Estudos Econômicos* 17, 2(1987): 151–173.

Franco, Carvalho. *Bandeiras e bandeirantes de São Paulo*. Brasiliana, vol. 181. São Paulo: Companhia Editôra Nacional, 1940.

Franco, Maria Sylvia de Carvalho. *Homes livres na ordem escravocrata*. 2d ed. Ensaios, no. 3. São Paulo: Atica, 1976.

Frazier, E. Franklin. *The Negro Family in the United States*. Rev. ed. New York: Dryden Press, 1948.

Freyre, Gilberto. *The Masters and the Slaves [Casa-Grande & Senzala]: A Study in the Development of Brazilian Civilization*. Trans. Samuel Putnam. 2d ed. rev. New York: Knopf, 1966.

Fukui, Lia Freitas Garcia. *Sertão e bairro rural: Parentesco e família entre sitiantes tradicionais*. Ensaios, no. 58. São Paulo: Atica, 1979.

Gama, Ruy. *Engenho e tecnologia*. São Paulo: Livraria Duas Cidades, 1983.

Genovese, Eugene. *The Political Economy of Slavery: Studies in the Economy and Society of the Slave South*. New York: Pantheon Books, 1967.

———. *Roll, Jordan, Roll: The World the Slaves Made*. New York: Pantheon Books, 1974.

Ginzburg, Carlo. *The Cheese and the Worms: The Cosmos of a Sixteenth-Century Miller*. Trans. John Tedeschi and Anne Tedeschi. New York: Penguin Books, 1982.

Godinho, Victorino Magalhães. *A economia dos descobrimentos henriquinos*. Lisbon: Liv. Sa da Costa, 1962.

Gongora, Mario. *Los grupos de conquistadores en Tierra Firme (1509–1530): Fisonomía historico-social de un tipo de conquista.* Santiago: Editorial Universitaria, 1962.

———. *Encomenderos y estancieros: Estudios acerca de la constitución social aristocrática de Chile después de la conquista, 1580–1660.* Santiago: Editorial Universitaria, 1970.

Goody, Jack. *The Development of the Family and Marriage in Europe.* Cambridge: Cambridge University Press, 1983.

———. "Bridewealth and Dowry in Africa and Eurasia." In Jack Goody and S. J. Tambiah, *Bridewealth and Dowry.* Cambridge Papers in Social Anthropology, no. 7. Cambridge: Cambridge University Press, 1973.

Goody, Jack, Joan Thirsk, and E. P. Thompson, eds. *Family and Inheritance: Rural Society in Western Europe, 1200–1800.* Cambridge: Cambridge University Press, 1976.

Gordon, Michael, ed. *The American Family in Social-Historical Perspective.* 2d ed. New York: St. Martin's Press, 1978.

Gorender, Jacob. *O escravismo colonial.* 2d ed. Ensaios, no. 29. São Paulo: Atica, 1978.

Graham, Richard. "Slave Families of a Rural Estate in Colonial Brazil." *Journal of Social History* 9(1976): 382–402.

Graham, Sandra Lauderdale. *House and Street: The Domestic World of Servants and Masters in Nineteenth-Century Rio de Janeiro.* Cambridge: Cambridge University Press, 1988.

Greene, Jack P. *Pursuits of Happiness: The Social Development of Early Modern British Colonies and the Formation of American Culture.* Chapel Hill: University of North Carolina Press, 1988.

Greene, Jack P., and J. R. Pole, eds. *Colonial British America: Essays in the New History of the Early Modern Era.* Baltimore: Johns Hopkins University Press, 1984.

Greer, Allan. *Peasant, Lord, and Merchant: Rural Society in Three Quebec Parishes, 1740–1840.* Toronto: University of Toronto Press, 1985.

Greven, Philip J., Jr. "Family Structure in Seventeenth-Century Andover, Massachusetts." *William and Mary Quarterly,* 3d ser., 23(1966): 234–256.

———. *Four Generations: Population, Land, and Family in Colonial Andover, Massachusetts.* Ithaca: Cornell University Press, 1970.

Gudeman, Stephen, and Stuart B. Schwartz. "Cleansing Original Sin: Godparenthood and the Baptism of Slaves in Eighteenth-Century Bahia." In *Kinship Ideology and Practice in Latin America.* Ed. Raymond T. Smith. Chapel Hill: University of North Carolina Press, 1984.

Gutman, Herbert G. *The Black Family in Slavery and Freedom, 1750–1925.* New York: Pantheon Books, 1976.

Habakkuk, H. J. "Family Structure and Economic Change in Nineteenth-Century Europe." *Journal of Economic History* 15(1955): 1–12.

Hall, Peter Dobkin. "Family Structure and Economic Organization: Massachusetts Merchants, 1700–1850." In *Family and Kin in Urban Commu-*

nities, 38–61. Ed. Tamara K. Hareven. New York: New Viewpoints, 1977.

Hallett, Judith P. *Fathers and Daughters in Roman Society: Women and the Elite Family.* Princeton: Princeton University Press, 1984.

Hanawalt, Barbara A. *The Ties that Bound: Peasant Families in Medieval England.* New York: Oxford University Press, 1986.

Hareven, Tamara K. "The Family as Process: The Historical Study of the Family Cycle." *Journal of Social History* 7(1974): 322–329.

————. "Modernization and Family History: Perspectives on Social Change." *Signs* 2(1976): 190–206.

Hareven, Tamara K., ed. *Transitions: The Family and the Life Course in Historical Perspective.* New York: Academic Press, 1978.

Harris III, Charles Houston. *A Mexican Family Empire: The Latifundio of the Sánchez Navarros, 1765–1867.* Austin: University of Texas Press, 1975.

Harris, Marvin. *Patterns of Race in the Americas.* New York: Walker, 1964.

Harris, Richard Colebrook. *The Seigneurial System in Early Canada: A Geographic Study.* Madison: University of Wisconsin Press, 1966.

Hemming, John. *Red Gold: The Conquest of the Brazilian Indians.* Cambridge: Harvard University Press, 1978.

Henretta, James A. "Families and Farms: *Mentalité* in Pre-Industrial America." *William and Mary Quarterly,* 3d ser., 35(1978): 3–32.

Herlihy, David. *Medieval Households.* Cambridge: Harvard University Press, 1985.

Herrmann, Lucila. *Evolução da estrutura social de Guaratinquetá num período de trezentos anos.* São Paulo: Instituto de Pesquisas Econômicas, 1986.

Higginbotham, A. Leon, Jr. *In the Matter of Color, Race and the American Legal Process: The Colonial Period.* New York: Oxford University Press, 1978.

Higgins, Kathleen Joan. "Iguatemí: A Brazilian Frontier Community, 1767–1777." M.A. thesis, University of Texas, Austin, 1980.

————. "The Slave Society in Eighteenth-Century Sabará: A Community Study in Colonial Brazil." Ph.D. diss., Yale University, 1987.

Higman, Barry W. "The Slave Family and Household in the British West Indies, 1800–1834." *Journal of Interdisciplinary History* 6(1975): 261–287.

————. *Slave Population and Economy in Jamaica, 1807–1834.* Cambridge: Cambridge University Press, 1976.

————. *Slave Populations of the British Caribbean, 1807–1834.* Baltimore: Johns Hopkins University Press, 1984.

Hirano, Sedi. *Pre-capitalismo e capitalismo.* São Paulo: Editôra Hucitec, 1988.

Hoberman, Louisa, and Susan Socolow, eds. *Cities and Society in Colonial Latin America.* Albuquerque: University of New Mexico Press, 1986.

Holanda, Sérgio Buarque de. *Raízes do Brasil.* 2d ed. Coleção Documentos Brasileiros, no. 1. Rio de Janeiro: José Olympio, 1948.

————. *Caminhos e fronteiras.* Rio de Janeiro: Livraria José Olympio Editôra, 1957.

————. "Movimentos da população em São Paulo no século XVIII." *Revista do Instituto de Estudos Brasileiros* 1(1966): 55–114.

————. *Monções*. 2d ed. São Paulo: Editôra Alfa-Omega, 1976.

————. *O extremo oeste*. São Paulo: Brasiliense; Secretaria de Estado da Cultura, 1986.

Holme, Oscar. "Ubatuba: Uma das primeiras vilas da Capitania de São Paulo a produzir café." *Boletim de Estudos Sociais* 1(1972): 17–28.

Howell, Cicely. *Land, Family and Inheritance in Transition: Kibworth Harcourt, 1280–1700*. Cambridge: Cambridge University Press, 1983.

Hughes, Diane. "Domestic Ideals and Social Behavior: Evidence from Medieval Genoa." In *The Family in History*, 115–143. Ed. Charles Rosenberg. Philadelphia: University of Pennsylvania Press, 1975.

Innes, Stephen. "Land Tenancy and Social Order in Springfield, Massachusetts, 1652 to 1702." *William and Mary Quarterly*, 3d ser., 35(1978): 33–56.

————. *Labor in a New Land: Economy and Society in Seventeenth-Century Springfield*. Princeton: Princeton University Press, 1983.

Instituto Histórico e Geográfico Brasileiro. *Catálogo de documentos sobre a história de São Paulo, existentes no Arquivo Histórico Ultramarino de Lisboa*. 13 vols. Rio de Janeiro: Instituto Histórico e Geográfico Brasileiro, 1956–1959.

"Inventário dos documentos relativos ao Brasil existentes na Biblioteca Nacional de Lisboa." *Anais da Biblioteca Nacional*. Vols. 75, 93.

Isaac, Rhys. *The Transformation of Virginia, 1740–1790*. Chapel Hill: University of North Carolina Press, 1982.

Johnson, Harold B. "The Donatary Captaincy in Perspective: Portuguese Backgrounds to the Settlement of Brazil." *Hispanic American Historical Review* 52(1972): 203–214.

————. "A Preliminary Inquiry into Money, Prices, and Wages in Rio de Janeiro, 1763–1823." In *Colonial Roots of Modern Brazil: Papers of the Newberry Library Conference*, 231–283. Ed. Dauril Alden. Berkeley, Los Angeles, and London: University of California Press, 1973.

Jones, Alice Hanson. "Estimating Wealth of the Living from a Probate Sample." *Journal of Interdisciplinary History* 13(1982): 273–300.

Jordan, David W. "Political Stability and the Emergence of a Native Elite in Maryland." In *The Chesapeake in the Seventeenth Century: Essays on Anglo-American Society*, 243–273. Ed. Thad W. Tate and David L. Ammerman. Chapel Hill: University of North Carolina Press, 1979.

Karasch, Mary C. "From Porterage to Proprietorship: African Occupations in Rio de Janeiro, 1808–1850." In *Race and Slavery in the Western Hemisphere: Quantitative Studies*, 369–393. Ed. Stanley L. Engerman and Eugene D. Genovese. Princeton: Princeton University Press, 1975.

————. *Slave Life in Rio de Janeiro, 1808–1850*. Princeton: Princeton University Press, 1987.

Keim, C. Ray. "Primogeniture and Entail in Colonial Virginia." *William and Mary Quarterly*, 3d ser., 25(1968): 545–586.

Keith, Robert B. *Conquest and Agrarian Change*. Cambridge: Harvard University Press, 1976.

Kennedy, John Norman. "Bahian Elites, 1750–1822." *Hispanic American Historical Review* 53(1973): 415–439.

Kent, R. K. "Palmares: An African State in Brazil." *Journal of African History* 6(1965): 161–175.

Kertzer, David I. *Family Life in Central Italy, 1880–1910: Sharecropping, Wage Labor and Coresidence*. New Brunswick: Rutgers University Press, 1984.

Kertzer, David I., and Caroline Brettell. "Advances in Italian and Iberian Family History." In *Family History at the Crossroads: A Journal of Family History Reader*, 87–120. Ed. Tamara Hareven and Andrejs Plakans. Princeton: Princeton University Press, 1987.

Kicza, John E. "The Great Families of Mexico: Elite Maintenance and Business Practices in Late Colonial Mexico City." *Hispanic American Historical Review* 62(1982): 429–457.

———. *Colonial Entrepreneurs: Families and Business in Bourbon Mexico City*. Albuquerque: University of New Mexico Press, 1983.

Kiernan, James Patrick. "The Manumission of Slaves in Colonial Brazil: Paraty, 1789–1822." Ph.D. dissertation, New York University, 1976.

Klein, Herbert S. *The Middle Passage: Comparative Studies in the Atlantic Slave Trade*. Princeton: Princeton University Press, 1978.

Knight, Franklin W. *Slave Society in Cuba during the Nineteenth Century*. Madison: University of Wisconsin Press, 1970.

Kocka, Jürgen. "Family and Class Formation: Intergenerational Mobility and Marriage Patterns in Nineteenth-Century Westphalian Towns." *Journal of Social History* 17(1984): 411–433.

Korth, Eugene H., and Della M. Flusche. "Dowry and Inheritance in Colonial Spanish America: Peninsular Law and Chilean Practice." *The Americas* 43(1987): 395–410.

Kottak, Conrad Phillip. "Kinship and Class in Brazil." *Ethnology* 6(1967): 427–443.

Kubler, George. *The Indian Caste of Peru, 1795–1940: A Study Based upon Tax Records and Census Reports*. Washington, D.C.: U.S. Government Printing Office, 1952.

Kulikoff, Allan. *Tobacco and Slaves: The Development of Southern Cultures in the Chesapeake, 1680–1800*. Chapel Hill: University of North Carolina Press, 1986.

Kuznesof, Elizabeth Anne. "Clans, the Militia and Territorial Government: The Articulation of Kinship with Polity in Eighteenth-Century São Paulo." In *Social Fabric and Spatial Structures in Colonial Latin America*, 181–226. Ed. David J. Robinson and David G. Browning. Syracuse: Syracuse University Press, 1979.

———. "An Analysis of Household Composition and Headship Rates as Related to Changes in Mode of Production: São Paulo, 1765 to 1836." *Comparative Studies in Society and History* 22(1980): 78–108.

———. "The Role of the Female-Headed Household in Brazilian Modernization: São Paulo 1765 to 1836." *Journal of Social History* 13(1980): 589–613.

———. "The Role of the Merchants in the Economic Development of São Paulo, 1765–1850." *Hispanic American Historical Review* 60(1980): 571–592.

———. *Household Economy and Urban Development: São Paulo, 1765 to 1836.* Boulder: Westview Press, 1986.

———. "Sexual Politics, Race, and Bastard-Bearing in Nineteenth-Century Brazil: A Question of Culture or Power?" *Journal of Family History* 16(1991): 241–260.

Ladd, Doris M. *The Mexican Nobility at Independence, 1780–1826.* Austin: University of Texas Press, 1976.

Lasch, Christopher. *Haven in a Heartless World: The Family Besieged.* New York: Basic Books, 1977.

Laslett, Peter. "The Study of Social Structure from Listings of Inhabitants." In *An Introduction to English Historical Demography*, 160–208. Ed. E. A. Wrigley. London: Weidenfeld & Nicolson, 1966.

———. "Size and Structure of the Household in England over Three Centuries." *Population Studies* 23(1969): 199–223.

Laslett, Peter, and Richard Wall, eds. *Household and Family in Past Time: Comparative Studies in the Size and Structure of the Domestic Group over the Last Three Centuries in England, France, Serbia, Japan and Colonial North America with Further Materials from Western Europe.* Cambridge: Cambridge University Press, 1972.

Lavrin, Asunción, and Edith Couturier. "Dowries and Wills: A View of Women's Socioeconomic Roles in Colonial Guadalajara and Puebla." *Hispanic American Historical Review* 59(1979): 280–304.

Lavrin, Asunción, ed. *Latin American Women: Historical Perspectives.* Westport, Conn.: Greenwood Press, 1978.

———. *Sexuality and Marriage in Colonial Latin America.* Lincoln: University of Nebraska Press, 1989.

Le Roy, Emmanuel Ladurie. "Family Structures and Inheritance Customs in Sixteenth-Century France." In *Family and Inheritance: Rural Society in Western Europe*, 37–70. Ed. Jack Goody, Joan Thirsk, and E. P. Thompson. Cambridge: Cambridge University Press, 1976.

———. *Montaillou: The Promised Land of Error.* Trans. Barbara Bray. New York: Vintage Books, 1979.

Leal, Victor Nunes. *Coronelismo: The Municipality and Representative Government in Brazil.* Trans. June Henfrey. New York: Cambridge University Press, 1977.

Leite, S.I., Serafim. *História da Companhia de Jesus no Brasil.* 10 vols. Lisbon: Livraria Portugália, 1938.

———. *Novas páginas de história do Brasil.* Brasiliana, vol. 324. São Paulo: Companhia Editôra Nacional, 1965.

Leonzo, Nanci. "As Companhias de Ordenanças na Capitania de São Paulo: Das origens ao governo do Morgado de Matheus." *Coleção Museu Paulista* 6(1977): 125–239.

————. "Defesa militar e controle social na Capitania de São Paulo: As milícias." Tese de Doutoramento: Universidade de São Paulo, 1979.

Levi, Darrell E. *The Prados of São Paulo, Brazil: An Elite Family and Social Change, 1840–1930.* Athens: University of Georgia Press, 1987.

Levine, David. *Family Formation in an Age of Nascent Capitalism.* New York: Academic Press, 1977.

Lewin, Linda. "Some Historical Implications of Kinship Organization for Family-based Politics in the Brazilian Northeast." *Comparative Studies in Society and History* 21(1979): 262–292.

————. *Politics and Parentela in Paraíba: A Case Study of Family-based Oligarchy in Brazil.* Princeton: Princeton University Press, 1987.

Lindley, Richard Barry. *Haciendas and Economic Development: Guadalajara, Mexico, at Independence.* Latin American Monographs, no. 58. Austin: University of Texas Press, 1983.

Lockhart, James Marvin. *Spanish Peru, 1532–1560: A Colonial Society.* Madison: University of Wisconsin Press, 1968.

————. "The Social History of Colonial Latin America: Evolution and Potential." *Latin American Research Review* 7(1972): 5–45.

Lockhart, James, and Stuart B. Schwartz. *Early Latin America: A History of Colonial Spanish America and Brazil.* Cambridge: Cambridge University Press, 1983.

Lockridge, Kenneth A. "Land, Population and the Evolution of New England Society, 1630–1790." *Past and Present* 39(1968): 62–80.

————. *A New England Town, The First Hundred Years, Dedham, Massachusetts, 1636–1736.* New York: W. W. Norton & Co., 1970.

Lomax, Derek W. *The Reconquest of Spain.* New York: Longman, 1978.

Love, Edgar F. "Marriage Patterns of Persons of African Descent in a Colonial Mexico City Parish." *Hispanic American Historical Review* 51(1971): 79–91.

Luis, Washington. *Capitania de São Paulo: Governo de Rodrigo Cesar de Menezes.* 2d ed. Brasiliana, vol. 111. São Paulo: Companhia Editôra Nacional, 1938.

Luna, Francisco Vidal, and Iraci del Nero da Costa. *Minas colonial: Economia e sociedade.* São Paulo: FIPE, Livraria Pioneira Editôra, 1982.

————. "Posse de escravos em São Paulo no incício do século XIX." *Estudos Econômicos* 13, 1(1983): 1–11.

MacFarlane, Alan. *The Family Life of Ralph Josselin, a Seventeenth-Century Clergyman: An Essay in Historical Anthropology.* Cambridge: Cambridge University Press, 1970.

Machado, Alcântara. *Vida e morte do bandeirante.* Coleção Reconquista do Brasil, vol. 8. Belo Horizonte: Editôra Itatiaia, 1980.

Madre de Deus, Frei Gaspar da. *Memórias para a história da Capitania de São Vicente.* Lisbon: 1797; repr. ed., Coleção Reconquista do Brasil, vol. 20. Belo Horizonte: Editôra Itatiaia, 1975.

Maeyana, Takashi. *Familiarization of the Unfamiliar World: The Family Networks and Groups in a Brazilian City.* Ithaca: Cornell University Latin American Series, 1975.

Magalhães de Gandavo, Pero de. *The Histories of Brazil.* Trans. J. B. Seton. New York: Cortes Society, 1922; repr. ed., Boston: Longwood Press, 1978.

Main, Gloria. "Inequality in Early America: The Evidence from Probate Records of Massachusetts and Maryland." *Journal of Interdisciplinary History* 7(1977): 559–581.

―――. *Tobacco Colony: Life in Early Maryland, 1650–1720.* Princeton: Princeton University Press, 1982.

Marchant, Alexander. *From Barter to Slavery: The Economic Relations of Portuguese and Indians in the Settlement of Brazil, 1500–1580.* Baltimore: Johns Hopkins University Press, 1942; repr. ed., Gloucester, Mass.: Peter Smith, 1966.

Marcílio, Maria Luiza. "Dos registros paroquiais à demografia histórica no Brasil." *Anais de História* 2(1970): 81–100.

―――. "Tendências e estruturas dos domicílios na Capitania de São Paulo (1765–1828) segundo as listas nominativas de habitantes." *Estudos Econômicos* 2, 6(1972): 131–143.

―――. *A cidade de São Paulo: Povoamento e população, 1750–1850, com base nos registros paroquiais e nos recenseamentos antigos.* São Paulo: Livraria Pioneira Editôra, 1974.

―――. "Crescimento demográfico e evolução agrária paulista, 1700–1836." Tese de Livre Docência: Universidade de São Paulo, 1974.

―――. *Caiçara: Terra e população: Estudo de demografia histórica e da história social de Ubatuba.* São Paulo: Edições Paulinas—CEDHAL, 1986.

Mariéjol, J. H. *The Spain of Ferdinand and Isabella.* Trans. and ed. Benjamin Keen. New Brunswick: Rutgers University Press, 1961.

Margolis, Maxine L. *The Moving Frontier: Social and Economic Change in a Southern Brazilian Community.* Latin American Monographs, 2d ser., no. 11. Gainesville: University of Florida Press, 1973.

Marques, A. H. de Oliveira. *A History of Portugal.* 2d ed. New York: Columbia University Press, 1976.

Marx, Karl. "The German Ideology: Part One." In *The Marx-Engels Reader*, 110-164. Ed. Robert C. Tucker. New York: W. W. Norton & Co., 1972.

Marzahl, Peter Gottfried. "The Cabildo of Popayán in the Seventeenth Century: The Emergence of a Creole Elite." Ph.D. diss., University of Wisconsin, 1970.

Mattoso, Katia M. de Queirós. *To be a Slave in Brazil, 1550–1888.* Trans. Arthur Goldhammer. New Brunswick: Rutgers University Press, 1986.

Maxwell, Kenneth R. *Conflicts and Conspiracies: Brazil and Portugal, 1750–1808.* Cambridge: Cambridge University Press, 1973.

Merrick, Thomas W. "Household Structure and Poverty in Families Headed by Women: The Case of Belo Horizonte." Paper presented at the Joint Meetings of the Latin American Studies Association–African Studies Association, Houston, November 1977.

Merrick, Thomas W., and Douglas H. Graham. *Population and Economic*

Development in Brazil, 1800 to the Present. Baltimore: Johns Hopkins University Press, 1979.

Metcalf, Alida C. "Recursos e estruturas familiares no século XVIII, em Ubatuba, Brasil." *Estudos Econômicos* 13(1983, Número Especial): 771–785.

——. "Families of Planters, Peasants, and Slaves: Strategies for Survival in Santana de Parnaíba, Brazil, 1720–1820." Ph.D. diss., University of Texas, Austin, 1983.

——. "Father and Sons: The Politics of Inheritance in a Colonial Brazilian Township." *Hispanic American Historical Review* 66(1986): 455–484.

——. "Vida familiar dos escravos em São Paulo no século dezoito: O caso de Santana de Parnaíba." *Estudos Econômicos* 17(1987): 229–243.

——. "Women and Means: Women and Family Property in Colonial Brazil." *Journal of Social History* 24(1990): 277–298.

Metraux, Alfred. *La civilizatión materielle des tribus Tupi-Guaraní*. Paris: Livrarie Orientaliste Paul Geuthner, 1928.

Mintz, Sidney W., and Eric R. Wolf. "An Analysis of Ritual Co-Parenthood (Compadrazgo)." *Southwestern Journal of Anthropology* 6(1950): 341–368.

Monteiro, John M. "São Paulo in the Seventeenth Century: Economy and Society." Ph.D. diss., University of Chicago, 1985.

——. "From Indian to Slave: Forced Native Labor and Colonial Society in São Paulo during the Seventeenth Century." *Slavery and Abolition* 9(1988): 105–127.

——. "Celeiro do Brasil: Escravidão indígena e a agricultura paulista no século XVII." *História: São Paulo* 7(1988): 1–12.

——. "Distribuição da riqueza e as origens da pobreza rural em São Paulo (século XVIII)." *Estudos Econômicos* 19(1989): 109–130.

Moog, Clodomir Vianna. *Bandeirantes and Pioneers*. Trans. L. L. Barrett. New York: G. Braziller, 1964.

Moreno Fraginals, Manuel. *The Sugar Mill: The Socio-economic Complex of Sugar in Cuba, 1760–1860*. Trans. Cedric Belfrage. New York: Monthly Review Press, 1976.

Mörner, Magnus, ed. *Race and Class in Latin America*. New York: Columbia University Press, 1970.

Morse, Richard M. *The Bandeirantes: The Historical Role of the Brazilian Pathfinders*. New York: Knopf, 1965.

——. *From Community to Metropolis: A Biography of São Paulo, Brazil*. Gainesville: University of Florida Press, 1958.

Motta, José Flávio. "A família escrava e a penetração do café em Bananal (1801–1829)." Paper presented to the Seminário Permanente de Estudo da Família e da População no Passado Brasileiro, IPE-USP, São Paulo, n.d.

Moura, Clovis. *Rebeliões da senzala (quilombos, insurreições, querrilhas)*. 2d ed. Rio de Janeiro: Conquista, 1972.

Moura, Margarida Maria. *Os herdeiros da terra: Parentesco e herança numa área rural.* São Paulo: Editôra Hucitec, 1978.

Mulvey, Patricia A. "Slave Confraternities in Brazil: Their Role in Colonial Society." *The Americas* 39(1982): 39–89.

Nazzari, Muriel. "Women and Property in the Transition to Capitalism: Decline of the Dowry in São Paulo, Brazil (1640–1870)." Paper presented to the American Historical Association, Chicago, December 1984.

———. "Women, the Family and Property: The Decline of the Dowry in São Paulo, Brazil (1600–1870)." Ph.D. dissertation, Yale University, 1986.

———. "Parents and Daughters: Change in the Practice of Dowry in São Paulo (1600–1770)." *Hispanic American Historical Review* 70(1990): 639–665.

Nielsen, Lawrence James. "Of Gentry, Peasants, and Slaves: Rural Society in Sabará and Its Hinterland, 1780–1930." Ph.D. diss., University of California, Davis, 1975.

Novais, Fernando A. *Portugal e Brasil na crise do antigo sistema colonial (1777–1808).* São Paulo: Editôra Hucitec, 1979.

O'Neill, Brian. "Dying and Inheriting in Rural Trás-os-Montes." *Journal of the Anthropological Society of Oxford* 14, 1(1983): 44–73.

Paes Leme, Pedro Taques de Almeida. *Nobiliarquia paulistana histórica e genealógica.* 5th ed. Belo Horizonte: Editôra Itatiaia, 1980.

Patch, Robert W. "Agrarian Change in Eighteenth-Century Yucatán." *Hispanic American Historical Review* 65(1985): 21–49.

Patterson, Orlando. *The Sociology of Slavery: An Analysis of the Origins, Development and Structure of Negro Slave Society in Jamaica.* London: MacGibbon & Kee, 1967.

Pedlow, Gregory W. "Marriage, Family Size, and Inheritance Among Hessian Nobles, 1650–1900." *Journal of Family History* 7(1982): 333–352.

Petersen, Dwight E. "Sweet Success: Some Notes on the Founding of a Brazilian Sugar Dynasty, the Pais Barreto Family of Pernambuco." *The Americas* 40(1984): 325–348.

Petrone, Maria Thereza Schorer. *A lavoura canavieira em São Paulo: Expansão e declínio (1765–1851).* São Paulo: Difusão Européia do Livro, 1968.

Petrone, Pasquale. "Os aldeamentos paulistas e sua função na valorização da região paulistana: Estudo de geografia histórica." Tese de Livre Docência: Universidade de São Paulo, 1964.

———. *Na baixada Santista, a porta e o porto do planalto.* São Paulo: Universidade de São Paulo, Instituto de Geografía, 1969.

Pierson, Donald. "Família e compadrio numa communidade rural paulista." *Sociologia* 17(1955): 113–131.

Prado, Caio. *The Colonial Background of Modern Brazil.* Trans. Suzette Macedo. Berkeley and Los Angeles: University of California Press, 1967.

Prado, J. F. de Almeida. *Primeiros povoadores do Brasil (1500–1530).* 2d ed. Brasiliana, vol. 37. São Paulo: Companhia Editôra Nacional, 1939.

———. *São Vicente e as Capitanias do sul do Brasil, as origens (1501–1531).* Brasiliana, vol. 314. São Paulo: Companhia Editôra Nacional, 1961.

———. *Jean-Baptiste Debret.* Brasiliana, vol. 352. São Paulo: Companhia Editôra Nacional, 1973.

Prefeitura do Município de São Paulo. *Bandeirantes no Paraguai Século XVII.* Coleção Departamento da Cultura, Vol. 35. São Paulo: Publicação de Divisão do Arquivo Histórico, 1949.

Price, Richard, ed. *Maroon Societies: Rebel Slave Communities in the Americas.* New York: Doubleday, 1973.

Putnam, Jackson K. "The Turner Thesis and Westward Movement: A Reappraisal." *Western Historical Quarterly* 7(1976): 379–404.

Queiroz, Maria Isaura Pereira de. *Bairros rurais paulistas.* São Paulo: Livraria Duas Cidades, 1973.

———. *O mandonismo local na vida política brasileira e outros ensaios.* São Paulo: Editôra Alfa-Omega, 1976.

Queiroz, Suely Robles Reis de. *Escravidão negra em São Paulo: Um estudo das tensões provocadas pelo escravismo no século XIX.* Coleção Documentos Brasileiros, vol. 176. Rio de Janeiro: Livraria José Olympio Editôra, 1977.

Rabb, Theodore K., and Robert I. Rotberg, eds. *The Family in History: Interdisciplinary Essays.* New York: Harper & Row, 1973.

Rabello, Elizabeth Darwiche. "As elites na sociedade paulista na segunda metade do seculo XVIII." Tese de Doutoramento: Universidade de São Paulo, 1973.

———. "Os ofícios mecânicos e artesanais em São Paulo na segunda metade do século XVIII." *Revista de História* 112(1977): 575–588.

Raboteau, Albert J. *Slave Religion: The "Invisible Institution" in the Antebellum South.* New York: Oxford University Press, 1978.

Ramírez, Susan E. *Provincial Patriarchs: The Economics of Power in Colonial Peru.* Albuquerque: University of New Mexico Press, 1985.

Ramos, Donald. "Marriage and the Family in Colonial Vila Rica." *Hispanic American Historical Review* 55(1975): 200–225.

———. "City and Country: The Family in Minas Gerais, 1804–1838." *Journal of Family History* 3(1978): 361–375.

———. "Consensual Unions and the Family in Nineteenth-Century Minas Gerias, Brazil." Paper presented to the Social Science History Association, Washington, D.C., November 1989.

———. "Single and Married Women in Villa Rica, Brazil, 1754–1838." *Journal of Family History* 16(1991): 261–282.

Reis, João José. "Slave Rebellion in Brazil: The African Muslim Uprising in Bahia, 1835." Ph.D. diss., University of Minnesota, 1982.

Reis, Paulo Pereira dos. *O Indígena do Vale do Paraíba.* Coleção Paulística, Vol. 16. São Paulo: Governo do Estado de São Paulo, 1979.

Ridge, Martin. "Frederick Jackson Turner, Ray Allen Billington, and American Frontier History." *Western Historical Quarterly* 19(1988): 5–20.

Rosen, Bernard C., and M. Tosta Berlinck. "Modernization and Family Structure in the Region of São Paulo, Brazil." *América Latina* 11, 3(1968): 75–96.

Rout, Leslie B. *The African Experience in Spanish America: 1502 to the Present Day*. Cambridge: Cambridge University Press, 1976.

Rowland, Robert. "Family and Marriage in Portugal (16th–20th Centuries): A Comparative Sketch." Paper presented to the Social Science History Association, Washington, D.C., October 1983.

Rubbo, Anna. "The Spread of Capitalism in Rural Colombia: Effects on Poor Women." In *Toward an Anthropology of Women*, 333–357. Ed. Rayna R. Reiter. New York: Monthly Review Press, 1975.

Russell-Wood, A. J. R. *Fidalgos and Philanthropists: The Santa Casa da Misericórdia of Bahia, 1550–1755*. Berkeley and Los Angeles: University of California Press, 1968.

———. "Local Government in Portuguese America: A Study in Cultural Divergence." *Comparative Studies in Society and History* 16(1974): 187–231.

———. "Women and Society in Colonial Brazil." *Journal of Latin American Studies* 9(1977): 1–34.

Russell-Wood, A. J. R., ed. *From Colony to Nation: Essays on the Independence of Brazil*. Baltimore: Johns Hopkins University Press, 1975.

Rutman, Darrett B. "Assessing the Little Communities of Early America." *William and Mary Quarterly*, 3d ser., 43(1986): 163–178.

Salmon, Marylynn. *Women and the Law of Property in Early America*. Chapel Hill: University of North Carolina Press, 1986.

Salvador, Frei Vicente do. *História do Brasil, 1500–1627*. Ed. Capistrano de Abreu, Rodolfo Garcia, and Frei Venancio Willeke, OFM. 6th ed. São Paulo: Edições Melhoramentos, 1975.

Salzano, Francisco M., and Newton Freire-Maia. *Problems in Human Biology: A Study of Brazilian Populations*. Detroit: Wayne State University Press, 1970.

Samara, Eni de Mesquita. "Aspectos de uma vila paulista em 1813 (de acordo com os dados fornecidos pelos maços de população de Itú)." *Anais do VII Simpósio Nacional dos Professores Universitários de História* (1973): 347–369.

———. "Uma contribuição ao estudo da estrutura familiar em São Paulo durante o período colonial: A família agregada em Itú de 1780 a 1830." *Revista de História* 105(1976): 35–45.

———. "O papel do agregado na região de Itú—1780 a 1830." *Coleção Museu Paulista* 6(1977): 13–121.

———. "O dote na sociedade paulista do século XIX: Legislação e evidências." *Anais do Museu Paulista* 30(1980/81): 41–53.

———. "Os agregados: Uma tipología ao fim do período colonial (1780–1830)." *Estudos Econômicos* 11, 3(1981): 159–168.

————. *As mulheres, o poder, e a família: São Paulo, século XIX*. São Paulo: Editôra Marco Zero, 1989.

————. "Famílias e domicílios em sociedades escravistas (São Paulo no século XIX)." Paper presented to the Conference on the Population History of Latin America, Ouro Preto, June 1989.

Samara, Eni de Mesquita, ed. *Família e grupos de convívio*. São Paulo: ANPUH/Marco Zero, 1989.

Samara, Eni de Mesquita, and Iraci del Nero da Costa. *Demografía histórica: Bibliografia brasileira*. São Paulo: Instituto de Pesquisas Econômicas, 1984.

Sant' Ana, Benevenuto Silverio de Arruda. *São Paulo histórico: Aspectos, lendas e costumes*. 6 vols. São Paulo: Coleção Departamento de Cultura, 1937–1944.

Sauer, Carl O. *The Early Spanish Main*. Berkeley and Los Angeles: University of California Press, 1969.

Schieber, Harry N. "Turner's Legacy and the Search for a Reorientation of Western History: A Review Essay." *New Mexico Historical Review* 44(1969): 231–248.

Schmidt, Carlos Borges. *O milho e o monjolo: Aspectos da civilização do milho: Técnicas, utensílios, e maquinaria tradicionais*. Documentário da vida rural, 20. Rio de Janeiro: Ministerio da Agricultura, Servico de Informação Agrícola, 1967.

————. *Técnicas agrícolas primitivas e tradicionais*. Rio de Janeiro: Conselho Federal de Cultura, 1976.

Schwartz, Stuart Barry. "The *Mocambo*: Slave Resistance in Colonial Bahia." *Journal of Social History* 3(1970): 313–333.

————. "Free Labor in a Slave Economy: The *Lavradores de Cana* of Colonial Bahia." In *Colonial Roots of Modern Brazil*, 147–197. Ed. Dauril Alden. Berkeley, Los Angeles, and London: University of California Press, 1973.

————. *Sovereignty and Society in Colonial Brazil: The High Court of Bahia and Its Judges, 1609–1751*. Berkeley, Los Angeles, and London: University of California Press, 1973.

————. "Elite Politics and the Growth of a Peasantry in Late Colonial Brazil." In *From Colony to Nation: Essays on the Independence of Brazil*, 133–154. Ed. A. J. R. Russell-Wood. Baltimore: Johns Hopkins University Press, 1975.

————. "Indian Labor and New World Plantations: European Demands and Indian Responses in Northeastern Brazil." *American Historical Review* 83(1978): 43–79.

————. *Sugar Plantations in the Formation of Brazilian Society: Bahia, 1550–1835*. Cambridge: Cambridge University Press, 1985.

Scott, Ana Silvia Volpi. "Dinamica familiar da elite paulista (1765–1836)." M.A. thesis, University of São Paulo, 1987.

Scott, Joan W., and Louise A. Tilly. "Women's Work and the Family in

Nineteenth-Century Europe." *Comparative Studies in Society and History* 17(1975): 36–64.

Searle, Eleanor. "Seigneurial Control of Women's Marriage: The Antecedents and Function of Merchet in England." *Past and Present* 82(1979): 3–43.

Seed, Patricia. "Social Dimensions of Race: Mexico City, 1753." *Hispanic American Historical Review* 62(1982): 569–606.

Segalen, Martine. *Nuptialité et alliance: Le choix du conjoint dans une commune de l'Eure.* Paris: Maisonneuve, 1972.

———. "The Family Cycle and Household Structure: Five Generations in a French Village." *Journal of Family History* 2(1977): 223–236.

Shammas, Carole. "The Domestic Environment in Early Modern England and America." *Journal of Social History* 14(1980): 3–24.

Shorter, Edward. *The Making of the Modern Family.* New York: Basic Books, 1975.

Silva, Antonio de Morais. *Diccionario da Lingua Portugueza.* 8th ed. Lisbon: Editôra Empreza, 1890.

Silva, Maria Beatriz Nizza da. "Casamentos de escravos na Capitania de São Paulo." *Ciência e Cultura* 32(1980): 816–821.

———. "O problema dos expostos na Capitania de São Paulo." *Anais do Museu Paulista* 30(1980/81): 147–158.

———. *Sistema de casamento no Brasil colonial.* Coleção Coroa Vermelha, Estudos Brasileiros, vol. 6. São Paulo: T. A. Queiroz, Editôra da Universidade de São Paulo, 1984.

Simonsen, Roberto C. *História econômica do Brasil (1500/1820).* 8th ed. Coleção Brasiliana, vol. 10. São Paulo: Companhia Editôra Nacional, 1978.

Simpson, Lesley Byrd. *The Encomienda in New Spain: The Beginning of Spanish Mexico.* Berkeley and Los Angeles: University of California Press, 1966.

Skidmore, Thomas E. *Black into White: Race and Nationality in Brazilian Thought.* New York: Oxford University Press, 1974.

Slenes, Robert Wayne. "The Demography and Economics of Brazilian Slavery, 1850–1888." Ph.D. diss., Stanford University, 1976.

———. "Slave Marriage and Family Patterns in the Coffee Regions of Brazil, 1850–1888. Paper presented to the American Historical Association, December 1978.

———. "Escravidão e família: Padrões de casamento e estabilidade familiar numa comunidade escrava (Campinas, século XIX)." *Estudos Econômicos* 17(1987): 217–227.

Smith, Daniel Blake. *Inside the Great House: Planter Family Life in Eighteenth-Century Chesapeake Society.* Ithaca: Cornell University Press, 1980.

Smith, Daniel Scott, and Michael S. Hindus. "Premarital Pregnancy in America, 1640–1971: An Overview and Interpretation." *Journal of Interdisciplinary History* 5(1975): 537–570.

Smith, David Grant. "The Mercantile Class of Portugal and Brazil in the Seventeenth Century: A Socio-Economic Study of the Merchants of Lisbon and Bahia, 1620–1690." Ph.D. diss., University of Texas, Austin, 1975.

Smith, Joan, Immanuel Wallerstein, and Hans-Dieter Evers, eds. *Households and the World Economy*. Beverly Hills: Sage Publications, 1984.

Smith, Raymond T., ed. *Kinship Ideology and Practice in Latin America*. Chapel Hill: University of North Carolina Press, 1984.

Smith, Richard M., ed. *Land, Kinship and Life-Cycle*. Cambridge: Cambridge University Press, 1984.

Snydacker, Daniel. "Kinship and Community in Rural Pennsylvania, 1749–1820." *Journal of Interdisciplinary History* 13(1982): 41–61.

Socolow, Susan M. *The Merchants of Buenos Aires, 1778–1810: Family and Commerce*. Cambridge: Cambridge University Press, 1978.

Soeiro, Susan A. "A Baroque Nunnery: The Economic and Social Role of a Colonial Convent, Santa Clara do Destêrro, Salvador, Bahia, 1677–1800." Ph.D. diss., New York University, 1974.

———. "The Social and Economic Role of the Convent: Women and Nuns in Colonial Bahia, 1677–1800." *Hispanic American Historical Review* 54(1974): 209–232.

Southey, Robert. *History of Brazil*. 3 vols. London: Longman, Durst, Rees, Orme & Brown, 1817–1822; repr. ed., New York: Greenwood Press, 1969.

Souza, Laura de Mello e. *Desclassificados do ouro: A pobreza mineira no século XVIII*. Biblioteca de História, vol. 8. Rio de Janeiro: Edições Graal, 1982.

———. *O diabo e a Terra de Santa Cruz: Feitiçaria e religiosidade popular no Brasil colonial*. São Paulo: Editôra Schwarcz, 1987.

Spalding, Karen. *Huarochirí: An Andean Society Under Inca and Spanish Rule*. Stanford: Stanford University Press, 1984.

Stack, Carol B. *All Our Kin: Strategies for Survival in a Black Community*. New York: Harper & Row, 1974.

Stein, Stanley. *Vassouras: A Brazilian Coffee County, 1850–1890*. Cambridge: Harvard University Press, 1957; repr. ed., New York: Atheneum, 1974.

Stein, Stanley, and Barbara Stein. *The Colonial Heritage of Latin America: Essays on Economic Dependence in Perspective*. New York: Oxford University Press, 1970.

Stolcke, Verena. *Cafeicultura: Homens, mulheres e capital (1850–1980)*. Trans. Denise Bottmann and João R. Martins Filho. São Paulo: Editôra Brasiliense, 1986.

Stone, Lawrence. *The Family, Sex and Marriage in England, 1500–1800*. New York: Harper & Row, 1977.

———. "Family History in the 1980s: Past Achievements and Future Trends." *Journal of Interdisciplinary History* 12(1981): 51–87.

Taunay, Affonso d'Escragnolle. *São Paulo nos primeiros anos (1554–1601), ensaio de reconstituição social*. Tours: Imprimerie E. Arrault, 1920.

———. *Collectanea de mappas da cartographia paulista antiga*. Publicação do Museu Paulista, vol. 1. São Paulo: Companhia Melhoramentos de São Paulo, 1922.

———. *História geral das bandeiras paulistas.* 11 vols. São Paulo: Typ. Ideal H. L. Canton, 1924–1950.

———. *A grande vida de Fernão Dias Pais.* São Paulo: Melhoramentos, 1977.

Taylor, William B. *Landlord and Peasant in Colonial Oaxaca.* Stanford: Stanford University Press, 1972.

———. *Drinking, Homicide and Rebellion in Colonial Mexican Villages.* Stanford: Stanford University Press, 1979.

Thompson, E. P. "Patrician Society, Plebeian Culture." *Journal of Social History* 7(1973/74): 382–405.

———. "The Grid of Inheritance: A Comment." In *Family and Inheritance: Rural Society in Western Europe, 1200–1800,* 328–360. Ed. Jack Goody, Joan Thirsk, and E. P. Thompson. Cambridge: Cambridge University Press, 1976.

Trumbach, Randolph. *The Rise of the Egalitarian Family: Aristocratic Kinship and Domestic Relations in Eighteenth-Century England.* New York: Academic Press, 1978.

Turner, Frederick Jackson. *The Frontier in American History.* Tucson: University of Arizona Press, 1986.

Tutino, John. "Power, Class, and Family: Men and Women in the Mexican Elite, 1750–1810." *The Americas* 39(1983): 359–381.

Van de Walle, Etienne. "Household Dynamics in a Belgian Village, 1847–1866." *Journal of Family History* 1(1976): 80–94.

Varnhagen, Francisco Adolfo de. *História geral do Brasil.* 3 vols. 10th ed. São Paulo: Editôra Itatiaia, 1981.

Venâncio, Renato Pinto. "Ilegitimidade e concubinato no Brasil colonial: Rio de Janeiro e São Paulo, 1760–1800." Estudos Cedhal no. 1. São Paulo: Centro de Estudos de Demografia Histórica de América Latina, 1986.

Vianna, Fransicso José de Oliveira. *Instituições políticas brasileiras.* 2 vols. 3d ed. Rio de Janeiro: Record, 1974.

Vives, Jaime Vicens. *An Economic History of Spain.* Trans. F. M. López-Morillas. Princeton: Princeton University Press, 1969.

Vries, Jan de. "Peasant Demand Patterns and Economic Development: Friesland 1550–1750." In *European Peasants and Their Markets: Essays in Agrarian Economic History,* 205–268. Ed. William N. Parker and Eric L. Jones. Princeton: Princeton University Press, 1975.

Wagley, Charles. "Kinship Patterns in Brazil: The Persistence of a Cultural Tradition." In *The Latin American Tradition: Essays on the Unity and the Diversity of Latin American Culture,* 175–193. Ed. Charles Wagley. New York: Columbia University Press, 1968.

Wall, Richard, ed. *Family Forms in Historic Europe.* Cambridge: Cambridge University Press, 1983.

Wallace, A. F. C., ed. *Men and Cultures: Selected Papers of the Fifth International Congress of Anthropological and Ethnological Sciences.* Philadelphia, September 1–9, 1956.

Walsh, Lorena S. "'Till Death do us Part': Marriage and Family in Seventeenth-Century Maryland." In *The Chesapeake in the Seventeenth Century: Essays on Anglo-American Society*, 126–152. Ed. Thad W. Tate and David L. Ammerman. Chapel Hill: University of North Carolina Press, 1979.

Waters, John J., Jr. "Hingham, Massachusetts, 1631–1661: An East Anglian Oligarchy in the New World." *Journal of Social History* 1(1968): 351–370.

———. "The Traditional World of the New England Peasants: A View from Seventeenth-Century Barnstable." *New England Historical and Genealogical Register* 130(1976): 3–21.

Weber, David. "Turner, the Boltonians, and the Borderlands." *American Historical Review* 91(1986): 66–81.

Weber, Max. *From Max Weber: Essays in Sociology*. Trans. and ed. H. H. Gerth and C. Wright Mills. New York: Oxford University Press, 1964; repr. ed., New York: Oxford University Press, 1973.

———. *The Theory of Social and Economic Organization*. Trans. A. M. Henderson and Talcott Parsons, ed. Talcott Parsons. New York: Free Press, 1964.

Wells, Robert V. "Quaker Marriage Patterns in a Colonial Perspective." *William and Mary Quarterly*, 3d ser., 29(1972): 415–442.

Wetherell, Charles. "Slave Kinship: A Case Study of the South Carolina Good Hope Plantation, 1835–1856." *Journal of Family History* 6(1981): 294–308.

Wheaton, Robert. "Family and Kinship in Western Europe: The Problem of the Joint Family Household." *Journal of Interdisciplinary History* 5(1975): 601–628.

Willems, Emilio. "The Structure of the Brazilian Family." *Social Forces* 31(1953): 339–345.

———. "On Portuguese Family Structure." *International Journal of Comparative Sociology* 3(1962): 65–79.

———. "Social Differentiation in Colonial Brazil." *Comparative Studies in Society and History* 12(1970): 31–49.

Wolf, Eric R. "Kinship, Friendship and Patron-Client Relations in Complex Societies." In *The Social Anthropology of Complex Societies*, 1–22. Ed. Michael Banton. New York: Frederick A. Praeger, Inc., 1966.

———. *Europe and the People without History*. Berkeley, Los Angeles, and London: University of California Press, 1982.

Wyntjes, Sherrin Marshall. "Survivors and Status: Widowhood and Family in the Early Modern Netherlands." *Journal of Family History* 7(1982): 396–405.

Yazawa, Melvin. *From Colonies to Commonwealth: Familial Ideology and the Beginnings of the American Republic*. Baltimore: Johns Hopkins University Press, 1985.

Yver, Jean. *Egalité entre héritiers et exclusión des enfants dotés*. Paris: Sirey, 1966.

Zuckerman, Michael. *Peaceable Kingdoms: New England Towns in the Eighteenth Century*. New York: Vintage Books, 1970.

Index

Abreu, Maria de, 185
Administração, 59, 75–78, 85, 131, 132, 165, 182–183
Agregados, 131–135, 145–147, 166–167; defined, 126–127
Agriculture: wheat, 32, 38, 52, 60; cattle, 32, 38, 58, 92, 93; seventeenth-century, 52–53; eighteenth-century, 60, 62–63, 79–82; nineteenth-century, 63–65; coffee, 64–65, 204; subsistence farming, 122–125; manioc, 124. *See also* Sugar
Ajuntamentos, 127
Aldeia: defined, 32–33, 38; crown policy of, 51, 69; Indians of, 69; *administração* and, 76–77; abolished, 82. *See also* Barueрí
Almeida, Guilherme Pompeo de, 182
Almeida, Fr. Guilherme Pompeo de, 59
Almeida, Maria de, 165
Almeida, Thomazia de, 185
Alvarenga, Aleixo Leme de, 71
Alveres, Clemente, 68
Alvres, Domingos, 68
American South: family patterns of, 17–19; slave families in, 160, 179–180; manumission in, 184
Anchieta, José de, 35–37, 124, 127
Andover, Massachusetts, 16
Andrade, Antonio Francisco de, 110–111, 165, 168
Andrade, Fernão Bicudo de, 77
Araçariguama: parish, 14, 77, 136, 143, 144, 148, 162–163, 168, 193, 208, 210; *fazenda*, 85, 115, 132, 182–183
Araujo, João Marques de, 77
Armação (pl. *armações*), 49–50, 57
Assumpção, Anna de, 166
Azevedo, Bernardo Pereira de, 142

Bahia, 19, 39, 42, 59
Bandeiras, 46–49, 57, 67–69, 200
Barcelos, Isabel de, 56, 70, 72, 73
Barros, Antonio Ribeiro de, 142

Barros, Fernão Pais de, 175–178
Barros, Luzia Leme de, 184
Barros, Pedro Vaz de, 47
Barros, Vicente Correa de, 166
Barueрí: parish and *aldeia*, 14, 78, 165, 201, 208, 210; population of, 41, 82; description of, 82–83; lands of, 132
Bicuda, Maria, 67
Bicudo, Antonio, 53, 70
Bicudo, Baltezar de Godoy, 79
Bicudo, Bernardo, 70, 71
Bicudo, Domingas de Godoy, 79
Birachoissava, 73
Borba, Antonio Gomes, 49, 50
Borba, Maria Gertrudes de, 84
Bororo, 77, 83
Brading, David, 5
Brito, Jeronymo de, 51
Brito, Miguel Bicudo de, 109
Bronner, Fred, 5

Caldeira, Ignacio Diniz, 89
Camacho, João de Gomes, 68
Câmara. See Town Council
Camargo, Anastasio Pereira de, 191
Camargo, Francisco Bueno de, 58
Camargo, Gabriella Ortis de, 78–79
Caminha, Pedro Vaz de, 26
Campos, Felippe de, 74
Campos, Mauricio da Rocha, 139
Campos, Pedro Vas de, 105
Cannibalism, 29, 33
Canto, Izabel da Rocha do, 115
Cardozo, Bento Joze, 152
Cardozo, Joze Alves, 152
Carvalho, Miguel Garcia de, 192
Castanho, Luis, 73
Castro, Anna Ribeira de, 167
Censuses: discussion of, 11–13, 80, 106, 128, 207–208; nuclear families in, 20; elite families in, 21; Barueрí census, 82–83; race in, 85–86, 149; planter families in, 87; peasant families in,